LADY EDITOR

Also by
MELANIE KIRKPATRICK

Thanksgiving:
The Holiday at the Heart of the American Experience

Escape from North Korea:
The Untold Story of Asia's Underground Railroad

MELANIE KIRKPATRICK

LADY EDITOR

A Biography

⟞⟐⟐⟐⟞

SARAH JOSEPHA HALE

and the

MAKING OF THE
MODERN AMERICAN WOMAN

ENCOUNTER BOOKS 𝑒 NEW YORK · LONDON

First American edition published in 2021 by Encounter Books,
an activity of Encounter for Culture and Education, Inc.,
a nonprofit, tax-exempt corporation.
Encounter Books website address: www.encounterbooks.com

Manufactured in the United States and printed on
acid-free paper. The paper used in this publication meets
the minimum requirements of ANSI/NISO Z39.48–1992
(R 1997) (*Permanence of Paper*).

FIRST AMERICAN EDITION

LIBRARY OF CONGRESS CATALOGING-IN-PUBLICATION DATA

Names: Kirkpatrick, Melanie, author.
Title: Lady Editor: Sarah Josepha Hale and the Making of the Modern
American Woman / Melanie Kirkpatrick.
Description: New York: Encounter Books, 2021. | Includes bibliographical
references and index. |
Identifiers: LCCN 2021003034 (print) | LCCN 2021003035 (ebook) | ISBN
9781641771788 (hardcover) | ISBN 9781641771795 (ebook)
Subjects: LCSH: Hale, Sarah Josepha Buell, 1788-1879. | Women periodical
editors—United States—Biography. | Godey's magazine. | Authors,
American—19th century—Biography. | Women social reformers--United
States—Biography.
Classification: LCC PN4874.H22 K48 2021 (print) | LCC PN4874.H22 (ebook)
| DDC 070.4/83470924 [B]—dc23
LC record available at https://lccn.loc.gov/2021003034
LC ebook record available at https://lccn.loc.gov/2021003035

Book design and illustration by Katherine Messenger

For Jack

"If I were asked, now that I am drawing to the close of this work, in which I have spoken of so many important things done by the Americans, to what the singular prosperity and growing strength of that people ought mainly to be attributed, I should reply—to the superiority of their women."

—ALEXIS DE TOCQUEVILLE,
Democracy in America (1840)

Contents

A Summer Snowstorm

I T IS A CLICHÉ to say that life can change in a single instant, but saying so doesn't make it any less shattering when the instant strikes in your own life.

For the pregnant young mother at home in a village in the hills of central New Hampshire, the moment arrived in mid-September 1822, when it began to snow. Sarah was a New Englander, born and bred, and snow didn't usually faze her. But this was different. It was too early in the season for the first snow. Leaves were still on the trees; only a few had turned red or gold. As she stood at her front door watching the snow transform the village green into a sheet of white, she was filled with worry about her husband.

David had left home that morning on horseback, heading for an appointment with a legal client eight miles away on Lake Sunapee. He was lightly dressed, unprepared for the storm that no one expected. When he finally staggered into the house that evening, he was soaked through to the skin, shivering with the cold. Sarah helped him undress and get into bed. The cold quickly turned to fever and then, ferociously, to pneumonia. By September 25, her beloved husband was dead. His funeral was held at the Baptist meeting house in a ceremony conducted by one of David's fellow Freemasons. A month after her husband's death, Sarah brought their fifth child into the world. Little William joined his now-fatherless brothers and sisters—David and Horatio, Frances and Josepha. The boys were seven and five; the girls three and not quite two.

The new widow had no illusions about what came next. David had made a good living as a lawyer, but like many young married couples, the Hales had no savings to speak of. Until the boys were old enough to go out to work, or until she remarried—an unthinkable prospect!—she and her children would have no choice but to rely on the charity that family and neighbors might offer. David's brother Freemasons would also provide assistance. Even so, it would be a struggle.

Sarah had had as fine an education as any American woman alive in the first quarter of the nineteenth century. Home-schooled by her mother and tutored by her brother, she had mastered the subject areas required for a college degree. But all that learning was of little use to her when it came to earning a living. Before marrying David, she had run a small school for young children. The teaching job barely covered her own expenses as a single woman, and it certainly wouldn't pay enough to provide for a family. Tutoring older boys to prepare them for entry into college, a more remunerative position, was out of the question. That was a position reserved for men with academic degrees—something no woman had obtained.

She liked to write poetry. David said she was good at it, and he had sold a couple of her poems to local publications. But poetry didn't put bread on the table. She knew of no woman who made a living as a writer.

It wasn't long before Sarah concluded, like countless widows before her, that she would have to rely on her sewing skills. Needlework was the only occupation open to a respectable lady who had fallen on hard times. While she was a fair hand at the needle, she didn't see how she could make a decent living as a seamstress. Laboring into the night sewing and mending garments for paying customers was mind-numbing, low-paying work. In any case, there weren't enough hours in the day or night to make enough money to pay for the superior education that she and David had envisioned for their children.

Many years later, Sarah came across a quotation that perfectly expressed her situation in the wake of David's death: The German poet Goethe wrote, "The excellent woman is she, who, if the husband dies, can be a father to the children."[1]

In the autumn of 1822, still grieving for her lost husband, she desperately wanted to be that excellent woman, one who could raise her children in the way that she and David had dreamed. As Thanksgiving Day approached, she had no idea how to accomplish that seemingly impossible goal.

SARAH JOSEPHA HALE was one of the most influential women of the nineteenth century, yet she is all but forgotten in ours. If she is remembered today, it is usually as the progenitor of our national Thanksgiving Day or as the author of the nursery rhyme "Mary Had a Little Lamb." Her essential role in shaping the way Americans thought about women and their place in society is largely forgotten.

She did so from her position as editor of two popular periodicals: the *Ladies' Magazine*, a serious intellectual journal and the first successful magazine for women; and *Godey's Lady's Book*, the most widely circulated magazine of the pre–Civil War period and one of the first publications to circulate nationwide. After her husband's death in 1822, she jump-started a career as a writer, made a name for herself, and, just six years later, accepted a job in Boston as founding editor of the start-up *Ladies' Magazine*.

Everyone knows about the 1848 Seneca Falls Convention and the Declaration of Sentiments listing women's grievances and demands. Less well known is that Hale's work laid the base on which the women who gathered at Seneca Falls, New York, rested their premises. Twenty years earlier Hale presented a vision of what women might become given education and encouragement. She used her powerful pen to help transform public perceptions about women's abilities and potential. In doing so, her work broadened public acceptance for educating women and provided intellectual legitimacy for reformers who shared her cause. Hale began her work before women could go to college, work as public schoolteachers, practice medicine, or even manage their own money.

As a member of the post-Revolution generation, born in 1788, Hale brought a deeply patriotic sensibility to her magazines. She believed that even though the thirteen former British colonies had won their war for independence, they would not be truly unified until the new nation developed its own cultural identity, one that was distinct from that of its former colonial masters. Women, she believed, played a leading role in shaping the new American culture, especially in their roles as homemakers and mothers.

Throughout her editorial career, Hale set out to publish content by American authors writing on American themes. From the perspective of the twenty-first century, this may seem an obvious aim—surely Americans want to read about America and their fellow Americans—but it was a radical idea in an era when most periodicals were cut-and-paste jobs, compiled by so-called scissors editors who clipped articles from British publications and republished them in their own periodicals.

Hale, in contrast, sought original, homegrown material. The bylines that appeared in the *Ladies' Magazine* and *Godey's Lady's Book* represented the best of the country's emerging literary talent: Washington Irving, Edgar Allan Poe, Nathaniel Hawthorne, James Fenimore Cooper, Henry Wadsworth Longfellow, William Cullen Bryant, John Greenleaf Whittier, and more. Hale also sought out talented women to write for her, and many female authors got their start in her magazines or built or enhanced their reputations there. Among them were Harriet Beecher Stowe, Lydia Sigourney, Catharine Sedgwick, and Frances Hodgson Burnett. When Hawthorne grumbled to his publisher about the "damned mob of scribbling women"[2] who were outselling male authors, his slur encompassed Hale and the popular female writers whose work she published.

Hale's all-American recipe for her magazines helped shape a common American aesthetic—creating a mass culture in literature, food, art, music, etiquette, and fashion. In *Godey's Lady's Book*, Americans north and south, east and west, found common cultural ground. Under Hale's tutelage in the *Lady's Book*, readers in every corner of the expanding nation were learning what it meant to eat like an American, dress like an American, behave like an American. They were quoting the same poetry, cooking the same recipes, sewing the same fashions, following the same child-rearing advice.

They were also reading the same essays and editorials on

what it meant to be a woman in America. Hale's greatest, and most lasting, legacy was how she used her magazines to reshape the way Americans thought about women and their roles. From her editorial perches at the *Ladies' Magazine* and *Godey's Lady's Book*, Hale was the genius presiding over the remarkable advancement in opportunities for American women in the nineteenth century.

Education for women was her paramount mission. "In this age of innovation," she wrote in the first issue of the *Ladies' Magazine*, "perhaps no experiment will have an influence more important on the character and happiness of our society than the granting to females the advantages of a systematic and thorough education."[3] The year was 1828, when only half of American women could read and there wasn't a single institution of higher education that admitted women.

Over the next half century no issue of Hale's magazines would go to press without at least one article hammering away at her revolutionary themes: Women are the intellectual equals of men. Women deserve to go to college. Women should be able to work for a living. Hale wasn't the only reformer pressing for advancements in women's roles in the first half of the nineteenth century, but she possessed something that her sister reformers lacked: an editorial megaphone.

The change in attitudes about educating women was one of the most rapid shifts in public opinion in American history. By the time of Hale's retirement in 1877, educational opportunities for women had exploded. More girls than boys attended high school, 30 percent of colleges were coeducational, and several all-female colleges offered an education for young women competitive with that which the Ivy League provided for young men.

As women became educated, Hale used the pages of *Godey's*

Lady's Book to champion their entry into the paid workforce. She believed that every woman should be able to support herself and her family should the need arise. This was a lesson she had learned the hard way when her husband died unexpectedly, leaving her with four small children and a fifth on the way. She fought for women to become public schoolteachers, nurses, typesetters, postmistresses, clerks, waitresses, professors, and other positions that heretofore had been held exclusively by the other sex. She published a monthly "Employment for Women" column in the *Lady's Book*, describing the kinds of work that could be suitable for women. In one of her editorial essays promoting female physicians, she expressed the expectation that she soon would "see the day when authoritative women will go about with their pills, prescriptions, and so forth, to deal with and diminish the majority of diseases that visit our households."[4]

Above all, she was the champion of the majority of her readers, who were wives and mothers—roles she thought were underappreciated and undervalued. She created the term "domestic science" as part of her effort to professionalize household skills and raise the status of homemakers. She started the first day nursery to care for the children of poor working women. She supported the establishment of kindergartens. She helped launch the first public playground. She encouraged the acceptance of washing machines, sewing machines, and other labor-saving devices. Her philanthropic work became a model for how women could acquire leadership skills and deploy them in the service of their communities.

Along the way, the editor took on a role that few American women had occupied before her: celebrity. As the circulation of *Godey's Lady's Book* grew, so did the fame of its editor.

Edgar Allan Poe was just one of the many literary figures who admired her. He called her a "lady of fine genius" and—pardon the sexism—"masculine energy and ability."[5] Dr. Oliver Wendell Holmes lauded her work, writing to her near the end of her life: "How much you have done, and always with a high and pure air!"[6] During his 1842 American tour, Charles Dickens sent her a note extending his respects. "Believe me," he wrote from Washington, D.C., "you will never find me departing from those sympathies which we cherish in common, and which have won me your esteem and approval."[7]

Hale, who avoided politics, nevertheless listed among her correspondents numerous governors, senators, members of Congress, presidents, and—in a curious choice for such a passionate American patriot—an English queen. Such was her celebrity—not to mention her chutzpah—that when James Buchanan was named ambassador to the Court of St. James's in London in 1853, she asked him to hand-deliver to Queen Victoria a copy of *Woman's Record*, her encyclopedic compendium of the history of women.[8] The future president of the United States was only too happy to comply with the famous editor's request.[9]

Presidents Millard Fillmore and Franklin Pierce wrote Hale to explain why they had rejected her proposal for a national Thanksgiving Day, a holiday she had been writing about since the 1820s and for which she had been lobbying since the 1840s. In 1863, Abraham Lincoln famously acted on Hale's proposal, put to him in a letter, thereby establishing the modern-day version of the holiday Americans celebrate today. After Lincoln's death, Hale successfully petitioned Andrew Johnson and Ulysses S. Grant to continue the Thanksgiving tradition that Lincoln had inaugurated. Her decades-long campaign for a national Thanksgiving illustrated two commanding traits of Hale's character: She was supremely self-confident and she was indefatigable when working on behalf of causes she championed.

SOME OF Hale's beliefs—such as her anti-suffrage views and her opinions about separate spheres of activity for men and women— show her to be, as we all are, a person of her time. Today these views are rightly seen as archaic. On other important women's issues, however—education, paid work, property rights—she was a radical, a woman ahead of her time. Hale's ideas about women's special obligations to family, their moral leadership, and how they should live useful lives remain relevant. They are worth considering, learning from, and adapting to a modern setting in which men and women are accepted as equals.

There is no contemporary analogue to Sarah Josepha Hale. But we can catch glimpses of her character, intelligence, drive, and influence in several notable women of the current day. Like Oprah Winfrey, she was culturally savvy and had a rare ability to connect deeply with her audiences. Similar to Nikki Haley, a former U.S. ambassador to the United Nations, she had a gift for delivering hard truths with poise and grace. Like the late associate Supreme Court justice Ruth Bader Ginsburg quoting her mother, Hale preached that women must be both independent and ladylike. Her dedication to empowering women through education is evident in the charitable work of former First Lady Laura Bush and philanthropist Melinda Gates.

It is a fitting moment to examine the life of Sarah Josepha Hale, the unsung prophet of women's march toward equality. She and her magazines changed the national conversation about women's roles, responsibilities, and power. In doing so, they laid the foundation for the women's suffrage movement of the post–Civil War period and the feminist revolution of the mid-twentieth century. Hale deserves her due as one of the most consequential figures in the narrative of American women's struggle for equality.

CHAPTER ONE

Daughter of the Revolution

SARAH JOSEPHA BUELL was born on October 24, 1788, on her family's farm in the picturesque hill country of central New Hampshire. Her hometown, Newport, had been founded just twenty-seven years earlier, in 1761, and it still had a frontier feel to it. The land was heavily forested, and settlements were widely separated. Old-timers remembered when wolves roamed the area and it behooved you to take your musket with you when you went out to the fields.

Among Newport's early settlers were a number of Buells who had emigrated from Killingworth, Connecticut, a coastal town almost two hundred miles to the south. Sarah's parents, Gordon and Martha Buell, moved to Newport shortly after the Revolution, settling on four hundred acres belonging to Gordon's grandfather along a slope of East Mountain in the southeast corner of the town. The house in which Sarah grew up does not survive, but a sketch depicts a classic New England farmstead with a main house connected to a series of outer buildings in

1

one continuous structure. In winter the family could walk from house to kitchen to buttery to barn without stepping outside into the snow.

The first U.S. Census, in 1790, counted only 132 households in Newport, 18 of which were occupied by families named Buell. The young Sarah grew up surrounded by an extended family of aunts, uncles, and cousins galore. Among her relatives were the town's first selectman, a popular singing master, and a housewife who was famous for her bear and pumpkin mincemeat pies, the recipe for which regrettably hasn't survived. Sarah's great-aunt Love Buell Nettleton was the local midwife. Aunt Love was admired both for her professional skills and for her dedication to duty, having once traveled three miles on snowshoes to attend a woman giving birth. Sarah, in short, came from a family of upright, hardworking citizens who possessed a high sense of duty to their community.

Two miles down a mountainside track from the Buell homestead stood the village of Newport. The village was so tiny that in the year of Sarah's birth it lacked that most familiar feature of New England towns: a church steeple. During Sarah's youth worshippers met at Proprietors' House, a rough-hewn, barnlike, multipurpose structure that functioned as meeting house, schoolhouse, and, on the rare occasions that it was necessary, courthouse. All public functions were held in Proprietors' House. It was there, in 1776, that townspeople gathered to hear the Declaration of Independence read aloud. The interior of the building was unfinished, with a primitive ceiling made of planks that had been nailed across the overhead beams. When an event drew a capacity crowd, the children would climb up and sit on the beams and boards, from where they would pay attention (or not) to the proceedings down below.

Edmund Wheeler, a mid-nineteenth-century chronicler of

the early history of Newport, extolled the area's natural beauty. "It is difficult to conceive of a more charming spot than that occupied by the main village," he wrote. He described the "gently-swelling verdant hills," the "wide-spreading branches of the elms," and the graceful waters of the Croydon and Goshen branches of the Sugar River that wind through town. He even had cheerful words to say about the village swamp, "in which the frogs, at certain seasons of the year, gave free concerts." In the 1820s, by which time Sarah was a wife and mother, the swamp, now drained, had become the town common. She lived in a house facing the common, where townspeople grazed their cows.[1]

Like Wheeler, Hale was moved by the beauty of her surroundings. In the summer of 1822, shortly before her husband's death, she wrote a poem titled "Address to Sugar River." The sentimental poem is perhaps not one of her better efforts, but it expresses her affection for the surroundings in which she grew up. She recalls halcyon childhood days spent reading on the bank of the Sugar and watching a little waterfall whose wonders she compared to Niagara's. Shakespeare had the Avon River, she writes, and Pope the Thames:

> *But my soft-gliding, native river raises*
> *A thousand images of home-felt joy;*
> *And though their* names *in lofty lays may shine,*
> *In* sweetness *they can ever equal thine.*[2]

SARAH BELONGED TO the eighth generation of Buells to call New England home. The family traced its American roots back to 1630, when a young carpenter called William Buell arrived from England aboard the ship *Mary & John*. William was a member of the religious community led by the Reverend John Warham, a Puritan pastor. Upon their arrival in the New World, Warham and his followers first founded Dorchester, now incorporated into the city of Boston. A few years later they helped establish the first permanent English settlement in Connecticut—the town of Windsor at the confluence of the Farmington and Connecticut Rivers. William's son Samuel eventually moved south to Killingworth, Connecticut, where his descendants stayed put for several generations. Sarah's mother's family— the Whittleseys—hailed from the town of Saybrook, adjacent to Killingworth. There had been Whittleseys in Saybrook since 1623, when the Dutch controlled the area.

Sarah's Puritan heritage is reflected in the given names of the ancestors found on the Buell family tree. The Puritans favored names from the Old Testament. In keeping with that tradition we find Buell men called Samuel, Nathaniel, and Asa along with women christened Mehitable, Hepzibah, Hannah, Abigail—and, of course, Sarah. Another Puritan naming practice was to call children after virtues. Sarah's ancestors include the sisters Mindwell and Freelove, the latter being a reference to God's free love for His believers, not the sexual revolution of the 1960s. Sarah's paternal grandmother was called Thankful, a name that turns up in Sarah's generation on another branch of the family tree. Sarah Josepha was named after her mother's parents, Sarah and Joseph Whittlesey, who were alive and living in Saybrook at the time she was born.

Sarah was Gordon and Martha Buell's third child and their first girl. Her older brothers—Charles Whittlesey Buell and Horatio Gates Buell—were born in 1784 and 1787, respectively. A younger sister, Martha Maria, arrived in 1793. The first Census records a third boy living in the Buell household in 1790, identity unknown. He might have been a hired hand, a visiting cousin, or even a third son who died when he was very young. All the children were close, but Sarah and Horatio—only nineteen months apart—were especially so. Both were highly intelligent, and there was a friendly spirit of intellectual competition between them. As the first daughter in the family, with two older brothers and a sister five years younger, Sarah was always trying to keep up with the boys.

OF THE MILLIONS of words that Sarah Josepha Hale wrote over the course of her long life, few were about her childhood in Newport or, for that matter, her personal life overall. If she wrote about herself, she preferred to focus on what she termed her literary life—her books, essays, poetry, and other prose. Even so, the attentive reader can catch glimpses of her personal life through her writing.

Hale lived at a time when it wasn't polite to talk too much about yourself, and in any case, she—ever the lady—would have felt uncomfortable doing so. In 1837, when she was approaching fifty, she wrote an essay about herself for inclusion in a collection of biographical sketches of female writers that she was editing. She opens the essay with an extended apology for writing about herself and later asks the reader not to think it "vanity or weakness" on her part when she praises her late husband.[3] Sarah would not have been comfortable as a member of the me generation.

Nearer to the end of her life, Hale explained her reticence to talk about her childhood in a letter to Edmund Wheeler, the Newport historian. Wheeler was writing a history of their mutual hometown, and he wanted to include a biography of its famous native daughter. "My birthplace will always be dear to

5

me," Hale wrote to Wheeler. "But I cannot expect the public to take interest in things whose places are in most instances probably now occupied by objects of greater beauty or usefulness. In short my dear townsman, I do not wish you to go at all into any details of my life or family. All that the public care to know is connected with my literary history."[4]

In reply, Wheeler did the sensible thing: Rather than attempt the impossible—writing an essay that would be acceptable to the famous editor—he invited Mrs. Hale to write the section on Mrs. Hale. The autobiographical essay that eventually appeared in Wheeler's book provides a window on Sarah's early life.

The most important influences on her childhood, she writes, were her parents, who had a love of learning and a deep religious faith. Their teaching, personal conduct, and life stories sparked her thinking on the two chief subjects that she championed throughout her half century as a writer, editor, and social reformer: women's education and America's emerging cultural identity.

The central event of Sarah's father's life was the Revolutionary War, and he passed along to his daughter a profound love of country. Gordon Buell served under the command of General Horatio Gates, after whom he named his second son. He fought with Gates at the Battle of Saratoga in 1777. The battle was a turning point in the war, with the American victory helping to persuade the French to enter the war on the side of the Americans. Gordon served four years in the Continental Army, rising to the rank of captain, the title by which he was addressed for the remainder of his life. During his military service he suffered an unspecified injury to his health, making the exhausting, relentless labor of farming difficult, especially as he grew older and less physically able. In 1810 the family gave up their farm on East Mountain and moved into town, where Captain Buell built the Rising Sun Tavern along the newly constructed Croyden Turnpike.

Gordon wasn't the only Buell to fight in the Revolution. Other Buells did so too—at Bunker Hill, Fort Ticonderoga, and elsewhere—and Sarah grew up in a household where Americans' newly won freedoms and the patriots who fought for them were deeply revered.

For the Buells in post-Revolution Newport, the valuable old-growth pine forest on the family farm was a potent symbol of American independence. Under the terms of the Newport town charter, granted by King George III, the original owners of the pine trees had been required to preserve the trees for the use of the Royal Navy, which commandeered them for masts for its ships. After the war, the property rights reverted to the owners of the forest. The Buells, not some faraway king, could now decide what to do with their pine trees. Sarah would spend hours lying on the forest floor gazing up at the towering treetops.

When she was ten years old, Sarah read David Ramsay's *The History of the American Revolution*, which affected her deeply. Ramsay was a cultural nationalist. He believed that it wasn't sufficient for the new nation to declare *political* independence. Americans must also liberate themselves from England by declaring *cultural* independence. That meant creating their own literature and art and conducting their own scientific research. He warned that the new nation would fracture if Americans weren't bound together by a common culture. Ramsay's book "made me a patriot for life," Hale wrote.[5] It provided the intellectual underpinnings of her future editorial vision to publish original works by American authors on American themes. It also helped explain her championship of a national Thanksgiving Day, a homegrown American holiday. She hoped that a shared holiday would draw together the nation, which was splitting over the issue of slavery, and prevent civil war.

Another book that had a large impact on the young Sarah was the Gothic novel *The Mysteries of Udolpho*, by Englishwoman Ann Radcliffe. The book represented two significant firsts for Sarah. It was the first novel she read, and it was the first book she read of any genre that had been written by a woman. She wrote: "Here was a work, the most fascinating book I had ever read . . . written by a woman! How happy it made me! The wish to promote the reputation of my own sex, and to do something for my own country, was among the earliest mental emotions I can recollect."[6]

Both sides of Sarah's family—the Buells and the Whittleseys—placed great value on education, as can be seen in the biographical sketches Wheeler provides of family members in his history of Newport. Among Sarah's relatives on the Buell side were a "lady of superior education and intelligence" and a man who was a "lover of books." Men and women on Sarah's mother's side of the family, the Whittleseys, receive similar accolades. Martha's brother, Arphaxad Whittlesey, was a schoolteacher, described by a former pupil as "a very competent teacher, an able writer, and a fluent and forcible speaker." Martha's sister Polly was "a lady of culture."

Wheeler reserved his highest encomium, though, for Martha Buell herself, whom he described as possessing "intellectual endowments of a high order." Martha appears to have been exceptionally well educated for a woman of her day, and she passed along her knowledge to her four children, whom she homeschooled. Girls weren't treated differently than boys in Mrs. Buell's schoolroom. Sarah received the same education as her older brothers.[7]

In her autobiographical profile, Sarah, without elaborating, describes her mother as having "enjoyed uncommon advantages of education." Martha possessed "a mind clear as rock-water, and a most happy talent of communicating knowledge." According to her daughter, Martha excelled, too, as a teacher, amusing and instructing her children at the same time. "She always contrived to teach us some serious *truth*, while she charmed us."[8]

The Puritans' emphasis on literacy meant that in New England in the late eighteenth century a high percentage of men—perhaps as high as 70 percent—could read, write, and do basic arithmetic. Literacy rates for women were lower but still strong when compared with England and other parts of Europe. While American women often were taught to read—principally so that they could read the Bible—they were not necessarily taught to write, which was considered a separate skill. If girls were educated, instruction often took place at home and was intermittent. Sewing, deportment, and household skills were taught, but it was uncommon for girls to pursue intellectual studies beyond basic literacy and numeracy.

Hale might have been thinking of her mother when she wrote in 1829, eighteen years after that lady's death, "There is no influence so powerful as that of a mother . . . but next in rank and efficacy . . . is that of a schoolmaster."[9] Martha Whittlesey Buell was both Sarah's mother and her first schoolteacher, and her influence was profound. Under Martha's tutelage, Sarah's education went well beyond the basic skills of reading, writing, and ciphering. The children studied the Bible, of course. They also read—and reread—*The Pilgrim's Progress*, which Sarah liked even more than *The Mysteries of Udolpho*. Their course of study included the works of John Milton, Joseph Addison, Alexander Pope, Ben Jonson, Robert Burns, and William Shakespeare.

Sarah credited her mother, too, for providing her children with a strong moral education. From Martha, Sarah learned how to live a virtuous life—how to be a responsible, loving wife and mother, how to be a good citizen, how to treat friends and neighbors. This aspect of Sarah's education would have included proper manners, about which she wrote a book published in 1868.[10]

It also would have included Sarah's religious education, about which little is known. Later in life she became a faithful Episcopalian, but she was brought up in the Congregational church, whose records list her mother as Member No. 101. Gordon's name does not appear on the church rolls, and there is probably an interesting story there that is lost to history. During her childhood or young adulthood, Sarah paid an extended visit to her maternal grandparents in Connecticut, where she encountered a stern, antiseptic version of New England Protestantism that didn't agree with her. In a fictionalized reminiscence of that visit she wrote that there was "a gloomy austerity about the Sabbath, as passed in my childhood, in Connecticut, that left unfavorable impressions on my mind." Sunday was a "day of gloom and dread."[11]

AT SOME POINT during her childhood, her brother Horatio started attending a preparatory school in town—boys only— to get him ready for entry to Dartmouth College, thirty miles from Newport and a two-day journey by horseback. When Horatio went off to Hanover, Sarah remained at home, pursuing a course of self-study and independent reading. Under Horatio's supervision, she strived to keep pace with what he was learning at college. During his long vacations from Dartmouth, Horatio oversaw his sister's progress in Latin, philosophy, and the other subjects that he was studying. "In childhood our studies had been pursued together," Hale later wrote, "and he seemed very unwilling that I should be deprived of all his collegiate advantages."[12]

Sarah's high-level course of self-study, enabled by Horatio, was about more than the acquisition of knowledge; it also had an impact on the development of her mind and her ability to think, reason, and write. "To my brother Horatio," she writes, "I owe what knowledge I have of Latin, of the higher branches of mathematics, and of mental philosophy. He often regretted that I could not, like himself have the privilege of a college education."[13] By the time of Horatio's graduation in 1809, Sarah Buell had received the rough equivalent of a Dartmouth education more than a century and a half before the first woman matriculated there in 1972. It was a singular accomplishment in an era when no American institution of higher education admitted women. Few women of her generation were as well educated as she.

In 1806, at the age of eighteen, with Horatio away at Dartmouth, Sarah made a decision that would have a deep impact on the course of her life: Life on the farm wasn't enough. She wanted to use the knowledge she had acquired by becoming a teacher, so she opened a school. Miss Buell's school was probably what was known in the parlance of the day as a dame school, a small, private school for young children that was run by a woman, often in her own home. Dame schools usually offered just the basics—the alphabet, beginner reading, addition and subtraction, perhaps writing. As a historian of the period has written, "In the early nineteenth century, women generally were not considered mentally suitable" for teaching anything beyond very elementary education. "A woman of a particular neighborhood, a widow or spinster perhaps, might

11

take small children into her home to teach them the rudiments of knowledge."[14]

Little is known about Sarah's school, including its location. The Buell residence on East Mountain would have been an unsuitable spot, too remote for youngsters to reach on foot. Local lore puts it in a section of Newport known as Guild, where the tiny one-room schoolhouse still stands. Legend further has it that this is the spot of the schoolroom incident that inspired Hale's most famous poem. It is not difficult to imagine a little lamb waiting outside the front door for a pupil by the name of Mary.

Sarah also taught briefly in the neighboring town of Croydon, which, if she took a shortcut through the woods and waded across the Sugar, was within walking distance of her home on East Mountain. A handwritten scholastic achievement certificate from Croydon, dated 1809, notes that one Sally Eastman "has learned her letters in six days." It is signed "Sarah J. Buell."[15] We know from Hale's later correspondence with Wheeler, the Newport town historian, that she spent six or eight weeks in Croydon. It is possible that she taught school to small children there, perhaps over the summer before opening her own school. Girls and small children were usually sent to school in the summer months, when the weather was fine and the walk to and from school was easier. Boys, who were needed for agricultural work at that time of year, attended school in winter.

Instruction in dame schools typically took the form of repetitive recitations of a set lesson, a style of learning called "blabbing." The teacher would stand in front of a class and spell a word or recite a sum. The boys and girls, speaking in unison, would then repeat the teacher's words. Sarah, however, set higher standards of achievement, using teaching methods that allowed students to advance at their own pace, much as she had done under her mother's supervision. Students were not allowed to blab.

Hale later drew upon her teaching experience for a short story titled "The Village Schoolmistress." "The business of instruction," the former schoolmistress writes, must be "esteemed amiable." It "must be divested of its associations of pretension and pedantry, and dullness and drilling." In her story, Hale presents the teacher's life as rewarding and enjoyable, and she encourages women to pursue teaching careers. A fictional character asks incredulously, "Whoever thought of associating pleasure with schoolkeeping?"[16] The enthusiasm with which the author answers that question makes it obvious that she found teaching a rewarding pursuit. As editor of the *Ladies' Magazine*, one of Hale's earliest campaigns on behalf of working women was to encourage communities to shake off old prejudices and hire women as teachers for the public schools.

Sarah's dame school was apparently successful, as it lasted four years. She stopped teaching in 1810, when her family moved to town and her parents presumably needed her help running the Rising Sun Tavern.

The year 1811 brought great sadness to the Buell family. Both Sarah's mother, Martha, and her younger sister, Martha Maria, died on the same day, November 25, probably of tuberculosis. It was four days after Thanksgiving. Martha was sixty years old and Martha Maria just eighteen. Early the following year, Gordon Buell decided that inn-keeping was too much for him, and he gave up the day-to-day management of the Rising Sun, eventually selling it. He and Sarah continued to live on the premises. It was there that Sarah met and fell in love with a fellow boarder, an amiable young lawyer who had newly set up practice in town. On October 23, 1813, the day before her twenty-fifth birthday, in the parlor of the Rising Sun Tavern, Sarah Josepha Buell, spinster, became Mrs. David Hale.

CHAPTER TWO

Wife and Widow

I N A LETTER to his sister at the time of her twenty-first birth-day, Horatio offered Sarah a piece of brotherly advice about marriage: Envy not young women who "flaunt and flutter," he told her. "It's true that these, generally speaking, get husbands the youngest." But "I am inclined to be skeptical whether their situation even after marriage is enviable." Horatio advised her to maintain her "dignity," to continue with her studies, and to wait for a man who will "soar above the worthless race of Poppin Jays" and "pleasure-seeking coxcombs."[1]

Sarah's choice of husband demonstrates that she took her brother's counsel to heart. David Hale was no more a popinjay or pleasure-seeking coxcomb than the cerebral Sarah could be said to flaunt and flutter. Theirs was a match made in heaven, a companionable union of intellectual equals. Years later, Sarah looked back on her marriage as a period of unbroken happiness.

David Hale grew up twenty-five miles south of Newport in the village of Alstead, New Hampshire. He was the eldest of fourteen children born to David and Hannah Hale. The Hales, like the Buells, came of Puritan stock and were ardent patriots. David's father fought in the Revolution and was a sentinel at the Battle of Bunker Hill. His mother, Hannah, was a descendant of Hannah Emerson Duston, a New England Puritan who, along with her newborn daughter, was famously taken hostage by Native Americans in 1697 in colonial Massachusetts. She escaped after killing and scalping her captors.[2] Cotton Mather recounted Hannah's abduction in 1702 in *The Ecclesiastical History of New-England*. More than a century later, Sarah Hale reimagined the attack on the Duston family in a poem that presented the perspective of Hannah's husband. "The Father's Choice"—like the twentieth-century novel *Sophie's Choice*—describes a parent's agonizing decision about which of his children to rescue from marauders. Nathaniel Hawthorne, Henry David Thoreau, and John Greenleaf Whittier also retold the story of the Native American attack on the Duston family.

Born in 1783, David Hale was five years older than Sarah. Like the Buells, the Hale family put a high value on learning. At least two of David's younger brothers graduated from Dartmouth. A third, Salma, became a U.S. senator from New Hampshire. In an era when the country had only one law school—in Litchfield, Connecticut— most would-be lawyers learned the law working side-by-side with an attorney. David studied with a lawyer in his hometown.

Upon being admitted to the bar in 1811, he set up practice in Newport, where he thrived. The town was growing rapidly, and the ambitious young attorney saw opportunities there that were not available in his hometown. He might have been lured to Newport by William Cheney, one of Newport's most successful businessmen. Cheney, who was seven years older than David, had also grown up in Alstead and moved to Newport in 1807.

So, too, Cheney may have helped David establish himself in Newport. In any case, the young lawyer soon developed a robust legal practice and became a justice of the peace. In 1819, he acted for the town in a petition to the state to divide the county in which Newport was located into two parts, with Newport as the seat of the new county. A biography of David found in a history of the judges and attorneys of New Hampshire remembers him thus: "Though he had not a collegiate education, his native thirst for knowledge and assiduous application enabled him to take rank with the best informed."[3] As with Sarah, the want of a college education appears to have been a major motivating factor for David. Both were lifelong learners. In his leisure time, David's passion was English literature, and he read widely in the classics.

After their marriage in 1813, the Hales moved into a spacious frame house in a new section of town. Their home was across from a marsh, which Cheney was instrumental in transforming into the village green. It was just a ten- or fifteen-minute walk from the Rising Sun Tavern in the town center. The two-story house in a classic New England saltbox design soon became known as Lawyer Hale's Mansion. Husband and wife established a satisfying joint routine of self-study. They would sit at a table in their sitting room every evening from eight o'clock to ten o'clock reading the classics, studying language and the sciences, and examining the prose style of the great English writers. "In this manner," Sarah later explained, "we studied French, Botany, then an almost new science in the country . . . and obtained some knowledge of Mineralogy, Geology, etc. besides pursuing a long and instructive course of reading."[4]

DURING THIS PERIOD Sarah, with her husband's encouragement, began to concentrate on her writing. Before her marriage, she had focused on writing poetry, but now she tried her hand at essays and short stories, writing under the pen name "Philo," Greek for "love." It was the first of several pen names she would adopt over the next few years to conceal her identity. Others were "Cornelia" and "A Lady of New-Hampshire." Pen names were the fashion of the day—men used them too—but they were especially handy for women who wished to remain out of the public eye, in keeping with prevailing standards of social decorum. Hale makes a telling point about the era's conventional views of marriage when she notes that her husband, not she, submitted several pieces of her writing to publications. If a lady had a husband, it was his responsibility to act for her in business matters.

Sarah also founded a local literary society in Newport. She dubbed it the "Coterie." The group was part book club, part writers workshop, and part current events discussion group. In some sense the Coterie was a forerunner of the lyceum movement, which promoted education through lectures, debates, classroom discussions, and entertainments. The lyceum movement took off in the 1820s, as lyceums and other cultural organizations with similar goals were founded in many American cities. One of the best-known lyceums opened in Boston in 1829 and hosted such literary lights as Edgar Allan Poe. The Coterie was a precursor, too, of the myriad women's organizations and private clubs for women founded after the Civil War for the purpose of discussing literature, history, and fine arts.

Members of the Newport Coterie would gather on pleasant afternoons in a meadow at the bend of a branch of the Sugar River, a short walk from the center of town. The group met in a tranquil spot along the water under the shade of two giant elms that had grown together so closely that they appeared as one. Newporters viewed the elms, with their intertwined branches, as a symbol of marriage and called them the "matrimonial tree." Situated on blankets under the matrimonial tree, members of the Coterie would read aloud, discuss current books and magazine articles, and critique the poems, essays, and fiction written by the aspiring authors in the group.[5]

The town of Newport was not home to any major cultural or educational institution, but it would be a mistake to think of it as an intellectual backwater. Other residents besides the Buells and the Hales were self-educated and well read and had access to family libraries, whose books they shared with neighbors. The Postal Act of 1792, which authorized low mailing rates for periodicals, made it possible for Newport residents to receive the newspapers and magazines published in the culturally more sophisticated urban centers of New York, Boston, and Philadelphia. So, too, the development of major roads brought Newporters in closer contact with the rest of the country. The Croydon Turnpike, built in 1806, and the Cornish Turnpike, finished in 1812, opened the town to travelers from the cities. Thanks to the turnpikes, Newport residents could travel more easily to Boston and elsewhere, carrying home books, periodicals, and new ideas. From her seat at the common table in the Rising Sun Tavern's dining room, Sarah listened to and learned from the stories of travelers who passed through Newport. It was an education in the wider world.

Despite these outside impressions, David was the most important influence on Sarah's early development as a writer. Looking back on her marriage at a time when she was well established as one of the country's leading editors, she wrote of David's "cool and sound judgment," his "refined taste," and his "perfectly balanced mind." She credited him for encouraging her to adopt a clear, forthright style of prose—that is, "pure idiomatic English." This wasn't always so, she confessed. She criticized her early writing as pompous and overblown, patterned on the eighteenth-century work of Samuel Johnson and, especially "Counselor Phillips," the nickname of the popular Irish writer and orator Charles Phillips, who was known for his florid prose. David set her the task of analyzing Phillips's prose, sentence by sentence, with the outcome that Sarah was persuaded to accept her husband's opinion that such writing was "sublime nonsense." David's feedback, coaching, and intellectual rigor along with his lawyerly insistence on clarity and concision were enormously valuable to her as she honed her writing skills.[6]

WRITING WASN'T the only activity that demanded Sarah's attention in the early years of her marriage. Babies arrived in the Hale household in quick succession. David Emerson was born in 1815. Horatio—named after her beloved brother—put in an appearance in 1817. Two girls—Frances Ann and Sarah Josepha—came along in 1819 and 1820, respectively. The younger Sarah Josepha would be known throughout her life as Josepha.

Up on the farm on East Mountain, Sarah's mother had seen to it that her daughter was well trained in cookery and the other essential arts of household management—skills that she would later call on for her writings on domestic science. Bringing up children and managing a household added up to a full-time job, or more. Lawyer Hale's household was prosperous enough to employ domestic help to assist Sarah in caring for the children and taking care of the house, allowing the mistress time to write as well as to pass the evenings in study with David.

Life for the Hale family was not without trials. In the autumn of 1818, when Sarah was pregnant with Frances, she fell seriously ill. She was diagnosed with consumption, the disease now known as pulmonary tuberculosis. TB is caused by bacteria that usually attack the lungs. As recently as the turn of the twentieth century, it was the leading cause of death in the United States, and in Sarah's time, it was considered a death sentence. It was the same disease that had taken her sister, Martha Maria, and probably their mother, in 1811.

David, however, was unwilling to accept his wife's fatal diagnosis. What happened next indicates the kind of man he was. Sarah's granddaughter gave the following account to Ruth Finley, whose biography of Sarah was published in 1931:

"It was the fall of the year," her granddaughter retells the story as Mrs. Hale told it to her listening grandchildren, "and the grapes were ripe. One evening David—your grandfather— had been reading aloud to me as I reclined on the sofa, when right in the middle of a sentence he suddenly closed the book and walked out of the house without a word. He was gone a long time. Where he went or what he did he never told me. But when he came back, he picked me up in his arms.

"'Listen,' he said, 'you are not going to die. I won't *let* you!'

"The very next morning we left the children . . . with their Aunt Hannah, and he and I started on a trip through the mountains in a gig. For six weeks we drove every day; it was beautiful weather; and I ate grapes. We had heard of the grape cure; so your grandfather decided to try it as a last resort. Also he had a theory that fresh air ought to be good for sick lungs. I remember we stopped at the doctor's house on the way out of town, and he vowed David would never bring me home alive. But David did bring me home, cured."[7]

David was ahead of his time. By the end of the nineteenth century, the fresh air cure that David had intuited was adopted as the most effective way to address the disease. TB sanitoriums located in the woods required their patients to adhere to a regimen of rest, a healthy diet, and outdoor exercise.

After Sarah's recovery, she and David had four more happy years together. Then, in the late summer of 1822, that September snowstorm hit. David contracted pneumonia and died on September 25. A month later, Sarah gave birth to the couple's fifth child, whom she named William George Hale.

SARAH JOSEPHA HALE, thirty-three years old, was now a widow with five children to support and educate. She was also penniless and in debt. While the family had lived comfortably on David's legal income, they had not put aside much in the way of savings. Nor could she turn to nearby male relatives for assistance. Her father had died in 1819. Her brother Charles, the sailor, had been missing for more than a decade and was presumed dead. Horatio, married with a family of his own in New York State, could not offer enough financial support to make a difference. Sarah, deemed insolvent by the probate court, had to endure the humiliation of having three court-appointed agents stationed in her home, where they negotiated financial settlements with the estate's creditors.[8]

As for self-support, the job prospects for a widow in a New England town in 1822 were limited, which is to say they were next to zero. Hale could have returned to teaching small children, but the pecuniary compensation, which might have been acceptable when she was a single woman living at home, would not have been sufficient to support a family. So she chose the only other option available to a woman of her class and background: sewing. With the financial backing of the Newport chapter of the Freemasons, of which David had been a popular member, she opened a millinery shop in her late husband's legal office. Her partner in the venture was David's unmarried, much younger sister, Hannah. A notice in the June 11, 1824, issue of the *Claremont Spectator* announced that "Mrs. & Miss H." have "obtained the latest and most approved fashions for Gowns, Spencers, Bonnets and Turbans, and intend keeping constantly for sale Fashionable Millinary" [*sic*]."

The business flourished—at least for Hannah. Sarah was a different story. The millinery trade held no charms for her. Her later tirades against fashion in the *Ladies' Magazine* and *Godey's Lady's Book* had their genesis during this unhappy period in her life. Another indication of her discontent is suggested in her 1833 short story "The Farmer and His Sons."[9] In this tale, a sailor son returns home a wealthy man after a long period away at sea. He arrives just in time to rescue from bankruptcy his brother, who has become blind, and his sister-in-law, who has been struggling to support the family by working as a milliner. Sarah frequently drew upon personal experiences for her fiction. Here, she was repurposing memories of her financial difficulties after David's death and daydreams that her lost brother Charles would miraculously reappear and rescue her.

Fifteen years after David's death, Hale remarked that during her marriage she wrote mostly for personal enjoyment and the "amusement of our own fireside," thereby giving the impression that she considered herself a mere dabbler at the craft of writing. "Till my husband's death . . . I had never seriously contemplated becoming an authoress," she explained.[10] That's probably true, even though the statement doesn't jibe with the fact that prior to David's death she had submitted her work for publication and remuneration. Much as she longed to write, a professional career as a writer would have been a near-impossible dream for a wife and mother of the era, even one who had her husband's backing. With the wolf at the door, however, Hale began to consider whether she could make a living doing what she loved best. The death of her husband was in some sense a personal liberation. If she hadn't been widowed, it is unthinkable that Hale—as talented as she was—would have risen to national prominence as a writer, editor, and social reformer.

In 1823 Hale's first book, a slim collection of poetry, was published in Concord, New Hampshire. The name of the author on the title page was, simply, "A Lady of New-Hampshire." She dedicated *The Genius of Oblivion* to "the friend and patrons of the author," by which she meant her late husband's brother Masons, who financed the book's publication. A dedicatory poem refers to the "Mystic Band . . . bending o'er a brother's early bier"—a reference to David's coffin—and ends with the lines

your patronage shall be my boast—
You kindly gave it when 'twas needed most.[11]

The volume sold for seventy-five cents. There is no surviving record of how many copies were sold or whether the author made any money on the book. In any case, the publication of *The Genius of Oblivion* seems to have provided a boost of self-confidence for Hale, who began to place her poems and short stories in popular periodicals in Boston, Philadelphia, and New York. She often wrote under the name "Cornelia." The pseudonym was a historical reference to the virtuous, cultured Roman wife and mother of the second century B.C. Hale identified with the Roman matron.

Among the periodicals for which she wrote were the *New-York Mirror*, a weekly devoted to arts and literature; the *American Monthly Magazine*, published in Philadelphia; and the *United States Review and Literary Gazette*, based in Boston. As the number of her publications mounted, "Cornelia" began to make a name for herself—to the extent that an editor might even announce to readers that there would be another offering by "Cornelia" in a coming edition. In 1826 she was invited to provide several entries in a popular annual gift volume titled *The Memorial: A Christmas and New Year's Offering*. A critic for the *United States Review and Literary Gazette* singled out her poem "The Muse's Hour" for praise.[12]

But it was the *Boston Spectator and Ladies' Album* that provided the biggest boost to Hale's career. Writing under the names "H.," "Cornelia," "Sarah," and "S.J.H.," Hale became a prolific contributor to the magazine. In 1826, she contributed seventeen poems, two short stories, and one critical review to the *Spectator*. She won twenty dollars—approximately five hundred dollars today—and a gold medal for her poem "Hymn to Charity," which the *Spectator* deemed the best poem in a contest it sponsored. She also won a volume of William Cowper's poetry for the best piece of prose contributed to the magazine and a volume of Milton's poetry for her poem "The Changing World."

Hale's early writing previewed some of the topics and themes she would take up as editor of the *Ladies' Magazine* and *Godey's Lady's Book*. Her 1824 poem "Stanzas: To a Deceased Husband" foreshadowed her deep interest in—obsession with, even—grief and mourning, subjects to which most women of the era could relate. She continued to write about death, and when she became editor of *Godey's Lady's Book*, she accepted and published numerous poems on the topic. Another poem, "The Patriot Mother," foreshadowed her interest in the Bunker Hill Monument, whose construction she championed in *Ladies' Magazine* in the 1830s.

Her editorial decision to focus the content of her magazines on American themes and American authors was explained in a short story titled "Country Literature." In the story a fictional character objects that too many Americans are importing their literary opinions from England. "Why this homage is worse than the 'tea tax,'" he complains, "and I am surprised that our literary men do not enter into a combination to resist such encroachments on the freedom of their minds."[13] It would fall not just to the nation's "literary men" but to Hale herself, a literary woman, to lead that resistance.

BY 1826, the reluctant milliner was spending less and less time sewing bows and ribbons on ladies' hats. She left the affairs of the millinery business in the hands of her sister-in-law while she toiled at her writing table. At the same time Hale was busy establishing herself as a popular writer of verse and prose, she also was at work on her first novel. *Northwood: A Tale of New England* came out in 1827, when William was four years old. Hale wrote in a preface to a later edition that the book "was written literally with my baby in my arms." The publisher was Bowles & Dearborn, in Boston, which published it in two volumes. This time the "Lady of New-Hampshire," also known as "Cornelia" or "S.J.H.," decided to come out of hiding. The title page bore the true name of the author: Mrs. S.J. Hale. It was a personal declaration of independence. From the publication of *Northwood* onward, Hale considered herself a professional writer.

Northwood holds a serious place in American literary history for several reasons. It was a milestone in early fiction by American women. It was one of the first novels to address head-on the issue of slavery. And, third, it painted a detailed, true-to-life portrait of the lifestyles and attitudes that prevailed in New England in the post-revolutionary period.

The novel recounts the story of Sidney Romilly, the oldest son of a New Hampshire farm family who has been sent away to be raised as a gentleman by wealthy slave-owning relations in South Carolina. At the age of twenty-four Sidney returns home, where he falls in love with a local girl and gains insights into her antislavery values. Most of *Northwood* is set in the actual town of that name, an obvious stand-in for Hale's hometown of Newport. Hale had never traveled to the South, and while it is possible that she may have encountered Southerners on one of her few trips outside Newport, her depictions of the South, slavery, and Southerners are wholly imagined and not always fully credible. With the exception of Harriet Beecher Stowe, whose best-selling *Uncle Tom's Cabin* came out in 1852, few novelists dared address the subject prior to the Civil War. Hale may have been the first American writer to set a novel against the background of slavery.

If *Northwood*'s depictions of the South were not always rooted in reality, those of a New England town during the post-revolutionary era were spot on. They were both historically accurate and cinematic in detail, from the portrait of Washington hanging over the fireplace in the Romilly sitting room to the description of the calico gowns worn by the Romilly girls. Historian Ernest L. Scott Jr. writes that *Northwood* replicates "old Puritan ways: the values, theological disputes, and the solidarity of family and the unity of family and town that had evolved in America."[14] The chapter devoted to a description of a Yankee Thanksgiving is captivating. Readers can practically smell the turkey and hear the children galloping through the parlor on their way to the dinner table. Twenty years later, in 1847, Hale would launch her campaign for a national Thanksgiving Day in the pages of *Godey's Lady's Book*. The love of the holiday she campaigned for was evident in *Northwood*.

Hale's views on women's education are glimpsed in *Northwood* as well. Of all of Hale's many causes, education for women was the one for which she fought longest and hardest—from the moment she took up the editorship of the *Ladies' Magazine* in 1828 until the moment she set down her pen as editor of *Godey's Lady's*

Book in 1877. In *Northwood*, Squire Romilly explains to an English visitor that "every child in the New England States has the privilege of attending free schools." Little Mary, one of the Romilly children, announces that she is "at the head of my class." Squire Romilly tells his visitor that "universal education" is the "foundation on which we are rearing the imperishable structure of our liberties and national glory." The singling out of Mary signals the importance Hale attaches to the education of girls, who will grow up to be mothers with the responsibility of molding their sons and daughters into patriotic, productive citizens.

Northwood was well received. Poet William Cullen Bryant gave it a glowing review in the *United States Review and Literary Gazette,* which he coedited. American books were beginning to be noticed across the Atlantic, he noted approvingly, and *Northwood* "adds another proof . . . that neither talents nor materials are wanting in our country." He praised Hale's "simple and expressive" writing style, which showed "very little affectation." He liked the "cheerful and benevolent spirit . . . that pervades the book, a disposition to find food for happiness, and not for discontent in the vicissitudes of life."[15]

These attributes—a declarative, direct prose style and an upbeat tone—were hallmarks of Hale's writing for the rest of her life, finding their greatest expression in her work in the *Ladies' Magazine* and *Godey's Lady's Book. Northwood* was published in England—a rare honor for an American novel. It was reissued in the United States in 1852, when, in the wake of the success of *Uncle Tom's Cabin,* Hale correctly perceived that it might attract a new generation of readers.

THE SUCCESS OF *Northwood* brought a flood of fan letters to Hale in Newport congratulating her on her novel. One such letter reached her hands toward the end of 1827. The name on the envelope was one she didn't know—the Reverend John Lauris Blake. Upon opening it, she was astonished to learn that Blake, an Episcopal clergyman in Boston and head of a school for girls, was writing to offer her a job. He was starting up a magazine, one aimed at women. He wanted her to come to Boston to edit it.

It is unclear why Blake picked Hale, whom he hadn't met, as the person best suited to be the founding editor of the *Ladies' Magazine*. The nascent American literary world was small, and it is possible that the Boston editors with whom Hale worked had spoken to Blake on her behalf. It might also have had something to do with the fact that Blake had grown up in Northwood, New Hampshire—the real Northwood, that is, not the fictional one. He would have had local contacts who could have assured him of Hale's character and abilities. Another possibility is that Blake's decision was connected with his membership in the Freemasons, the Newport lodge of which had supported the widow Hale after the death of her husband. Perhaps word of Hale's talent had reach him through one or more of David's brother Masons.

Whatever Blake's reasons for offering her the editorship, Hale accepted. She later wrote that her main reason for taking the job was that it would give her the means to educate her children as their father would have done. The immediate consequence of her decision, though, was that she couldn't afford to keep the family together. All but one of the children were dispersed to live with relatives while Hale made the move to Boston. Hannah, Hale's sister-in-law the milliner, took in the eldest, David. He was twelve. Horatio, ten years old, went to live with his Uncle Horatio in New York State. The two girls, Frances (age nine) and Josepha (age eight), were sent to Keene, New Hampshire, to stay with their father's younger brother Salma and his wife. The baby of the family, William, was the only child who accompanied his mother to Boston.

The heartbreak of being separated from four of her children was compounded by the pain inflicted by friends who disapproved of her decision to accept the job. A contemporary of Hale's later remarked that many of the editor's Newport friends considered it an "absurd project." They warned Hale that when she failed in Boston, as she inevitably was destined to do, and was forced to return to Newport, she would have lost the sympathy and patronage of "those who had generously employed her to trim their old bonnets."[16]

Hale edited the first four issues of the *Ladies' Magazine* from Newport, before packing up, taking Willie by the hand, and boarding a stagecoach for Boston in the spring of 1828. The stagecoach departed from the Rising Sun, the tavern her father had built and the place where she met and married David. It was a potent symbol of all she was leaving behind.

In a few months she would turn forty. She was a relatively novice writer; the first of her work had debuted in the serious metropolitan journals only five years previously. The variety of intellectual topics with which she was conversant was limited by her life experience in a small New England town. The only editing she had done was that of the amateur writers who belonged to the Newport Coterie. She had little clue about the practicalities of running a magazine—commissioning articles, setting deadlines, supervising printers, meeting budgets. She was launching a project—a magazine for women—that hadn't succeeded in the past. In the world of journalism, her place—as the female editor of an intellectual journal—was unheard of, and she was criticized, condemned even, for daring to accept it. In short, she was an unlikely editor, as well as an untutored one, which made the success of the *Ladies' Magazine* all the more remarkable.

CHAPTER THREE

The Ladies' Magazine

S ARAH JOSEPHA HALE was wont to say that she was the
first woman to edit an American magazine. That is not
strictly accurate, but it is close to the truth. Hale was the first
woman to *succeed* in the risky business of running a magazine.
While there were lady editors before Hale, their publications
were short-lived, their influence was slight, and their names are
now mostly forgotten.[1]

In the early years of the American Republic and into the first
quarter of the nineteenth century, magazines came and went
with great rapidity. But by 1825, three years before the first issue of the *Ladies' Magazine* rolled off the presses, there were
212 magazines in print, compared with just 82 in 1810 and a
mere 16 in 1793.[2] A tiny number were aimed at women. Most of
those offered trivial fare such as lurid short stories about separated lovers, villainous seducers, and romances that ended in
tragedy. Flowery poetry and advice columns on acquiring and
keeping husbands were other staples of the genre. Some of the

popular general-interest magazines published women's pages, with similar non-serious content.

An exception to this model was the *Boston Spectator and Ladies' Album*, which debuted in 1825 with a promise "to entertain the hours of leisure with original essays on life, manners, religion, and morals."[3] It lasted just two years, but not before making an important contribution to the nation's literary life by introducing to its readers a poetess called Cornelia. Cornelia was revealed as Sarah Josepha Hale when she won the magazine's annual literary prize in 1827. The unmasking likely helped her get the job as editor of the *Ladies' Magazine*.

As a writer who had spent the past several years seeking outlets for her work, Hale was aware of the precarious nature of the magazine industry and the string of start-ups and shutdowns. As she embarked on her new career as editor of the *Ladies' Magazine*, she was either confident enough in her abilities or desperate enough in her personal financial straits to believe she had a chance of making her magazine a success. In any case, she chose to ignore the warning of Noah Webster—he of later dictionary fame—who remarked about the start-up of his own magazine forty years earlier that "the expectation of failure is connected with the very name of a Magazine."[4]

HALE'S *Ladies' Magazine* debuted in January 1828. From the inaugural issue, it was clear that it was something different from the women's fare that had preceded it. It was a serious intellectual journal with an editor who was intent on exploring the potentially explosive topic of the role of the American woman in modern society. The editorial philosophy that Hale would advance over the next fifty years of her editorships was evident from the first issue: advocacy of female education, encouragement of American writers and American subject matter, and promotion of female leadership in charitable causes.

In introducing the *Ladies' Magazine* to readers, Hale announced on the first page that "no experiment will have an influence more important on the character and happiness of our society, than the granting to females the advantages of a systematic and thorough education." Why? An educated woman would be a "rational companion" to her husband and a "competent" mother to her children, teaching them from infancy to love "all that is great and good" and to practice "piety and virtue."[5] This, in essence, was the doctrine of republican motherhood, which took hold around the time of the American Revolution. It centered on the belief that women needed to be educated so they could better instruct their children in the new republic's civic virtues.

Over the next half century at the *Ladies' Magazine* and *Godey's Lady's Book*, Hale didn't waver from her view that marriage and motherhood were the primary responsibilities and largest sources of satisfaction for women, even as she fought to advance educational and professional opportunities for them. On this point, she was a woman of her time, reflecting the prevailing views about women's paramount duties to their families. So, too, she concurred—but only up to a point—with the popular opinion that men and women should operate in separate spheres, with the principal zone of operation for women being the home.

Hale was conservative, but she wasn't closed-minded. As time passed, she would expand her list of the benefits of educating women to include useful work by which they could make contributions to society. She campaigned for the entry of women into many jobs that heretofore had been closed to them. This line of thinking was previewed in the first year of her editorship of the

Ladies' Magazine, when she wrote that she was in the process of formulating her views on how educated women should use their learning. She posed the question: Are the young women who were studying in private academies or seminaries being educated for learned professions rather than to be good wives and mothers? Using the editorial "we," she replied to her own question: "We [shall] have more to say on this particular, at a future time."[6] Later that year she opined on women and happiness: "I would have them seek some employment, have some *aim* that will, by giving energy to their minds, and the prospect of honorable independence, should they choose to continue single, make them less dependent on *marriage* as the means of *support*."[7]

Hale would develop these ideas more fully in future issues of the *Ladies' Magazine* and then at the *Lady's Book*. But in her introductory essay for the inaugural issue of the *Ladies' Magazine*, perhaps in part because she saw it as the winning argument, Hale kept her focus on educating women for the purpose of ensuring that they would be better wives and mothers.

In an era when it was common for a man to control what his wife and daughters read, Hale used the introduction to make a pitch for her new magazine to the men who had the authority to allow it into the house and the financial resources to buy subscriptions: that is, fathers, husbands, brothers, suitors. Yes, this was a magazine for women, but she invited gentlemen to examine it and judge its contents. The father will find nothing "to weaken parental authority." The husband "may rest assured that nothing found on the pages of this publication shall cause [his wife] to be less assiduous in preparing for his reception or less sincere in welcoming his return." As for the "favored lover," ah, he can win the affection of his lady by buying her a subscription. Instead of gazing on "that inconstant thing, the moon, so often obscured by clouds," his lady love will cast her eyes on the "pure pages" and improving content of Hale's magazine.[8]

Hale employed a light touch and a smattering of humor when asking male readers for their stamp of approval. Even so, her deferential language and acceptance of men's authority over their female relatives can raise hackles when read in the twenty-first century. Put in the context of the social mores of the day, though, her reasons for reaching out to the men were pragmatic. No women's magazine could succeed if men objected to it. If she wanted to persuade the public of the value of female education, she first had to get the attention of men, who could make it happen.

The *Ladies' Magazine*'s first issue was a trumpet fanfare for what was to come. Over the following nine years, Hale never let up. Every issue of the *Ladies' Magazine* had something to say on the subject of women's education. The magazine quickly became the national bulletin board for developments in women's education around the country. It was the go-to place for learning about new schools for women, educational philosophy, teaching techniques, innovative educators, and more.

She urged women to study chemistry, biology, geology, physics, minerology, and other sciences—subjects that traditionally were considered too taxing for the female intellect. She published reading lists and self-study advice for readers who wished to extend their knowledge and improve their minds. She cited the benefits of physical activity for girls and women, pooh-poohing prevailing notions that women were too delicate for exercise or that it was improper for girls to behave like boys.

In an 1830 letter to Catherine Fiske, head of the school Frances Ann and Josepha attended in Keene, New Hampshire, Hale showed that she practiced what she preached when it came to her own family. "I have written to my daughters many directions respecting their exercises," she told Miss Fiske, "and I wish you would use particular care that they do exercise. . . . Children will play if it is allowed them, but young misses who are studiously inclined need some stimulus to active exercises."[9]

Hale vigorously defended learned women who were derided as "bluestockings," a derogatory term for women with intellectual or literary interests. She found the word repulsive—reflecting prejudices that should be stamped out. She rejected it, too, as injurious to the cause of higher education for women in that it demeaned their intellectual accomplishments, discouraging others from pursuing academic learning. She spoke bluntly about the "evil" to which educated women are subjected. "It is to have cultivated minds, and yet be confined to a society that does not understand and cannot appreciate their talents and intelligence. This frequently occurs."[10]

She pushed for public funding of institutions of higher education for women. Of the 131 American colleges that received public support, she noted despairingly in 1835, the number that admitted women was zero. She urged private donations to women's schools, excoriating Mrs. Christopher Gore of Boston—widow of a former governor of Massachusetts—for leaving a bequest of $50,000 to Harvard University rather than for the purpose of founding an institution that educated women. She asked, "When will women learn that the most effectual way in which they can promote the great interests of literature, morality and piety, is to provide for the instruction of their own sex?"[11] She pressed this cause for the rest of her life, including in connection with her work on the founding of Vassar College in the late 1860s.

As for female employment, she advanced the idea of vocational training for women that would lead to remunerative work, and she published articles advocating that women be trained for jobs as nurses and cooks—occupations traditionally filled by men. She railed against schools for women that emphasized such traditional feminine pursuits as singing, drawing, fancy needlework, and playing the piano while neglecting academic excellence. Students at such schools might master fashionable accomplishments, in her opinion, but they didn't receive an education.

STARTING IN 1829, the *Ladies' Magazine*'s second year of publication, Hale began to publish profiles of the best schools for young ladies around the country, delineating their educational philosophy, curriculum, staff, and rates. One example will suffice to show Hale's method. In December 1833, she devoted four and half pages to a description of Miss Fiske's Young Ladies Seminary in Keene, New Hampshire—a school she knew well since her two daughters attended it. Miss Fiske's school offered a four-year curriculum that included astronomy, geology, chemistry, botany, algebra, geometry, and other subjects not usually considered suitable for women. Miss Fiske is quoted approvingly on her goals for her students: "We expect woman to be qualified to think with candor—act with justice—counsel with kindness—and direct with wisdom." This is a magnificent mission statement for any school—then or now, for women or for men. The cost of attending Miss Fiske's school was one hundred dollars for forty-eight weeks of tuition and board plus six dollars for fuel. There were extra charges for languages, music, and art.[12]

Hale gave similar treatment to numerous other schools for girls, including Catholic schools, whose academic rigor she admired but which she saw as in competition with schools run by Protestants, the country's dominant faith. Her aim was twofold:

to provide information to parents considering schools for their daughters and to share information with teachers and administrators who could learn from the examples of others. In addition to profiling schools, she also published articles by or about the prominent female educators of the day, including Emma Willard of Troy, New York; Catharine Beecher of Hartford and later Cincinnati; and Sarah Pierce of Litchfield, Connecticut. Willard, whom Hale met when their sons were cadets at West Point, became a close friend. Hale wrote admiringly of Willard's work in the *Ladies' Magazine* and published several of Willard's essays. Their friendship foundered when Hale appeared to favor Willard's estranged second husband, who proved to be a reprobate.

By 1835, Hale began to write optimistically about the pace of change regarding attitudes on educating women in a new column bearing the headline, "Progress of Society." Using the editorial "we," she commented:

> Seven years ago when our Magazine was first commenced but very little public attention was paid to this subject. We would not be understood as boasting that our labors alone have wrought this change, but we may claim that we have pursued a systematic and persevering course in endeavoring to do this—and now we scarcely open a newspaper, a periodical or a new book that does not contain sentiments respecting the capacities and powers of women.[13]

By June 1835 she was ecstatic to report about the progress made toward the establishment of Mount Holyoke Female Seminary in South Hadley, Massachusetts. Reporting that $10,000 had been raised for that project, she enthused that "the great work of *beginning* is accomplished. . . . Soon, very soon, a permanent system of Female Education will be established in our land."[14] Mount Holyoke received its charter as a teaching seminary in 1836 and opened its doors in 1837.

HALE'S INTRODUCTION in the first issue of the *Ladies' Magazine* also promised that the new magazine would be thoroughly American. It would contain "well written communications, whether poems, letters, sketches, tales, or essays, descriptive of American scenery, character, and manners."[15]

The newbie editor didn't yet have the contacts or the budget to commission as many original articles as she would like, so she ended up writing much of the content of the early issues herself—as much as 50 percent in some months. The inaugural issue contained poetry, fiction, and essays by the editor. She even penned a letter to the editor—and replied to herself.

Despite her goal of publishing only original content, Hale occasionally reprinted material that had appeared elsewhere. She always did so with due credit and usually with extensive analysis and editorializing. She would use the reprinted material as a jumping-off point from which to present her own thoughts. In the first issue, she published lengthy excerpts of a lecture delivered by a minister in New Hampshire making the case for "Female Education," as she titled the excerpt. In her commentary, Hale took the opportunity to deplore the fact that state legislatures had not established colleges or endowed professorships for the education of young women. She also vehemently expressed her dissatisfaction with Boston's recently announced decision to close its public high school for girls. She acerbically noted that the public high school helped the poor, not just the rich, to get an education. Girls from rich families could afford to attend one of Boston's many private academies for young women. With the closure of the public high school, girls from families of lesser means were now out of luck.[16]

Hale has sometimes been criticized for not paying enough attention to the plight of poor women and their special difficulties in obtaining an education and finding work. It is true that middle-class women were the main readers of her magazines. But she wrote frequently about the poor and devoted much of her philanthropic work to organizations aimed at helping them rise out of poverty. To give a single example of the kind of empathetic articles she published about poverty, in 1834 she recounted a poignant anecdote about an illiterate frontier mother who taught her children to read with a hymnal, the only book she owned other than the Bible. The mother, who knew the hymns by heart, would sing the words and the children would spell them out.[17]

A monthly feature by Hale titled "Sketches of American Character" debuted in the *Ladies' Magazine*'s inaugural issue. A literary sketch was a term popularized by Washington Irving and referred to short, descriptive pieces of fiction or nonfiction. Hale's column was a huge hit with readers—so popular that Putnam & Hunt, publisher of the magazine, couldn't meet the demand for a complete set of the twelve issues of *Ladies' Magazine* published in 1828. Responding to public demand, Putnam & Hunt collected the sketches in a book, which it published in 1829. The book—titled, like the column, *Sketches of American Character*—was also popular, going into several editions. A later *Ladies' Magazine* series with a similar approach, *Traits of American Life*, was similarly collected and sold in a single volume. *Sketches of American Character* sold almost one hundred thousand copies, the definition of a best seller in the 1820s.[18]

Each sketch was an original short story, written by Hale,

that recounted the tale of a fictional character who exemplified some aspect of the national character. Every entry in the series carried a moral, often about good citizenship. The first sketch, "Walter Wilson," told the story of a wild, idle boy who grew up to be a successful, honored man thanks to the tutelage of his grandfather, who had fought in the Revolution. The story concludes with a patriotic message about how any person who works hard can succeed in America. It was a paean to the country's founding generation—a theme that would appear repeatedly throughout Hale's editorial career.[19]

Later sketches that year explored more contentious subjects, including women's financial dependence on men, the difficulties women faced in securing an education, and working women. It sometimes seemed that Hale was able to let loose in her fiction, drawing on her own personal experiences and frustrations. She often spoke more forcefully about women's issues in her short stories than in her essays and editorials. She seemed able to free herself to express her inner outrage over women's lack of opportunities even while presenting positive depictions of marriage, motherhood, and family life.

Three sketches published in 1828 condemned laws or practices that denied women financial independence and the ability to make decisions for themselves. In one sketch, a woman forfeits her personal fortune when she marries without the consent of her uncle, who controls her money. A second story tells of a young widow who is left penniless after her brother, who didn't approve of the man she married, refuses to hand over the annuity that their father left her. In a third story, two sisters, untutored in financial matters, blow through their inheritance and are reduced to relying on relatives to support them.[20]

Another sketch, "The Village Schoolmistress," made the case

for the suitability of women as teachers.[21] Teaching in 1828 was not a women's profession. In the prevailing view, women were intellectually inferior to men, capable of teaching very young children but not older ones. Hale argued that the two sexes had equal intellectual capabilities but lacked equal educational opportunities. A correctly educated woman could teach as well as an educated man, she believed, and she was an early proponent of opening the profession to women. Her advocacy in the *Ladies' Magazine*, and later in *Godey's Lady's Book*, helped build public support for her favored outcome. By the 1840s, women were entering the teaching profession in large numbers.

THE FIRST YEAR of the *Ladies' Magazine* signaled Hale's debut as a lady of letters. The intellectual journals of the day reviewed the latest books, and Hale's magazine followed suit—with an important difference. She paid special attention to offerings by American writers, especially women, whose work she showcased. "There is no sex in talents, in genius," she wrote.[22]

Hale was a confident literary critic. She had read widely, studied the classics, and spent many hours critiquing literature with her late husband at the worktable in their Newport sitting room. She had high standards, she knew what she liked, and she expressed her views forcefully. She tartly told aspiring contributors to the *Ladies' Magazine* that she wasn't interested in publishing "long, lovesick, lamentable tales, written without plan or aim, and only concluded when the author has exhausted every five syllable word to be found" in the dictionary.[23]

Over the nine years of the existence of the *Ladies' Magazine*, Hale published, reviewed, or excerpted dozens of books by women, many of whose careers she helped launch and whose thinking—especially on female education—she helped popularize.

She took pride in publishing a high standard of literary work. In an 1834 essay titled "Literature for Ladies," she excoriated most published prose aimed at female readers as "trashy and vapid." The press is "teeming" with publications for ladies, which are "poured forth in one weak, washing, everlasting flood" of frivolity.[24] She encouraged women to read nonfiction, especially American political history.

In January 1834, as the magazine was entering its seventh year of publication, Hale noted that her contributors included "almost all the distinguished literary ladies of our country." She singled out for mention Lydia Sigourney, Catharine Sedgwick, Caroline Gilman, Emma Embury, Lydia Maria Child, Hannah Flagg Gould, Anna Maria Wells, Emma Willard, Almira Phelps, "and others who have preferred to remain incognito." Most of these writers and their work will not be familiar to modern readers, but they were popular and influential in their day.[25]

She frequently cited Lydia Maria Child, a prolific writer, ardent abolitionist, and champion of the rights of women and Native Americans. Hale called Child "a lady of the first literary achievements" and praised many of her books, including the best-selling *Frugal Housewife*. Hale especially liked the message that *The Frugal Housewife* sent to sophisticated young women who thought they were above housework: "Here then is proof that learning, imagination, genius, do not unfit a lady for domestic usefulness."[26]

Another Lydia often appeared in the *Ladies' Magazine*, beginning in its first year of publication, cloaked in the initials L.H.S.—for Lydia Huntley Sigourney. Sigourney contributed numerous poems, almost always under her initials, as there was a Mr. Sigourney back home in Hartford who disapproved of his wife's name appearing in print. In 1830, Hale published Sigourney's essay "Comparative Intellect of the Sexes," giving it the publication's most prominent front-page placement. "The sexes are intended for different spheres and constructed in conformity to their respective destinations by Him," wrote "L.H.S.," "but disparity does not necessarily imply inferiority."[27]

The two Lydias—Child and Sigourney—were, like Hale, among the first American women to earn their livings by their pens. Hale's recognition of the value of their writing helped to establish their reputations as among the finest female writers of the first half of the nineteenth century.

When it came to literature—written by women or men—Hale was something of a talent spotter. In 1828, the *Ladies' Magazine* was one of only a handful of periodicals to notice *Fanshawe*, the first novel of an anonymous young author. She gave it a rave review. Don't borrow it from a library, she advised. Rather, "Purchase it, reader. There is but one volume, and trust me that is worth placing in your library." The unnamed author was Nathaniel Hawthorne, then twenty-four years old.[28]

Two years later she singled out for praise a work by another unknown young writer, Edgar Allan Poe. Poe's book of verse, *Al Aaraaf, Tamerlane, &c*, had gone largely unremarked by other critics. "The author, who appears to be very young, is evidently a fine genius; but he wants judgment, experience, tact," Hale wrote, comparing him to Shelley.[29]

Not long after Hale's review of *Tamerlane* appeared, Poe entered the U.S. Military Academy at West Point, where Hale's eldest son, David, also a cadet, made his acquaintance. In early February 1831, David wrote his mother about Poe, telling her that he had "communicated what you wrote to Mr. Poe," referring to her review of *Tamerlane*. He "is thought a fellow of talent here," David wrote, "but he is too much a poet to like Mathematics."[30] Shortly after David wrote these words, Poe—who had stopped attending classes and participating in cadet parades—was court-martialed and expelled. The army's loss was literature's gain. Poe and Hale went on to develop a close working relationship.

A third young writer who caught Hale's eye was Nathanial Parker Willis, better known by his byline N.P. Willis. Willis was a prolific author of prose and poetry in the mid-nineteenth century. He was one of the best-known and best-paid writers of his day. Willis was in his early twenties and just out of Yale when Hale wrote favorably about him in 1828. In 1829, when she invited him to write for the *Ladies' Magazine*, he responded, with more than a touch of youthful arrogance, that she couldn't afford him. "You could not afford . . . the price which my poetry brings me," he wrote in reply. "I get for every article five dollars and often more." Willis was probably right that Hale wouldn't be able to pay him what he wanted. She settled for reprinting several pieces of prose that he had written for other publications.[31]

Hale published works by other eminent authors. The Quaker poet John Greenleaf Whittier contributed "Metacom," a stirring poem about the heroic death of the Native American chief—also known as King Philip—in King Philip's War. James Fenimore Cooper—the celebrated author of the 1826 novel *The Last of the Mohicans* and many other works set on the American frontier—contributed a short story about Europeans' humorous misunderstandings of Americans. Hale translated the story from the French in which Cooper had written it. She reprinted William Cullen Bryant's mournful poem "June" about a man contemplating his own grave, calling him "one of the brightest lights of American genius" and his work an exemplification of "the kind of poetry we need in our country."[32]

Hale had a broad set of interests, and the books she selected for review or excerpt ranged widely. Fiction and poetry loomed large, and she paid special attention to the annual gift volumes such as *The Token* and *The Atlantic Souvenir,* which collected prose and poetry by American authors—sometimes including Hale. Such compilations helped foster and elevate the literary tastes of Americans, she believed, as well as display the talents of American writers.

She reviewed numerous books on science, a heretofore-neglected area of study for girls and young women. In keeping with her campaign for public schools to hire female teachers, she recommended books on teaching techniques. She published reviews of the annual reports of the American Institute of Instruction, which she routinely lambasted for failing to acknowledge and support the growing number of female teachers. Native American history and lore constituted another subject of interest; she was highly sympathetic to their plight, in one review referring to the "unfeeling rapaciousness of the white man."[33] Juvenile literature held great interest for her too, and she admired works for children that both entertained and instructed them. Travel literature that offered insights into foreign countries—especially other societies' treatment of women—also caught her eye.

HALE'S BREADTH of interests curiously didn't extend to a topic that one would think would be *de rigueur* for the editor of a women's magazine: fashion. She abhorred fashion, refusing at first even to cover it in the *Ladies' Magazine.*

Her antipathy to fashion—"that ever-changing, fantastical Divinity"—predated her move to Boston. Perhaps it was linked to her unhappy stint in the millinery business, when she earned her living by sewing bows on bonnets for condescending town matrons. While still in Newport, she touched on the subject of American fashion in *Northwood,* her 1827 novel. She described with approval the simple attire of two "neatly dressed" young ladies in her fictional New England village. The sisters

> were habited precisely alike, in dresses of American calico, in which deep blue was the prevailing color. The frocks were fitted closely to the form, fastened behind with blue buttons, and displaying the finely rounded symmetry of the shape to the greatest advantage. The frocks were cut high in front, concealing all the bosom but the white neck, which was un-covered and ornamented—when does a girl forget her or-naments?—with several strings of braided beads, to imitate a chain; and no eye that rested on those lovely necks would deem they needed richer adornments. The only difference in their costume was in the manner they dressed their hair. Sophia, the eldest and tallest, confined hers on top of the head with a comb, and Lucy let hers flow in curls around the neck. Both fashions were graceful and becoming.[34]

As editor of the *Ladies' Magazine,* Hale wanted to encourage an American style of attire—just as she wished to cultivate an indigenous American literature. "Are we always to be indebted to Paris and London for our mode of dress?" she asked readers in 1830, the outrage obvious in her question. "Shall the taste-ful and elegant ladies of Boston and New-York never venture to decide on the proper and becoming for themselves? Shall we never be fashionably independent—republicans in costume as well as character?"[35]

At the *Ladies' Magazine,* she kept returning to the themes of neatness and simplicity as the appropriate American style of dress. "We would not have ladies despise or neglect dress," she wrote. "They should be careful to be always fit to be seen— personal neatness is indispensable to agreeableness—almost to virtue." But—and here she reveals a deeper objection to fash- ion—"There are objects more worthy to call forth the energies of rational beings than the tie of a cravat, or the trimming of a bonnet."

In short, Hale believed that fashion was a waste of time and money. The lady who devotes herself to following fashion "has wasted her time, lost opportunities of moral and mental im- provement, neglected the education of her children and the du- ties of benevolence, and most probably disturbed her husband's peace by her caprices, if she have not seriously embarrassed him by her extravagances." Sometimes her tirades against fash- ion bordered on the silly, as when she opined that the Empress Josephine would have been happier after her divorce from Na- poleon had she consoled herself with more useful activities than "decorating her person for admiration."[36]

She also objected to the health and safety risks taken by "fashionists"—a precursor of the word "fashionista," a mod- ern-day appellation for women who love clothes. She raged against heels that were too high, dresses that were too flimsy for winter weather, and corsets that were laced too tightly. She lamented the craze for unnaturally small waists.

When the *Ladies' Magazine* was first established, Hale had resolved not to publish fashion plates. But in 1830, she changed her mind and included a fashion engraving in the November is- sue. By the beginning of 1832 she was promising that more fash- ion plates would appear in the coming year. She explained that "reflection and the counsel of judicious friends" had changed her mind. She now deemed it wise to publish fashion plates for the purpose of explaining why women shouldn't worship the gods of fashion. She informed her readers that she would take the opportunity of publishing fashion plates so that she could occasionally give readers "a lecture on these evils."[37]

Talk about contrived reasoning. The real reason she allowed fashion plates to darken the pages of the *Ladies' Magazine* was that she had been persuaded they were a necessary evil. Hale realized that if her publication was going to compete effectively with the new magazines challenging the *Ladies' Magazine*'s preeminent place in the women's market, she would have to give readers what they wanted, including fashion.

In personal life, Hale's single concession to fashion was her hairstyle. Like most women of her era, she parted her long hair in the center and pinned it up in the back. On the two sides, she wore "pipe curls," also known as "rag curls." The curls, which dangled over her ears, resembled short lengths of pipe. They were fashioned from rags, which the wearer knotted into strands of hair and wore overnight. Pipe curls first became popular early in the nineteenth century, and Hale was faithful to them for the rest of her life—apparently indifferent to the fact that the hairstyle had long since gone out of fashion by her twilight years.

Hale's style of dress was far removed from the elaborate European fashions she railed against, but neither was it simple American calico. After David's death in 1822 until her own passing in 1879, she wore black as a sign of perpetual mourning. She would sometimes add a touch of white—a style known as half mourning—as seen in an 1831 portrait in which a narrow border of a white under-blouse peeks out from under Hale's black dress.[38] Bombazine—a dull black fabric made of silk and wool—was a typical fabric for ladies' mourning dresses. Dr. Oliver Wendell Holmes referred to Hale as the "lady in bombazine" in his 1858 best seller, *The Autocrat of the Breakfast Table*, which relates conversations among the residents of a Boston boardinghouse in the 1830s. Holmes, then a young medical student in Boston, lived at the same boardinghouse as Hale and her son William.[39]

Under the social conventions regulating mourning in the nineteenth century, widows were expected to wear black for two years. Some bereaved women, such as Hale, chose to remain in black for the rest of their lives. First Lady Sarah Polk similarly wore mourning from the time her husband, President James Polk, died in 1849 until her own passing in 1891.

WHEN SHE MOVED to Boston in 1828, Hale had been widowed for six years, long past the time that widows were expected to remain in black. She may have had a reason beyond honoring the memory of her late husband for her decision not to put aside her mourning garb. She was moving to an unfamiliar city to assume a role that society didn't recognize as belonging to women. Widows, however, were afforded a special position of respect and courtesy.

So, too, widows had a special place in the eyes of the law. Widows enjoyed most of the same legal rights as men. They could enter into contracts, sue and be sued, write wills, buy and sell real estate, control their earnings, and accumulate property. A married woman, however, was subject to the legal doctrine called coverture. As soon as a woman married, she became dependent on her husband, who acted for her and in most instances controlled the property she brought to the marriage or earned during it. Married women could not own property, sign legal contracts, or have legal rights to their children in case of the dissolution of their marriage. As a widow, Hale knew that her mourning garb would deflect awkward questions about the whereabouts of her husband and signal that she could act on her own behalf in business matters.

HALE WAS A CONFIDENT, self-assured writer and editor, and she had no trouble working with men in her editorial capacity. She could reject a manuscript from a man or pan a book written by a man. Consider her biting comments about N.P. Willis, editor of *American Magazine*: "He is not sufficiently *manly* in his style," she opined. "His reminiscences are too often of his college life, and his descriptions of 'lady's love' are seldom happily done."[40]

Commenting on literature, critiquing submissions, and making decisions about what to publish or review were her principal duties as editor of the *Ladies' Magazine,* and she relished the work. She found herself on less sure ground when it came to business matters rather than literary ones. This meant operating in the "public sphere," a world from which women were largely excluded.

Writing to Bostonian David Henshaw in October 1829, she noted that while she was "sometimes obliged to intrude on the notice of strangers," she never did so "without fear" and much preferred meetings where she could be respected as a mother rather than as an author.[41] A few months later, in a letter to Henry A.S. Dearborn, Hale expressed her "dread" of the possibility of being present at a public meeting attended by gentlemen.[42]

Hale's worries about the appropriate behavior for a working woman in the man's world of business were matched by her concerns about the proper behavior of a working mother in a world that expected mothers to stay home with their children. She had addressed that question in the case of four of her five children. Before she left Newport to move to Boston, she found homes for David, Horatio, Frances, and Josepha and arranged for their schooling. But little Willie, her six-year-old, was to accompany her to Boston, serving as a blessing to her but also posing an altogether new challenge.

CHAPTER FOUR

Mary's Lamb

--≈◉-▪-◉≈--

WHEN HALE MOVED to Boston in 1828 to edit the *La-dies' Magazine,* one of her first priorities was finding someone to care for Willie while she was working. It wasn't long before she set upon a good option: Establish an infant school. Hale hired a teacher to instruct Willie and a few other small children at the boardinghouse where the Hales resided. According to family tradition, Hale provided the space for the school in her suite of rooms. In lieu of payment for taking care of Willie, the teacher pocketed the tuition paid by the other families.[1]

Infant schools were the forerunners of schools that came to be known as kindergartens, providing for the education of children aged roughly four to seven. Their mission was to prepare young children for entry into primary schools by teaching them the rudiments of reading and writing, helping them develop behavioral skills, and inculcating them with a sense of right and wrong. Infant schools were a new idea at the time of Hale's move to Boston, the first ones having opened in

England in 1818 and 1820, and Hale's infant school for Willie in the boardinghouse is sometimes credited with being the first kindergarten in the United States. There is no doubt that it was one of the first. Around the same time that Hale established the infant school for William, the Infant School Society was launched in Boston. The society's aims were twofold: educate poor children who otherwise had no access to schooling and provide working mothers with a day care facility for their children. One such infant school enrolled only African American children.

Unlike dame schools, whose curriculum varied with the skills and interests of the women who ran them, infant schools operated under a set of educational principles regarding how to prepare children for upper grades. At both types of schools, the teachers were overwhelmingly women. Hale was emphatic that women were uniquely qualified to teach the very young. Men, she believed, rarely possessed the patience, intuitiveness, and compassion necessary for instructing small children.

Hale wasn't alone in this view. Many years later, Elizabeth Peabody, founder of the American kindergarten movement, shared an amusing anecdote from her childhood in a letter to her old friend Sarah Hale, then eighty-nine years old and living in Philadelphia. "The education of the young American," the venerable Peabody wrote to the equally venerable Hale, "was presented to my childish imagination by my mother when I was so young that, mistaking the word *ancestors* for *Ann-sisters*, I got an impression that I never have quite lost that women were the originators of the American nation and *responsible for its education.*"[2] The two women, both early proponents of education for very young children, were united in the opinion that women were the best teachers of this age group.

Having spent seven years running a successful dame school in Newport—not to mention her experience as the mother of five children—Hale had developed strong ideas about how to instruct young children. She believed that children learned best when they developed at their own pace and that self-instruction, guided by a teacher, was the most effective way to absorb knowledge. Good teachers helped pupils learn how to learn—a lesson Hale had absorbed from her mother, who was her first teacher. She believed, too, that young children learned best when they were entertained—that is, with music or lively stories that held their attention. She vehemently opposed corporal punishment.

Hale's interest in infant schools is evident from her first years as an editor, when she wrote approvingly in the *Ladies' Magazine* of the establishment of the charitable infant schools in Boston. As she said of one, "It is absolutely necessary [that] right feelings be cultivated, and good habits formed. This can be done only by early and effective instruction."[3] She saw infant schools, too, as a way to help disadvantaged children rise out of poverty. A child who attended an infant school would be better placed to succeed when he entered a common—that is, public—school at the age of eight or so. She advocated that all children—not just those from poor families—would benefit from attending infant schools. She also pointed out the advantages of infant schools for mothers who worked outside of their homes.

Hale's educational theories aligned with those of Swiss pedagogue Johann Heinrich Pestalozzi, whose work she often cited in the *Ladies' Magazine*. The two never met—Pestalozzi died in 1827, before Hale's magazine was launched—yet that didn't stop her from referring to him as the "amiable Pestalozzi" and employing his name as an adjective when she wished to praise a teaching technique—as in the Pestalozzian method of teaching music. She was particularly enthusiastic about singing being introduced into school curriculums as a method of reinforcing what children learned.[4]

HALE'S THEORIES about how to teach children were based on her concept of childhood, which she idealized as a time of vulnerability, openness, and freedom. She believed that children were not mini-adults—as had been a prevailing assumption until recently. They were, rather, unformed beings receptive to a variety of influences, good and bad. It was a period of life when mothers, teachers, and other adults with whom a boy or girl interacted had a responsibility to help shape the character of the growing child and set them on the right path. Hale filled the pages of the *Ladies' Magazine* with articles, short stories, and poetry that expounded on these ideas, which were progressive in her day, along with her theories about the value of self-instruction and entertaining pedagogical techniques.

It was in her writing for children, however, that Hale put her beliefs into action. Her juvenile poetry and short stories were a departure from the moral didacticism that characterized most writing for children until the early nineteenth century. Rather, they were child-centered and provided an engaging blend of entertainment and moral instruction. They almost always carried a message or provided some factual information, but they also engaged the imagination. The natural instincts of childhood were good, not evil, she believed. She saw the job of the writer of children's literature as reinforcing the positive feelings and attitudes that children were exploring for themselves. As she wrote in the preface to one of her numerous collections of stories for youngsters, she aimed to enlist the "feelings and fancies" of children to lead their "affections the right way, to fix habits of just thought, and thus make the will obedient to the moral feelings."[5] While Hale spent her career writing principally for women, her work for children is also worthy of note. It—and the work of several of her female contemporaries—contributed to a shift in children's literature of which generations of young readers were the beneficiaries.

At first, the chief outlet for Hale's writing for children was the *Juvenile Miscellany*, a bimonthly magazine edited by Lydia Maria Child. Hale supplemented her income from editing the *Ladies' Magazine* by contributing articles to the children's magazine. Child was a prolific writer of novels, advice books, and children's literature, as well as an impassioned human rights activist—abolitionist, feminist, and advocate for rights for Native Americans. Like Hale, she thought that writing for children should be entertaining and educational. The *Juvenile Miscellany* proclaimed its mission in its subtitle: "For the instruction and amusement of Youth."

Writing for the *Miscellany* was also appealing to Hale because the children's publication, like the *Ladies' Magazine*, shared the objective of publishing articles by Americans on American subjects. In the words of one historian, the *Juvenile Miscellany* was "a landmark in the history of story-writing for the American child. Here at last was an opportunity for the editors to give to their subscribers descriptions of cities in their own land in place of accounts of palaces in Persia; biographies of national heroes instead of incidents in the life of Mahomet; and tales of Indians rather than histories of Arabians and Turks."[6]

Child's editorial approach to the *Juvenile Miscellany* was to publish a mix of short stories, poetry, biographical sketches, puzzles, and, at the end of each issue, a "conundrum," or verbal puzzle, the answer to which appeared in the following issue.

Many of the leading female writers of the day contributed to the *Miscellany*—including those who also wrote for Hale's magazines: Lydia Huntley Sigourney, Anna Maria Wells, Hannah Flagg Gould, Eliza Leslie, Caroline Howard Gilman, and others. Child herself wrote a substantial portion of the content of each issue, including an occasional message to readers, such as the one that appeared in her 1827 New Year's issue titled "Value of Time." In it she counsels boys and girls that "it is your duty—a solemn, and serious duty—to make good use of the time God has given you." Virtually every story, poem, and biographical sketch that Child published contained a moral for the magazine's young readers.

The magazine, which debuted in 1826, was an immediate hit, signing up 850 subscribers within a few months. Hale rapturously reviewed several issues in the *Ladies' Magazine*, urging every family with children to subscribe. She added that "grown people would not find their time misspent while perusing its pages, which is more than we would be willing to say in favor of, at least, one half of the new publications that are thronging us."[7]

Decades later, women's rights activist Caroline Healey Dall recalled the hubbub in the Boston neighborhood where she grew up on the day the *Juvenile Miscellany* was delivered to her childhood home in the 1820s. "No child who read the Juvenile Miscellany . . . will ever forget the excitement that the appearance of each number caused," Dall wrote. "The children sat on the stone steps of their house doors all the way up and down Chestnut Street in Boston, waiting for the carrier. He used to cross the street, going from door to door in a zigzag fashion; and the fortunate possessor of the first copy found a crowd of little ones hanging over her shoulder from the steps above. . . . How forlorn we were if the carrier was late!"[8]

The *Ladies' Magazine* and the *Juvenile Miscellany* both were published by Putnam & Hunt, which may explain why, in 1834, Hale was invited to take over from Child as editor of the *Juvenile Miscellany*. The magazine's circulation was plummeting in the South after the 1833 publication of Child's antislavery book, *An Appeal in Favor of That Class of Americans Called Africans.* Outraged parents, too, were canceling subscriptions in protest of the antislavery and antiracism stories that Child published in the *Miscellany.*[9]

The new editor oversaw the magazine in much the same vein as the old, minus the antislavery message and with a greater emphasis on science, on which Hale was keen. An early issue under her editorship contained a biographical essay on the life of Benjamin Franklin and the story of a Native American massacre of an English settlement in Maine, as well as short stories, poetry, and puzzles. Readers would have been hard-pressed to notice a difference between Child's editorship and that of Hale.

In an effort to drum up subscribers, Hale conducted a personal letter-writing campaign, sending copies of the magazine to what we would today call opinion makers, inviting them to subscribe. In 1835 she edited a book—*Tales for Youth*—that was a compilation of items that had appeared in the magazine. In the end, though, there was nothing Hale could do to rescue the *Juvenile Miscellany*. By 1836, the country was on the brink of a recession, the *Miscellany*'s circulation in the South hadn't revived, and the magazine closed.

Editing two magazines would have been a Herculean task even for Hale, whose energy seemed boundless. But she was nothing if not hardworking and she was motivated by a need for money. She frequently told her readers that she went to work in order to pay for the education that her late husband would have wanted their children to have. The extra income from *Juvenile Miscellany* was helpful in meeting the costs of her children's school fees.

By the time she began to edit the *Miscellany*, Hale had already begun to write children's books, perhaps motivated in part by a wish to enter the growing and lucrative market of literature for young readers. The production of children's books became more profitable as the population of American children grew, more women became literate, and public schools opened across the land. The population of the United States increased by a third or more every 10 years in the decades between 1820 and 1840—from 9.6 million in 1820 to 12.8 million in 1830 to 17.1 million in 1840. The next decade saw the population grow by a whopping 35.9 percent to 23.2 million in 1850. Not long after the successful launch of the *Juvenile Miscellany*, Lydia Maria Child sent a message to a friend that she had recently discovered that "children's books are more profitable than any others."[10] Hale apparently reached the same conclusion.

THE *Juvenile Miscellany* represented a milestone in Hale's career for another reason. The magazine was the first to publish her most famous poem—"Mary Had a Little Lamb." Yes, it was Sarah Josepha Hale—not Mother Goose—who wrote the beloved nursery rhyme. It is hard to think of a better-known verse in the English language. Hale's lines are more universally recognizable than anything even Shakespeare wrote. They have been translated into just about every language known to modern man, from Armenian to Zulu.

The poem appeared in the September–October 1830 issue of the *Juvenile Miscellany* under its original title, "Mary's Lamb." Today, the first stanza is the one that generations of five-year-olds have sung. The original poem, however, had three stanzas of eight lines each:

Mary had a little lamb,
Its fleece was white as snow,
And everywhere that Mary went
The lamb was sure to go;
He followed her to school one day—
That was against the rule,
It made the children laugh and play,
To see a lamb at school.

And so the Teacher turned him out,
But still he lingered near,
And waited patiently about,
Till Mary did appear;
And then he ran to her and laid
His head upon her arm,
As if he said—"I am not afraid—
You'll keep me from all harm."

"What makes the lamb love Mary so?"
The eager children cry—
"O, Mary loves the lamb, you know,"
The Teacher did reply;—
"And you each gentle animal
In confidence may bind,
And make them follow at your call,
If you are always kind."

It is rare today to hear of a child having a lamb as a pet, but at the time Hale wrote her poem it was an ordinary occurrence. Sheep are poor mothers, sometimes rejecting their newborns and abandoning them to die. Feeding a motherless lamb is a time-consuming task, which farm families traditionally entrusted to a small boy or girl. For the child, caring for a lamb was both an amusement and an early lesson in how to take responsibility for a farming task. Lambs are docile and playful, and until they are grown and join their flock they happily adopt the person who feeds them. That a naughty little lamb might have followed its mistress to school one day would have been instantly understandable—and amusing—to children of Hale's day.

The last stanza, not well known today, carries the moral of the poem: Be kind to animals. The poem's publication corresponded with the period when Americans were beginning to awaken to the issue of cruelty to animals. Its message would have resounded with readers.

Hale wrote "Mary's Lamb" for her volume *Poems for Our Children*, also published in 1830 and designed, as the subtitle says, "for Families, Sabbath Schools, and Infant Schools." In the preface, addressed to "all Good Children in the United States," she explains that she wrote the verses "to furnish you with a few pretty songs and poems which would teach you truths, and, I hope, induce you to love truth and goodness." Children "who love their parents and their home, can soon teach their hearts to love their God and their Country."[11]

The poems' titles indicate their subject matter. Several—"Birds," "Spring," "Summer Morning," "The Stars"—extol the beauty of nature. Others—"My Mother's Sweet Kiss," "The Bright Hearth"—teach the value of a stable, loving home. The patriotic poem "My Country" concludes with the lines, "I bless my God that I was born / Where man is *free*!" "The Boy, the Bee, and the Butterfly" exhorts children to be more like the disciplined, hardworking bee than the butterfly, which flits from place to place. If that all sounds rather dull and didactic, it's not. The verses are charming, with sweet story lines and colorful images.

Hale wrote the fifteen poems in the anthology at the suggestion of Lowell Mason, a composer and music educator who is
credited with introducing music education in the public schools.
Mason believed that singing had a "happy influence . . . upon
the feelings and manners and morals of the rising generation, on
whose character the future destiny of the country depends."[12]
In 1831, a year after the publication of *Poems for Our Children*,
Mason put "Mary's Lamb" and other verses in Hale's collection
to music. Her poems were included in a textbook with a lengthy
but descriptive title: *Juvenile Lyre, Or, Hymns and Songs, Religious, Moral, and Cheerful, Set to Appropriate Music, For the
Use of Primary and Common Schools. Juvenile Lyre* was one of
the first school songbooks in the United States.

Hale's name appeared as the author on the title page of *Poems
for Our Children*. In *Juvenile Lyre*, however, Mason failed to give
her credit for "Mary's Lamb" or the other poems of hers that he
put to music.

Mason wasn't alone in neglecting to credit Hale for "Mary's
Lamb." Next up in a long line of poetry thieves were McGuffey's
first and second Eclectic Readers—out in 1836—which published "Mary's Lamb" as Lesson Forty-Seven, still without acknowledging the author. The McGuffey Readers were widely
used in elementary schools across America from the middle of
the nineteenth century until the middle of the twentieth century. Thanks to their popularity, "Mary's Lamb" was memorized
by generations of young readers. Few of those young scholars,
though, would have been able to pass a quiz that asked them to
provide the name of the poem's author. Subsequently, "Mary's
Lamb" was published without credit to the author by virtually
every nineteenth-century juvenile poetry anthology, according
to the *Dictionary of Literary Biography*.[13]

Copyright protection wasn't commonplace in the 1830s, and it was far from unusual for a short piece of literature to be re-printed without credit or compensation to the author. As the years went by, and the poem's popularity grew, Hale apparently felt no need to assert her authorship—especially since her name was attached to the first appearance of "Mary's Lamb" in *Poems for Our Children.*

HALE'S CONTRIBUTIONS to children's literature didn't end when the *Juvenile Miscellany* folded in 1836. She went on to write or edit numerous volumes of poetry and prose for boys and girls. The early 1840s saw the publication of the Little Boys' and Girls' Library, a series of ten titles published by Edward Dunigan of New York City. Each book was issued simultaneously in two editions, one with illustrations in black and white and the oth-er where the illustrations had been colored by hand. The books were printed in a small format—easy for little hands to hold—and bound in paper or boards. Hale was the editor of the series. The authorship of the individual books has not been confirmed, but it is assumed that Hale wrote some, if not all, of them.

The series—and Hale—received plaudits in the *United States Magazine and Democratic Review,* a well-regarded periodical and publisher of literary works by Hawthorne, Whitman, Whit-tier, and others. "These excellent little works for children have already become highly popular," the magazine wrote in its re-view. "Indeed the endorsement of the well-known editor offers so strong a guarantee for their internal excellence, while their brilliantly colored embellishments add so essentially to their exterior attractions that the public would be at fault were the result otherwise."[14] Hale's imprimatur was a mark of the book's quality—and a reputational asset to her publishers.

Edward Dunigan published numerous other books for children written or edited by Hale. Just how many is difficult to establish, since many of the books went into two or more printings or were reprinted in omnibus volumes, sometimes under new titles. Suffice it to say that Hale was prolific.

While she wasn't above writing an occasional fairy tale, most of her fiction for children had contemporary settings and realistic storylines. One of her approaches was to recount the everyday exploits of good children versus naughty children with an eye—of course!—to demonstrating the superiority of the well-behaved child. In "The Wise Boys," we meet, among others, Matt Merrythought, who is always cheerful, and his counterpart, Sulky Joe. Similarly, Fred Forethought always thinks before he acts, Luke Lovebook is a diligent student, and the industrious Ben Bee understands that

By honest industry, men rise
To wealth and high degree;
While idleness begets contempt,
Ill health, and poverty.

Another example of Hale's work for children is *Spring Flowers, or the Poetical Banquet*, a collection of poems on flowers and nature that is intended to inspire a respect for nature in young readers. One of the verses inveighs against the killing of birds with bows and arrows. Also in the volume are a few poems aimed at raising awareness of children in need. One tells the story of a poor chimney sweep who is left out in the cold; another recounts an encounter with a beggar girl.

In *The Countries of Europe and the Manners and Customs of Its Various Nations*, published in 1843, Hale provides young readers with information about European life in seventeen poems and accompanying hand-colored illustrations. She hadn't been to Europe, and the information she presented was highly subjective. It generally accorded with the views she also expressed in her writing for women. Her impassioned criticism of the treatment of women in Muslim countries in articles written for the *Ladies' Magazine* is reflected in the chapter on Turkey in *The Countries of Europe*, where she writes:

> *Now we travel south to Turkey,*
> *And for all the world I've seen,*
> *I would not be a Turkish girl,*
> *Nor a little Turkish queen.*

The chapter is accompanied by a drawing of a subservient young woman kneeling at the feet of a man who is seated on a cushion. Point made.

Turkey isn't the only country she criticizes in *The Countries of Europe*. In the chapter on England, Hale takes the opportunity to harp on one of her favorite themes: the superiority of American ideals to those of the old country.

> *But we hope better things for the land of our sires;*
> *That the spirit of Freedom will kindle her fires*
> *From our altar, which Washington hallowed and blessed.*
> *And Old England, revived by the breath of the West,*
> *May live (if she'll raise up her down-trodden poor)*
> *As long as the earth and the ocean endure.*

WHEN HALE BEGAN writing for children during the 1830s, her own children were growing up. Her oft-stated goal was to educate them as their father would have wished—a formidable task for a woman without private means in the first half of the nineteenth century. Her husband though, had he lived, could have succeeded no better than she did in providing the best education available to their three sons and two daughters. She always considered it her life's finest achievement. They were a brilliant quintet, and they did their parents proud.

David, the eldest, was thirteen years old when his mother left Newport for Boston in 1828. At fourteen, he received an appointment to West Point. He graduated in 1833, the youngest in his class, ranking thirteenth in his class of 150 cadets.

A letter to his mother, written in 1831 when he was sixteen, suggests a warm, sometimes playful, mother-son relationship. The letter is clearly a continuation of an ongoing epistolary conversation, with references to the latest issue of the *Ladies' Magazine*, which had just arrived in David's mailbox; to a coming family trip up the Hudson River; and to the boy's studies, which weren't going as well as usual. "You were right in thinking that I had not obtained the standing I expected," he confesses. Hale was something of Tiger Mom, setting high academic standards for her children.

David recounts a bit of hometown gossip about a friend in Newport who has just gotten married, making "an honest woman" of his wife, and imagines his mother's response: "Fie! My son, thou art not yet old enough to say such things. Leave them to be discussed by the women of N. at the tea table, that altar of slander at which so many unfortunate characters are torn in piecemeal." The comment about the slanderous women of Newport may be a not-so-subtle reference to the nasty treatment given his mother when she made the decision to accept the editorship of the *Ladies' Magazine*.[15]

Sarah and David's second son, Horatio, was eleven years old when his mother took up the editorship of the *Ladies' Magazine*. He lived, first, in Glens Falls, New York, with his maternal uncle, Judge Horatio Buell, and then, in Keene, New Hampshire, with his paternal uncle, Salma Hale, later a member of the U.S. House of Representatives. The boy then spent a year in Newport, working at a printing office, before joining his mother in Boston at the age of thirteen. With financial assistance from two of his mother's friends, Gideon Thayer and Abbott Lawrence, he enrolled in the Chauncy Hall School, which educated the sons of prominent Bostonians.[16] He then entered Harvard College, graduating in 1837 at the top of his class. Among his classmates was Henry David Thoreau.

Horatio had a remarkable ear for languages—a course of study in which, he later wrote, "my mother encouraged me."[17] During his freshman year at Harvard, a group of Native Americans from Maine camped near the college grounds. Intrigued by their customs and language, Horatio undertook a field study of their language, a then-unknown Algonkian dialect. Drawing on his knowledge of printing, he published a pamphlet about his findings, which he distributed to fifty friends. That monograph and the overall high quality of his academic work led to an invitation to join the U.S. Exploring Expedition, a five-year expedition sponsored by the federal government for the purpose of exploring and surveying islands and countries bordering the Pacific Ocean. Horatio was the group's philologist, responsible for recording the vocabularies and sketching the grammars of the Oceanic languages the expedition encountered. In the final year of the voyage, he went ashore in the Oregon Territory to record the ethnic and linguistic varieties of the native peoples from California to British Columbia.

True to her commitment to higher education for women, Hale made sure that Frances Ann" (called "Fanny") and Sarah Josepha ("Josy") were also well educated. After they completed their studies at Miss Fiske's Young Ladies Seminary in Keene, she sent them to the Troy Female Seminary, established in 1821 by her friend Emma Willard. By the time the Hale girls arrived in Troy, the school enrolled more than three hundred students, including the daughters of many prominent figures.

As for little William, the six-year-old who had accompanied his mother to Boston in 1828, he, too, received a superior education during his years there. He followed his brother Horatio to the Chauncy Hall School and then on to Harvard College, where he graduated second in his class.

WHEN THE *Ladies' Magazine* merged with *Godey's Lady's Book* at the close of 1836, Hale struck an agreement with publisher Louis Godey that she would edit the new publication from Boston while William was at Harvard. She wanted to remain nearby during his undergraduate years. The *Lady's Book* was published in Philadelphia, more than three hundred miles distant.

In preferring to stay in Boston, she might have been thinking, too, of the charitable and civic projects there to which she was committed. As editor of the *Ladies' Magazine*, Hale was deeply enmeshed in the intellectual life of Boston. She was also at the center of two large philanthropies in which she assumed leadership roles that normally would have gone to men. The Seaman's Aid Society, which aided the families of absent sailors, became a model for charitable organizations in port cities around the United States, as well as an example of how to provide jobs for women that paid a living wage. At the Bunker Hill Monument Association, Hale demonstrated that women could successfully build and lead large public-service organizations. Her example of philanthropic leadership helped pave the way for the women's rights movement, launched in 1848 at the convention in Seneca Falls, New York, and the Women's Christian Temperance Union, one of the most influential social institutions of the nineteenth century.

CHAPTER FIVE

Let the Ladies Do It

⸺⊙⸺⊙⸺

HALE COVERED philanthropy frequently in her magazines, with special attention paid to educational organizations and charities that served women. The first issue of the
Ladies' Magazine in January 1828 carried a short item bearing
the headline "Fatherless and Widows' Society, Boston." It announced the establishment by a small group of Boston ladies of
an organization to provide assistance to women and children
who had lost their husbands and fathers. The article wasn't
signed, but the prose style is unmistakably Hale's.

So, too, was the writer's compassion for indigent widows and
children, whom she described as "the most forlorn and destitute of any class of people in the world."[1] This was a subject on
which the widow Hale had painful personal experience. She
didn't stint in expressions of respect for the work of the Fatherless and Widows' Society, which had raised $4,000 for the relief
of widows and children during the winter months.

In her devotion to helping the less fortunate, Hale was very much a woman of her time. In the early nineteenth century, wealthy and middle-class women were active in the numerous new charities to help the urban poor. Men led the charities and raised the needed funds, but women often were the worker bees, usually in the form of auxiliary committees, which offered as many opportunities for socializing as for doing good. In a letter to a friend, Hale once expressed her frustration with the do-gooder ladies of Boston society: "It is so discouraging to listen to the observations and doubts and objections of those who would not be reported as backward in any charitable measure—but yet do not *feel* the warmth and zeal of true charity that 'hopeth all things, believeth all things, endureth all things.'"[2]

In his travels around the United States in the 1830s, Alexis de Tocqueville famously observed that Americans were constantly forming voluntary organizations for the purpose of mutual aid and support. This activity was nurtured by Americans' religious faith and the Judeo-Christian values on which the nation was founded. In her writing, Hale frequently referred to women's Christian duty to help the less fortunate. This was in keeping with her personal religious beliefs. Raised in the Congregational church, she became an Episcopalian when she moved to Philadelphia, where the Congregational church, the offshoot of seventeenth-century New England Puritanism, had limited activity.

Like millions of Americans of the period, Hale was profoundly influenced by the Second Great Awakening, the religious revival that swept the country in the late 1700s and early 1800s. The Second Great Awakening taught that all individuals are responsible for perfecting their own souls as much as possible and for lifting up their neighbors whenever they are able. During the antebellum period, this religious commitment translated into social action—freeing the slaves, feeding the poor, slaying demon drink, and more. In the felicitous phrase of Karl Zinsmeister, author of a history of American philanthropy, the Second Great Awakening "rooted the golden rule in American breasts."[3]

Hale didn't just write about helping the less fortunate— though she did that frequently—she put her faith into action. First in Boston and later Philadelphia, she involved herself deeply in local charities. As an editor, she was smart enough to recognize the difference between reporting and advocacy, and she was careful not to overdo the promotion of the charities she supported. She understood that there is a line between providing information and empathetic commentary to her readers and boring them, offending them, or turning them off with solicitations. She used her position to advance her views, but she didn't want to take advantage of it. She also understood human nature, as evidenced by her shrewd observation in a letter to a friend that "there exists a wide difference between admiring benevolence and practicing it."[4] The publicity she provided in the *Ladies' Magazine* for various charities wouldn't necessarily result in public support for them.

A PRIME BENEFICIARY of Hale's hands-on charitable work was the Seaman's Aid Society, which Hale founded with several other women in Boston in 1831 and presided over for several years. The women's organization was intended to be an auxiliary to the work of the Port Society of Boston, led by the charismatic Methodist preacher Edward Thompson Taylor. Father Taylor, as he was universally known, had run away to sea as a boy. That experience gave him a firsthand understanding of the sailor's life and an ability to reach out to seamen in terms that would be familiar to them. In Boston, he provided charitable assistance and religious support to sailors and maritime workers on the docks of the North End.

Visitors of all faiths flocked to Father Taylor's ecumenical chapel, the Seamen's Bethel, to hear his compelling Sunday sermons. Walt Whitman called him an "essentially perfect orator."[5] Herman Melville used him as the model for the character of Father Mapple in *Moby Dick*. Charles Dickens went to hear him preach during his 1842 American tour. Ralph Waldo Emerson, another fan, said of Taylor: "How puny, how cowardly, other preachers look by the side of this preaching! He shows us what a man can do."[6]

Deeply impressed with Father Taylor's ministry, Hale was inspired to create the Seaman's Aid Society. The society's mission was to assist seamen and their left-behind wives and children, who often endured terrible privations when the family breadwinner was away at sea. If the husband or father failed to return, the family was left permanently in poverty. Hale described the dire conditions under which a sailor's family lived in an account of the exploitative system under which sailors were paid:

The lot of the sailor's wife is one of extreme hardship. The highest wages which, in the best times, a common seaman can obtain is *eighteen dollars* per month—often he is obliged to accept ten or twelve only: but we will take the highest rate, eighteen dollars. Of this sum he is usually obliged to take up two months' pay in advance for his outfit. He can then leave only half-pay—*or nine dollars per* month—for the support of his family; and, as he had received his wages for the first two months, his wife must wait three months, and then can only draw *nine dollars* to pay the expenses of the preceding thirteen weeks.

We will allow this woman only two children to support, for we seek not to invest this subject with any over-wrought coloring—the real picture is sufficiently dark. But how can three persons subsist on such small means? . . .

With the strictest economy and best possible manage-ment, a sailor's wife cannot, from her husband's half pay, do more than meet her rent for one room and provide fuel for the year. The food and clothing for herself and children she must earn.

But . . . if the ship is wrecked, the common sailor loses all his pay! and even on learning the news of any accident to, or detention of a vessel, the owner generally refuses to pay the order of the sailor's wife, and she is thus, not unfrequently, deprived of any benefit of her husband's wages.[7]

In Boston in the 1820s and 1830s, numerous charities pro-vided relief for the sick and destitute, unwed mothers, orphan children, and other needy members of the community. The relief took the form of handouts: food for families, shoes for children in winter, orphanages, hospices for the dying, and so forth.

Hale deplored almsgiving to the healthy and able-bodied—by which she meant the traditional way of assisting the needy through handouts. A woman might be industrious, ambitious, and reliable, but once she was accepted as a charity case, Hale argued, she lost the incentive to work, her self-respect disap-peared, and she was branded as a pauper. All hope of improv-ing her situation in life was gone.

Under Hale's leadership, the Seaman's Aid Society decided to try a different kind of philanthropy. The animating idea of the society was to help seamen's wives and daughters help themselves. She wanted to empower individual women to break out of the cycle of poverty in which sailors' wives were usually trapped.

Hale believed that the most effective way to help the women of seamen's families escape lifelong poverty was to teach them skills that would help them find jobs. Armed with a marketable skill, they then would be able to provide for their own support—with luck, on a permanent basis. If their husbands never returned from sea, the widows and their families would be in a position to take care of themselves. In the *Ladies' Magazine*, she applauded the British system of vocational schools for boys, and she wrote of her admiration for Jews, who, she said, ensured that their young men were taught a trade. Now she was applying the same principle to indigent women in Boston. The trade she had in mind was needlework, which was one of the few culturally acceptable occupations for women.

Hale understood that her idea of putting poor women to work was bound to be controversial. Her plan's best chance of success, she realized, was to secure Father Taylor's imprimatur. The pastor, however, was traveling in Europe, so she decided to wait for his return before activating her plan. In the meantime, the members of the Seaman's Aid Society met in members' homes and sewed garments to give away to the poor. It was almsgiving as usual, and Hale was scornful:

Yes—the ladies left their families, gave up useful occupations, elegant pursuits, or improving studies, to assemble themselves together, and make coarse garments, to be distributed gratuitously; while poor women, who ought to have been employed in needle-work, and to whom, probably, these very garments were given, were spending their time in idle gossip, or vicious indulgences!⁸

Upon his return to Boston, Father Taylor expressed enthusiasm for Hale's proposal. Over the next few years, the Seaman's Aid Society racked up a number of accomplishments. An early step was to open a nonprofit clothing store in the basement of Taylor's church. Women from seamen's families staffed the store and made the garments that were sold there. The new store competed favorably with the local slopshops, which had had a monopoly on seaman's garments and were notorious for selling overpriced clothes of poor quality. An advertising circular addressed to the seamen of Boston promised that the new store's garments were made of good materials, in the best manner, with strong seams, and "will not be blown apart in the first gale."⁹

A second tenet of Hale's philanthropic philosophy was that women deserved to be paid a fair wage. The wives and widows who made the garments for the Seaman's Aid Society were paid nearly twice as much as the women who sewed for the slop shops. A full-time seamstress for the Society could earn a minimal living for herself and her children.

Many of the work-women, as they were called, were mothers, and the Society hit upon the idea of setting up a day nursery for their children. The nursery enabled the work-women to do their jobs secure in the knowledge that their children were being well cared for. This was an incalculable emotional boon at a time when poor mothers who went outside the home to work often had to leave their young children home alone, sometimes tied to a bed or a chair for their safety or put under the care of siblings who were barely older than their charges. The Society's day nursery was the first day care center for the children of working women in the United States.

The Society opened a free school for mariners' daughters. In addition to studying the regular subjects taught at public schools, the girls learned needlework, which (to Hale's dismay) wasn't taught in the public schools. The aim was to provide the girls with a marketable trade in the expectation that they would be able to support themselves upon graduation. The girls were also given the opportunity to earn some money by sewing items for the clothing store. The Society operated a lending library, which provided books to seamen's children. Finally, the Society established, with the Port Society, an alcohol-free boardinghouse for seamen. The mission of Mariners House, which continues to operate into the twenty-first century, was—and is—to provide a safe, comfortable, and inexpensive home for seamen when they come ashore.

Hale's work with the Seaman's Aid Society deeply influenced her views on two economic issues impacting women: the exploitation of poor, working women and the lack of property rights for married women, rich and poor.

For the rest of her life, she would return again and again to the subjects of female poverty and fair wages for women. She challenged readers of the *Ladies' Magazine* and *Godey's Lady's Book* to take personal action by paying adequate compensation to the women they hired to cook, sew, and launder for them. She published the work of Mathew Carey, a prominent Philadelphia publisher and author who wrote movingly about the suffering of indigent women in American cities, and asked Carey for help in identifying issues she should address. "If you have any communications respecting charitable objects, especially those connected with female suffering," she wrote him in 1831, "I shall be happy to give them a place and commendation in my work. I intend to devote my own attention more deeply to the subject."[10] She turned to the topic in her fiction, too, in short stories—often with tragic endings—that realistically portrayed the lives of poor women who wanted to work but were unable to find employment.

Hale's experience working with the families of seaman exposed her to the inequities of coverture, the common-law system under which married women were required to hand control of their financial affairs, including any money they earned, to their husbands. Hale had already inveighed against coverture in the *Ladies' Magazine*, and her experience with the Seaman's Aid Society intensified her outrage at the system that denied women control of their own money.

She had previously focused on the harm coverture did to wealthy and middle-class women who had the misfortune to marry men who were dishonest or incompetent in managing their wives' money. Now her attention was caught by the impact that coverture had on poor women. In a no-holds-barred article titled "Rights of Married Women," published in the *Lady's Book* in 1837, she wrote about the "barbarous custom of wresting from woman whatever she possesses, whether by inheritance, donation or her own industry." The "most disgusting feature of this law is its operation on the poor, taking from the wife the poor earnings of her own hands, and putting them in the hands of a husband to waste as he pleases." The law thus "degrades the woman to the condition of a slave."[11]

She went on to give a real-life example of how the law hurt a sailor's wife and family:

Sometimes the husband, after spending all his living, is gone for months, or years, contributing nothing to the family; the wife, meanwhile, for she is a mother, and rarely does a mother give up the ship in which her children are embarked, labors and saves, and finally succeeds in furnishing her little room comfortably. The husband returns. He pleads to be admitted, promises amendment, and she, womanlike, receives him. For a short time all goes on happily; but the mania of intoxication seizes him—he is a madman—but still, unless his wife will appear against him in a criminal prosecution, she has no shield from his injustice. He can take all her furniture, even her clothing, and that of her children, and sell them, legally for *rum*. And there are in this city, dealers in that moral poison, who will encourage him in doing this; and receive the last cent of her earnings, though they knew she and her children were perishing with cold and hunger![12]

The news peg for "Rights of Married Women" was a bill pending in the New York State legislature that extended property rights to married women. The New York bill passed in 1848. By the end of the century coverture was weakened or eliminated in the rest of the country.

HALE WAS A visionary philanthropist, and the Seaman's Aid Society was just one example of her philanthropic leadership during the years she lived in Boston. Her decade-long effort on behalf of the Bunker Hill Monument was another spectacular success story, though it began poorly.

When the men of New England failed to raise enough money to complete the proposed monument to the American heroes who fought in the first major battle of the American Revolution,

Hale stepped forward. The ladies of New England, she declared, would finish the job. So they did—but not without enduring criticism for stepping out of line. Raising money, Hale was informed, was man's work. Her campaign to rally the women of New England to rescue the stalled effort to complete the Bunker Hill Monument was the first time that American women played a prominent public role in a major philanthropic endeavor.

The Bunker Hill Monument was one of the first historic monuments in the United States. It was the brainchild of the Bunker Hill Monument Association, founded in 1823 by a group of notable Bostonians—all men—each of whom put up five dollars toward the project. By 1825, the association had raised enough funds to purchase the site of the battle—fifteen acres in Charlestown, across the Charles River from downtown Boston. It sponsored a competition for design of the monument to be built there. The winning entry was submitted by Solomon Willard, a local architect and stone carver. He envisioned a 221-foot-high granite obelisk. It was to be the first obelisk built in the United States.

The cornerstone of the monument was laid on the fiftieth anniversary of the Battle of Bunker Hill—June 17, 1825—in the presence of the Marquis de Lafayette, the French aristocrat and general who served in the Continental Army during the Revolution. Lafayette was in the United States for a lengthy tour set to culminate with his participation in celebrations marking the fiftieth anniversary of the Declaration of Independence the following year. Famed orator Daniel Webster, at the time a congressman from Boston—and later senator and secretary of state—delivered a stirring address. He blessed the construction of the monument and bade it "rise till it meet the sun."[13] The event drew an astounding 100,000 spectators, including 190 aged veterans of the Battle of Bunker Hill. A dinner for 4,000 guests followed in a massive tent that had been erected on the building site.

The dinner lasted several hours, during the course of which thirteen toasts were offered, the number corresponding to the original number of states. Guests lifted their glasses to, among others, the men who died at the Battle of Bunker Hill, the surviving veterans of the battle, the memory of Washington, the president of the United States, the governor of Massachusetts, and, of course, the yet-to-be-built monument itself. The campaign was off to a grand start.

And then it all fell apart.

Despite the monument's appeal to New Englanders' abundant patriotism, the project wasn't popular in all quarters. There were businessmen who thought the site on which the monument was to be built could be better used for commercial activity in the burgeoning Charlestown area. Some clergymen preached against donating to the construction fund, arguing that the money would be more usefully spent on charities that helped the poor. It wasn't long before the directors of the Bunker Hill Monument Association were reduced to squabbling, contributions lagged, and construction proceeded only in fits and starts. For one four-year period the unfinished structure was left untouched, covered by a temporary roof.

Enter Mrs. Hale.

Deeply patriotic, Hale had several personal connections to the Battle of Bunker Hill. Growing up in Newport, she had heard firsthand accounts of the events of June 17, 1775, from veterans who had survived the battle. In the words of Edmund Wheeler, the Newport historian, "at the first sound of war," Hale's relation Matthew Buell had "left his plow in the furrow, and hastened to the defense of his country."[14] Her father-in-law served as a sentry during the battle, while other members of the Hale family fought.

In 1830, this daughter of the Revolution, by now a prominent member of Boston society, decided to enter the fray over the erection of the monument. The proximate cause of her decision was the Bunker Hill Monument Association's last-ditch scheme to hold a lottery to raise the $50,000 needed to finish the project. True to her Puritan heritage, she found gambling of any sort anathema—the work of the devil. She viewed the proposed lottery as immoral and totally inappropriate for what she saw as a sacred cause. Not only was the lottery unlikely to succeed in raising the necessary funds, she wrote in the *Ladies' Magazine*, it was unworthy of the patriotic nature of the proposed monument. She decried the proposal as "humiliating, even degrading" in its appeal to "avarice and gambling propensities."[15]

Hale proposed, instead, a radical alternative: Let the women of New England raise the funds to rescue the monument. Under her proposal—put first in a letter to the association's Building Committee and then in an article in her magazine—the money was to come "solely from the ladies." She instructed women not to turn to their husbands, fathers, or brothers with requests for contributions. Rather, they were told to raise it themselves either by economizing on household expenses or depriving themselves of luxuries. She reached back into ancient history and cited the example of the women of Rome, who gave up their gold jewelry to pay the ransom demanded by the Gauls who had captured their city.[16]

Critics of Hale's plan pointed out that since the law gave husbands control of their wives' financial affairs, contributions by married women would ipso facto come from men, who might already have donated as much money as they wished. Hale countered by imposing a limit of one dollar—about twenty-seven dollars today—on the amount of individual contributions. Just about every woman who wished to make a donation would have at least that amount at her disposal from her housekeeping budget, she explained. Contributions from children under the age of twelve—both girls and boys—would also be accepted. What better way for mothers to instill a love of country in their sons and daughters? she asked.

Hale's proposal caused a predictable stir. It was condemned in the Boston press in editorials thundering that women were stepping out of their proper sphere. Joseph Buckingham of the *Commercial Gazette* accused Hale of interfering in the affairs of men by telling them how to manage their money. Hale responded to the attacks with extreme tact—but without conceding an inch. She replied sweetly that her proposal was never intended to contradict the opinions of men. She declared that no woman should join the society formed to accept contributions "without the consent of her immediate protector." But patriotic women want to do their part, she insisted. Such assistance was women's God-given responsibility, citing a higher authority than the Boston *Commercial Gazette*. In the biblical book of Exodus, the women of Israel offered their jewelry for the building of the tabernacle. So, too, the women of New England were willing to sacrifice to do their patriotic duty. Her argument won the day.

On April 6, 1830, the board of directors of the Bunker Hill Monument passed a resolution accepting Hale's proposal. The resolution praised the "patriotic ladies" for their "generous zeal" in wishing to participate in the completion of the obelisk that would give "honor to the names of their gallant countrymen" who had died "in the cause of freedom."[17]

And so the ladies' campaign began. Hale kept up the pressure in the *Ladies' Magazine,* printing updates on the fundraising and publishing sentimental poems written by herself and Lydia Sigourney commemorating the heroes of the Battle of Bunker Hill. The ladies' committee she assembled in Boston sent circulars to every town in Massachusetts encouraging women to form local fundraising committees. The Boston committee placed notices in newspapers soliciting funds, and it invited donors to personally deliver their contributions to the homes of committee members. That invitation was a clever marketing move. A woman might not feel comfortable walking into the atmosphere of an all-male office to deliver her contribution, but ringing the bell of the private residence of a committeewoman would be another matter. Paying a house call was a familiar, non-intimidating activity.

DESPITE HALE'S EFFORTS, by the end of 1830 it was clear that the fund drive, which had raised less than $3,000, was a bust. The Bunker Hill Monument Association struggled on for another decade, when Hale and the ladies of New England again rose to the occasion. By 1840 the association was out of money and in debt. At their annual meeting on the anniversary of the battle in June of that year, the directors received a discouraging report: $40,000 was needed to clear the association's debts and finish the monument. The report dolefully concluded, "Under all these circumstances, it must be confessed that it is extremely doubtful whether the present generation will have the pleasure to see the Monument completed."[18]

Yet there was still a glimmer of hope. Two donors were prepared to each give $10,000, but only if the association had a viable plan to raise the additional funds. At a follow-up meeting eight days later, someone hit upon the notion of the association sponsoring a ladies' fair at which donated goods would be sold. The minutes of the meeting record that the proposal for a fair had been suggested by an unnamed lady.

The idea didn't go over well at first. It was remarked that the most that had previously been raised from a ladies' fair in Boston was only $2,000 or $3,000. But no one had a better idea, and after vigorous discussion, the directors voted unanimously to give it a try. The next step was to enlist the help of Hale—probably the unnamed woman who had recommended a ladies' fair.

It was by now the end of June 1840. Hale immediately formed an executive committee of five women, including the wife of the mayor of Boston, for the purpose of organizing the fair. Ladies' fairs were a commonplace fundraising activity at the church or community level. But Hale had a grander vision. She proposed a weeklong fair in a lavishly decorated space smack in the heart of the city. The goods sold at the fair would be handmade items contributed by women not just from Boston but from all of Massachusetts and the neighboring states. Soon the women of New England were sewing, knitting, crocheting, embroidering, and otherwise using whatever skill they possessed to make items to sell in aid of the monument. A familiar question around Boston in the summer of 1840 was: What are you doing for the fair?

A place and a date were soon selected. The fair would take place in Quincy Hall, opposite Faneuil Hall. It would open on Tuesday, September 8, and run for a week. The date was selected to coincide with the New England Whig Party's political convention, which was scheduled to take place on Bunker Hill during that period. The president of the convention was Daniel Webster, by then a senator. Webster declined a request to solicit contributions from convention attendees, saying that doing so would threaten to politicize the fair. That year was a presidential election year—William Harrison, a Whig, would go on to defeat incumbent Martin Van Buren, a Democrat—and political sentiments ran high. Tensions were such that summer that the ladies' committee banned party emblems from the fair.

The timing of the fair turned out to be propitious. The Whig convention drew attendees from every part of the country, many of whom attended the fair and made contributions. The Louisiana delegates combined their resources to purchase a large-scale model of the monument. They carried the model back to New Orleans, where it was publicly displayed in honor of Judah Touro. Touro, a transplanted New Englander, was one of the two philanthropists who had pledged to donate $10,000 to the monument's construction fund.

The ladies' fair succeeded beyond the Bunker Hill Monument Association's wildest expectations, raising $30,000, after expenses, for the monument fund. The board of directors of the association passed a resolution commending the ladies for their "enthusiasm, industry, ingenuity and untiring activity" in designing and running the fair.[19]

Work on the unfinished obelisk resumed at a quick pace. Less than two years later, on Saturday, July 23, 1842, at six o'clock in the morning, several hundred people gathered to witness the laying of the topstone of the monument. Hale was not present, having moved the previous year to Philadelphia to edit *Godey's Lady's Book*.

BY THE MIDDLE OF 1832, the *Ladies' Magazine* had reached an important milestone: It had survived longer than any previous publication for women. The subscription list was steadily increasing. The magazine's reach extended beyond New England, circulating in every one of the twenty-four states then in the Union. Hale felt confident enough to report to readers that improvements in the state of female education had been made thanks in part to the influence of the *Ladies' Magazine*.

Also in 1832, the magazine expanded its review and criticism section and decided to give itself a new name: *Ladies' Magazine and Literary Gazette*. In 1834, Hale changed the name again, this time to the *American Ladies' Magazine*. There was a *Ladies' Magazine* in Britain, and she wanted to make sure that there was no confusion between the two publications.

Under all of its various appellations, the *Ladies' Magazine* was well regarded by the public. Both the publication and Hale received numerous accolades, including from the *New-York Mirror*, which called the editor a lady of "intelligence" and "decided talent" and praised the "sterling merit of her work." It urged every lady in America to buy a subscription to her magazine.

By the end of 1834, though, the *American Ladies' Magazine* was in financial trouble. In her usual end-of-the-year report to readers, Hale confided, "My list of subscribers has much diminished and my profits, in consequence, are quite small." She blamed the decline on two factors—the country's economic woes and publication of a number of new, competing periodicals. Note her use of the first-person pronoun "my." Hale now had a financial stake in the *American Ladies' Magazine*. The terms aren't known.

In 1835 her annual report was mixed. Hale reiterated her belief that her magazine's campaign on behalf of female education, now concluding its eighth year, was having a significant impact nationwide. So, too, she wrote, female talent and genius were commanding greater notice and more respect—noting that America's most gifted female writers appeared in the *Ladies' Magazine*. The finances of the magazine, however, were still not in good shape. She implored readers for prompt payment of the "many small sums due" for the subscription year that was closing—"It would be to us a great advantage"—and she asked them to encourage their friends to take out subscriptions for the coming year. There was a whiff of desperation in her appeals.

The following year's update brought tidings of big changes at the magazine. In a longer-than-usual annual report, Hale announced that she could no longer sustain the magazine in its present form. She made acerbic reference to subscriptions that were "tardily paid" or even "wholly neglected." This would be the final issue of the *American Ladies' Magazine* in its current form, she informed her readers. It was merging with another magazine for women, a competitor known as the *Lady's Book*.

As editor of the combined periodical, Hale pledged to continue her work "on behalf of our own sex," and she expressed enthusiasm for the opportunity of working in a "wider field," presumably a reference both to Philadelphia, where the *Lady's Book* was headquartered, and to the *Lady's Book*'s somewhat different readership, which tended to be less intellectual than that of the *Ladies' Magazine* and more interested in the practical aspects of homemaking. On the business side, the new publication would be superior to that of the *American Ladies' Magazine*, she promised. One could almost hear her sigh of relief at the prospect of relinquishing responsibility for dunning delinquent subscribers and other duties relating to the business aspects of running a magazine.

Hale didn't provide the name of her partner in this new venture. He was someone who would have as great an influence on her life's course as her brother Horatio, who educated her, and her husband David, who encouraged her to write. He was the owner and publisher of the *Lady's Book* and the man with whom she was going to create one of the most successful and influential publications in U.S. history: Louis A. Godey.

CHAPTER SIX

The Prince of Publishers

L ouis Antoine Godey was born in New York City in
1804, the son of French immigrants. His parents, Louis
and Margaret, hailed from Sens, a cathedral town seventy-five
miles south of Paris in the Burgundy region. They fled to the
United States at the end of the eighteenth century during the
bloody upheaval of the French Revolution.

The Godey family was of humble means, and young Louis
didn't have the benefit of many years of formal education. He
spent enough time in school to learn how to read, write, and
cipher. He learned, too, how to write a beautiful hand, a skill
that would serve him well in his chosen profession, where good
penmanship was an asset.

At fifteen, like many boys of his era, he set out on his own to
seek his fortune. He worked first as a newsboy and then—the
record is unclear—in a small bookstore or newsstand, possibly
owned by his father. The jobs sparked his lifelong fascination
with the publishing trade.

When Godey was in his mid-twenties, he left New York City for Philadelphia, drawn by that city's thriving printing and publishing industry. Philadelphia had been the book printing and publishing capital of the country since the late seventeenth century—well before the days of the city's most famous printer, Benjamin Franklin. It would retain that position until the middle of the nineteenth century, when New York City took the lead.

In 1828, the year Hale launched the *Ladies' Magazine* in Boston, Godey got a job working for Charles Alexander, whose firm traced its origins back to the printing company founded by Franklin in 1728. Godey was a scissors editor for the *Daily Chronicle*, a local newspaper that Alexander had recently established. A scissors editor was a journalistic pirate. His job was to scour magazines and newspapers from London, Paris, and around the United States looking for items to reprint in his own publication. If the original publishers were lucky—and they usually weren't—they received credit for the pilfered material. They never were fortunate enough to be remunerated for the unauthorized republication of their own articles. It would take more than a half century before the International Copyright Act of 1891 provided a measure of protection to foreign writers and publications from American pirates like the young Godey.

The energetic scissors editor from New York City must have made an impression on his boss, for just two years after joining the *Daily Chronicle*, in 1830, Godey and Alexander teamed up to start a monthly magazine for women. Magazines for women had multiplied during the late 1820s—Hale's *Ladies' Magazine* was the most prominent—and Godey sensed opportunity. Never mind that most of the ladies' magazines were short-lived, ceasing publication after just a year or two. Like every entrepreneur, Godey believed he could do better.

His magazine began as a low-cost, patchwork operation. He purchased a dozen old fashion plates from the owner of a defunct publication, clipped a batch of articles from copies of out-of-date British, French, and American magazines, and launched the inaugural issue of the *Lady's Book* in July 1830. The word "Godey's" did not get added to the magazine's name until more than a decade later.[1]

The title page of the first issue grandly announced that the *Lady's Book* was published by L.A. Godey & Co. at 112 Chestnut Street in Philadelphia. The next page displayed a hand-colored fashion plate, depicting a woman of the period in a gown and bonnet and carrying a sunshade. This was one of the "embellishments" that Godey would go on to trumpet as a special feature of his *Lady's Book*.

The content of the first issue consisted largely of articles from past issues of British and French periodicals, some of which were duly credited. The lead story, titled "The Latest English Fashions," came from the London magazine *La Belle Assemblée* and gave detailed descriptions of fashionable evening gowns. A generous use of French words in the copy provided a certain panache.

Fashion was the chief preoccupation of the *Lady's Book*, but there were also other items of interest. The first issue contained several sentimental poems, including two by Sir Walter Scott, published, it should go without saying, without remuneration to the Scottish poet. There were several brief sketches of life in exotic lands. "The Giraffe," reprinted from the *Magazine of Natural History*, describes the habits of that animal and the dress of his keeper, a man called Ati, in Darfur, a region in what is now Sudan. "Recollections of China" recounts the Chinese love for the peony, the "king of flowers," of which, readers learn, there are 250 species in that country. The first issue also contained columns offering practical advice. A reader could learn techniques for embroidering on muslin, how to hold her arms properly while dancing, and the correct way to mount a horse gracefully.

The only item in the first issue identified as original to the *Lady's Book* was a lurid short story titled "The Leper's Confession." The author, R. Penn Smith, was a minor Philadelphia writer who went on to pen the fictitious journal of Davy Crockett and the Alamo. It became a best seller in the 1850s largely because most readers believed Smith was recounting the real-life exploits of Davy Crockett, not the products of his own vivid imagination.

The formula Godey came up with for the first issue of the *Lady's Book*—fashion plus a smattering of poetry, fiction, sketches of life abroad, and a few how-to articles—remained largely unchanged for the next six years. Needless to say, it didn't have a great deal in common with Hale's *Ladies' Magazine*. For several years, Godey had a corner on the market for female readers in Philadelphia, and the *Lady's Book* faced no serious local challengers there. The mid-1830s saw the launch of several new women's magazines but nothing to knock the *Lady's Book* from its ranking as a favorite read of Philadelphia women.

GODEY OCCASIONALLY tried his hand at literary writing. ("May, favourite child of Spring" in the May 1836 issue is one example of his uninspired poetic endeavors.) But he was wise enough to realize that he was neither an able writer nor a good judge of literature. He was a better publisher than editor, and he soon accepted that his talents lay in the direction of business, not journalism or literature.

As the 1830s progressed, Godey's ambitions grew. Toward this end, he followed the success of Hale's magazine with admiration and a touch of awe. Not only did he recognize that the *Ladies' Magazine*, with its high-quality original content and a focus on American themes, was a superior publication. He noted that it also was one of the first American periodicals to build a national circulation—something he hadn't been able to accomplish for his magazine. As he examined the reasons that contributed to the *Ladies' Magazine*'s success, he concluded that all pointed to a single factor: its editor.

While Godey's magazine had little to differentiate itself from the array of magazines that catered to ladies, Hale's magazine was something else. Not for her the "fluff and flounce" found in other ladies' magazines, as one scholar has put it. Hale's readers were middle-class women, "women of the sewing circle rather than of the salon, and of the lyceum rather than of the theater, women coping with life on serious terms, earnest about philanthropies and progress, proud of their new country, busily endowing the old-fashioned religion with a new outlook."[2] Godey reckoned that as the country grew and prospered, the market for a serious ladies' magazine would grow with it. He wanted to be ready to take advantage of that opportunity.

Unlike Godey, Hale was what we would today call an opinion leader. She identified, examined, and publicized issues that she thought her readers needed to know. She didn't just report on cultural attitudes, she helped shape them. Hale also had literary judgment and taste—attributes Godey lacked. At the *Ladies' Magazine*, Hale had been sharp enough to recognize the talents of the young Poe and Hawthorne and to seek out talented female writers. The literary quality of the poems and short stories in the *Ladies' Magazine* was superior to anything Godey published.

There was another reason Godey wanted Hale to run his magazine. He was growing increasingly busy with publishing ventures outside the *Lady's Book*. In 1836, his publishing house was the first American publisher to bring out the popular seafaring novels of the English author Frederick Marryat, a Royal Navy officer turned writer. Around the same time, he teamed up with his friends Morton McMichael and Joseph C. Neal to launch the *Saturday News*, a weekly magazine for families. He would go on to start up the *Lady's Dollar Newspaper* in 1847, the *Lady's Musical Library* in 1842, and *The Young People's Book* in 1841.

At some point in the mid-1830s, Godey began to court Hale to move to Philadelphia and run the *Lady's Book*. At first she declined. But Godey wouldn't take no for an answer. Operating on the principle that flattery will get you everywhere, he took his suit public, pursuing it in the pages of his own magazine. It is amusing to trace how he made his play for Hale.

In 1835, he praised a recently published collection of Hale's columns for the *Ladies' Magazine*, adding that he read anything from Mrs. Hale's pen with avidity.[3] A few months later, he took the unusual step of publishing a poem written by a fourteen-year-old—and then extolling the young author to the skies. The poem, titled "The Eagle's Speech," was undistinguished except for one aspect: the poet's mother. The author was Horatio E. Hale, second son of Sarah Josepha Hale. "The poetic talents of Mrs. Hale," Godey gushed, "have descended to her son."[4] Sweet words indeed for a proud parent.

In the same item, Godey offered yet another tip of the hat to Hale by promoting her forthcoming book, *The Ladies' Wreath*, a collection of verse by British and American female poets. Godey confessed that he hadn't read *The Ladies' Wreath*, but no matter. He was nevertheless confident that the book will be "both interesting and valuable" due to Hale's "acknowledged good taste."[5]

Finally, an item in Godey's monthly column in July 1836 provided a strong hint that change was in the air. Godey announced that he was now seeking original contributions for the *Lady's Book*. "The Lady's Book will be principally composed of original matter of the best kind to be procured in this country," he wrote, "and purely American in its character." He spoke of the "large expense" he was willing to incur to secure such articles that were exclusive to the *Lady's Book*,[6] following up two months later by promising to pay authors "the highest rates of remuneration offered by any periodical in this country."[7] This extravagant promise was directed at Hale, who had started her own magazine with a similar pledge about original material but was facing hard times fulfilling that promise now that the *Ladies' Magazine* had fallen into financial straits. Godey was offering Hale an arrangement that every editor dreams of: You find the talent, he was saying, and I'll pay for it. There was also a subtle threat. With or without Hale, Godey was hinting, he was determined to remake his magazine into a serious competitor to the *Ladies' Magazine*.

By the close of the year, Godey's suit was successful. Hale accepted his offer to combine the two magazines. Her title would be literary editor but she would have charge of the bulk of the content. Godey's name remained on the title page as editor, but he would devote most of his attention to business functions.

In securing Hale's services, Godey had to concede an important point: She would edit the *Lady's Book* from Boston. Hale would not join Godey in Philadelphia until William, then fourteen years old, had graduated from Harvard. Perhaps recalling how she had left Willie's brothers and sisters in the care of others when she moved to Boston, Hale was determined to provide a home for her youngest child until he was ready to leave the family nest.

Agreeing to let his editor live in a distant city, some 350 miles from where he resided and where the magazine was published, was no small concession on Godey's part. In a decade when railroads were just beginning to supplant stagecoaches as mail carriers, it could take as long as two weeks for a letter from Boston to travel the distance to Philadelphia. Godey had won the services of the editor he wanted, but as he was to discover, the logistics of producing the magazine on time every month provided frustrations he hadn't anticipated.

Thus began the golden age of the *Lady's Book*. When Godey announced the merger of the two magazines in December 1836, he called it the beginning of a new era. The partnership between Hale and Godey would last forty-one years. Together they would create the most influential magazine in antebellum America.

HALE'S FIRST ISSUE as editor of the *Lady's Book* was January 1837. In an opening editorial titled, a bit pretentiously, "The *Conversazione*," Hale pledged "to carry onward and upward the spirit of moral intellectual excellence in our sex." She described the merger of the two publications as "pleasant voices blended in one sweet melody."[8] That was an appropriate image—if a little flowery. The embellishments that Godey loved—engravings, fashion plates, needlework patterns, sheet music—now kept company with Hale's passions for original American literature and women's empowerment issues such as education, property rights, philanthropy, and increased opportunities for employment.

Hale apparently felt the need to take a public stand regarding the colorful fashion plates on which the *Lady's Book* had built its reputation. In her "*Conversazione*," she reiterated the principles that she had laid down in the *Ladies' Magazine*. Readers shouldn't imitate the styles depicted in the fashion plates willy-nilly, she preached. Rather, the reader should adapt them to "her own figure, face, and circumstances." And then came a sermon: "This exercise of individual taste is sadly neglected by our fair countrywomen," she wrote. "We seem willing to adopt almost any and every frippery ornament, invented by French and English milliners." In the "Editor's Table" at the end of the same issue, the new editor denounced that month's fashion plate, which pictured a mother and little girl, who, in Hale's words, "has already imbibed the poison of vanity."[9] It was Hale's declaration that she was going to stand by her principles—and that that was fine with Godey.

For the next four decades, Godey would handle the business operations of the *Lady's Book* while Hale oversaw the magazine's contents. The exception was fashion, which remained under Godey's aegis. As the years passed, Hale's animus toward fashion softened—at least to the extent that she wasn't as vociferous in her condemnations. In 1838, the fashion plate became a monthly feature. It eventually expanded to a long, foldout page featuring colorful crowds of fashionable women. The hand-tinted fashion plates were so popular that readers removed them from the magazine for scrapbooks or display.

When Godey was asked—as he often was—why the fashion plates appeared in different colors in the same issue of the magazine, he came up with an ingenious reply: "We now colour our plates to different patterns," he informed readers, "so that two persons in a place may compare their fashions, and adopt those colours that they suppose may be most suitable to their figures and complexions."[10] This was Godey speaking in his capacity of quick-witted public relations man. The true reason for the differently colored engravings had to do with the work habits of the women he hired to color them. Many of the women worked from home, and if they ran out of the specified color, they simply substituted another.

In a friendly jab at Hale, who was quick to praise opportunities for women to enter new occupations, Godey also liked to note that the fashion plates created jobs for the women hired to do the hand-coloring. He boasted in 1851 that the magazine employed 150 women in the coloring and binding departments alone.

Readers didn't always understand Hale's and Godey's separation of editorial duties. You can detect the note of annoyance in the voice of the person—possibly Hale—who wrote the following notice that appeared repeatedly in the *Lady's Book*: "Mrs. Hale is not the Fashion Editress. Will our subscribers please remember that?"

GODEY WAS by all accounts a gifted and energetic man of business. At the *Lady's Book* he implemented numerous moneymaking schemes. One was a service by which readers could order books, copies of the engravings published in the magazine, and many household items. This was a forerunner of the mail-order catalog that became popular later in the century. Perhaps Richard Sears, born in 1863, and Alvah Roebuck, born in 1864, got the idea for their famous mail-order catalog from reading copies of the *Lady's Book* that their mothers left around the house.

Another Godey innovation was premiums—in his grandiose words, "magnificent and expensive premiums," or gifts that he offered to new subscribers and those who renewed their subscriptions. He promoted the use of "clubs," by which he set reduced subscription rates to groups of individuals who pooled their money for multiple copies. In 1857, the advertised annual subscription rates were $3 for one copy, $5 for two copies, $6 for three copies, and so forth. He also offered reduced rates for subscriptions to both the *Lady's Book* and *Arthur's Home Magazine,* another monthly published in Philadelphia that was aimed at female readers.

GODEY WAS a consummate showman, never shy about pitching his product in a string of superlatives. He delighted in trumpeting the *Lady's Book* success, such as his assertion in 1841 that "from Maine to the Rocky Mountains there is scarcely a hamlet, however inconsiderable, where it is not received and read."[11] Advertisements for the *Lady's Book* made lavish promises. A full-page house ad at the back of the January 1850 issue promised that that year's *Lady's Book* "SHALL SURPASS THAT OF 1849, And exceed all magazines past, present, and to come." Recognizing that Hale's reputation helped attract subscribers, he often touted her name in his advertisements. The magazine's contents are always "moral and instructive," he vowed in a typical comment, thanks to "Mrs. Sarah Josepha Hale, whose name alone is a sufficient guarantee for the propriety of the Lady's Book."[12]

To get his magazine noticed in more communities, he sent complimentary copies of the *Lady's Book* to a long list of newspapers and periodicals in the expectation that in return for the free copies they would write favorably about the magazine—thereby encouraging their readers to subscribe. When the papers obliged with flattering notices, Godey was only too happy to reprint their adulations, filling his monthly column with these accolades. In March 1871 he quoted papers from Maine, Illinois, Connecticut, Iowa, Michigan, Indiana, Pennsylvania, and Massachusetts with such tributes as:

> "GODEY'S LADY'S BOOK for January surpasses in brilliancy all previous efforts."[13]
>
> "Godey is continually astonishing us with some new enterprise, some additional attraction."[14]
>
> "The best ladies' magazine in the country."[15]

And the *pièce de résistance*:

"When we examine the numbers of this matchless periodical, monthly, as they are received, we think surely Godey has
reached the highest attainable point in his department of literature. Yet, behold! the succeeding number shows that he
has climbed still higher. The January number for 1871 sur-
passes all that have preceded it. It should be in every family,
as it is an invaluable assistant to every housewife."[16]

Godey was perfectly happy to do his own boasting too. In the
February 1858 issue, he bragged that "the *Lady's Book* is the best
work for ladies published in this country." Just in case readers
didn't get his message, he also wrote, "Remember that the *Lady's Book* is not a mere luxury; it is a necessity." So, too, he encouraged readers to write to him and then published their complimentary letters—thousands of them over the years.[17]

The zenith of Godey's self-promotional declarations may have
come in 1849, when he published a short item titled "We." "The
word is almost exclusively restricted to royalty and the press,"
he wrote. "We, therefore, may justly appropriate it. We not only
belong to the press but . . . we are so repeatedly called 'the Prince
of publishers,' 'the Napoleon of the press'—and our magazine is
so often termed 'the Queen of the monthlies' and 'Princess of
magazines'—that our royalty even presses upon us."[18]

THE PRINCE OF PUBLISHERS' biggest innovation was his controversial decision, in 1845, to copyright the contents of the *Lady's Book*. The U.S. Constitution protects authors' interest in
their work, and in 1790 Congress legislated that protection into
the nation's first copyright law. After that, American publishers

routinely took out copyrights for books under the 1790 law, but for some reason they didn't bother to do so for periodicals. Godey's decision created a furor.

It is improbable that Godey made his copyright decision without consulting his editor. We can infer Hale's views on the subject of copyright from what she wrote much earlier at the *Ladies' Magazine*. As early as 1828, she argued that "the time has arrived when our American authors should have something besides empty praise from their countrymen."[19] Also that year, in a review of Hawthorne's novel *Fanshawe*, she urged readers not to borrow the book from a library or a friend but to buy it.[20]

The *Baltimore Saturday Visiter* [*sic*] called Godey's decision to copyright the *Lady's Book* an "insulting proposition," writing, "It pains us to see that Mr. Godey has resorted to the narrowly selfish course of taking out a *copyright* for his book."[21] Godey defended his action by explaining that he paid good writers good money for original articles and that he, the publisher, had a right to protect his investment from being stolen by other periodicals. The former scissors editor knew how the game was played. Fifteen years earlier, when he was working at the *Philadelphia Daily Chronicle*, he had spent hours poring over magazines looking for articles to steal.

In an explanation to readers of his decision, Godey asked only that newspapers that wished to reprint articles from his magazine wait one month before doing so. As an example of the indignities he had endured, he mentioned an unnamed weekly paper that, having received an early copy of the *Lady's Book*, had pirated nearly half its contents, publishing them before the *Lady's Book* had reached subscribers.

Edgar Allan Poe came to the defense of Godey and George Graham, who had also announced that he would copyright his

Graham's American Monthly Magazine. Writing in the *Broadway Journal*, which he owned and edited, Poe said:

> It is really very difficult to see how any one can, in conscience, object to such a course on the part of Messrs. Godey and Graham. To our comprehension, a mere statement of the facts of the case should stand in lieu of all argument. It has long been the custom among the newspapers—the weeklies especially—to copy Magazine articles in full, and circulate them all over the country—sometimes in advance of the magazines themselves. In other words, Godey and Graham have been at all the cost, while the papers have enjoyed, if not the advantage—at least the most important item of it—the origination of the articles.[22]

The *Baltimore Saturday Visiter* wasn't alone in criticizing Godey. Other papers took shots at him too, and it took courage for Godey to stand by his copyright decision. He relied on local newspapers to promote the *Lady's Book.* By risking their approbation he risked both the reputation of his magazine and its circulation.

Godey's PR skill and editorial innovations helped build the *Lady's Book*'s circulation and made him a rich man. At the time of his death in 1878, his estate was valued at about $1 million, roughly $26 million today.

BEING THE ASTUTE businessman that he was, Godey must have had some trepidation when, in 1836, he agreed that his editor-to-be would run the *Lady's Book* from several hundred miles away. The long-distance relationship between the Philadelphia-based publisher and the editor in Boston worked well, albeit with bumps along the way. Godey complained that Hale didn't always deliver her copy for "Editor's Table" on time, and he was upset when authors he thought wrote exclusively for the *Lady's Book* appeared in other publications. (Lydia Sigourney was the biggest offender.) For her part, Hale was annoyed at not always receiving the page proofs in time to get her markups back to Philadelphia before the magazine went to press. They also clashed over money matters, with Godey responding angrily at a comment by Hale about her "small" salary.[23]

Hale had an extensive circle of friends in Boston, where she was involved in multiple philanthropies—the Bunker Hill Monument, the Perkins School for the Blind, the Seaman's Aid Society, the first public children's playground, and more. It is possible that she didn't always give as timely attention as she might have to communicating with Godey in faraway Philadelphia. Relations between the two deteriorated to the point where in 1839 Godey proposed that Hale give up editing the magazine. He didn't want to sever the relationship completely; Hale's national reputation and influence were too important to the continuing success of the *Lady's Book*. Rather, he offered to pay her for the use of her name as editor on the title page along with an agreed-upon number of pages of her own writing each month. They were able to smooth over their differences, but it was clear that the long-distance relationship wasn't always easy to manage.

At the same time, their friendship was deepening. When Godey's young daughter Fanny died at the end of 1837, he responded to Hale's condolence note in a highly personal way, with the sort of information one would only share with a close friend:

Fanny was not my only child. I have one older—but I am almost ashamed to confess it that I thought her the favourite.

Perhaps the feeling may be natural that we should feel for the most helpless. Of course, as is every parent, she was a perfect being—That she was beautiful I could not help but see. A more than usual interest seemed to gather around her. She came into this world . . . three days after my poor brother's death. She came perhaps a little unexpectedly—and restored our little family into its former state. Perhaps our smiles were a little tempered with sadness, but she brought with her relief to my mother, who was in a very desponding way until this, as it now appears, transient vision, floated before us.[24]

GODEY WAS, by many accounts, a well-loved and respected citizen of Philadelphia. On the twenty-fifth anniversary of the founding of the *Lady's Book*, in 1855, Godey's colleagues in the publishing business held a grand dinner in his honor to which they invited local notables and old friends of the honoree.

Never one to overlook a marketing moment, Godey published a detailed account of the dinner, along with transcripts of the speeches, in the *Lady's Book*.[25] The dinner was catered by Thomas J. Dorsey, an African American who had been born a slave, fled to Philadelphia, and was now a high-society caterer to the elite of city. American flags hung on the walls of the banquet hall, and "rare" flowers decorated the table. Among the speakers was the mayor of Philadelphia, who called Godey "a man of honor, courage, and virtue . . . with a heart the warmest that ever flowed in a human bosom." Another speaker praised him as a patron of literary talent, defining the word *patron* as "the man who pays [the author] well for his labor," a designation that perfectly fit the honoree. A friend who had known him since their shared schooldays in New York City said of him, "a more genial, lovable, and sterling man does not live."

The tribute dinner was an all-male affair, but four women who were closely associated with Godey received glancing references: Godey mentioned his wife, though not by name, who was back home "with her little family beside her." He thanked his hosts on her behalf for honoring him. He also thanked the binder of the *Lady's Book*, an unnamed woman who had been working with him since the magazine's founding in 1830 and had now brought her son into her business. Godey did not mention Hale, but the presider of the dinner made an indirect reference to her and Emma Embury, a Philadelphia writer and (in 1855) an assistant editor of the *Lady's Book*. They were described as Godey's "accomplished collaborators."

Even in an era when women were expected to remain in the background and it was considered disrespectful for men to mention their names in public settings, the short shrift accorded Hale and her dominant role in the *Lady's Book*'s success seems unjust. This was especially so when it came to the wording of the first toast: "The health of our friend, Louis A. Godey, the most widely and permanently successful among the educators of American ladies." Left unsaid was that it was Hale, not Godey, who introduced the topic of educating women when she became editor in 1837. It should be noted that Godey's silence on Hale's role was a rare occasion. He usually was unstinting in his praise of Hale, whose work he lauded frequently in the pages of the *Lady's Book*. Hale's salary and other terms of her employment are unknown other than the fact that on the thirtieth anniversary of her editorship, in 1867, Godey gave her a bonus of $5,000.[26]

HALE'S DECISION to close the *Ladies' Magazine* and merge it with the *Lady's Book* could not have come easily to her. But as much as she may have wanted to retain full control of her own magazine, she was wise enough to read the writing on the wall. Godey was determined to upgrade his *Lady's Book* with or without her help. Her magazine was struggling financially, and it would have had a difficult time surviving competition with Godey's better-funded publication.

Godey's offer came at a time when her personal financial pressures were intensifying. David had graduated from West Point in 1833, but her other children were still completing their studies and she was struggling to pay their school fees. David sent her what he could to help with expenses, but it wasn't much. He anticipated being able to send her several hundred dollars a year once he was promoted to lieutenant.[27]

She was especially worried about how to pay for her daughters' education at Emma Willard's school, the Troy Female Seminary in Troy, New York, near Albany—in Hale's view, the country's best school for young women. She told Willard in March 1834 that she would not be able to afford to send Fanny and Josy to her school that year. Necessary improvements to the *Ladies' Magazine*—she possibly meant the purchase of engravings—meant that she would not "realize as much from my labors this year as usual." She proposed that the girls enter Willard's school the following year. Once they were enrolled she expressed the hope that Willard would give Fanny a job teaching Latin and Greek in partial payment for her school fees. (Fanny's teacher "says she has the best knowledge of Latin of any female he ever knew," Hale wrote.) As for Josepha, Hale proposed sending her to live with a sister of her late husband in Concord, New Hampshire, for a year to learn domestic skills. "My second daughter was thirteen last Dec.," she wrote Willard. "She can do nothing for herself yet." Willard's reply has not survived, but we know that Fanny and Josy were enrolled at the Troy Female Seminary by 1836.[28]

In a retrospective essay at the time of his fiftieth reunion at Harvard, Horatio pointedly noted his mother's "scant means" during the years he was in college.[29] As the year 1837 commenced, though, Hale's financial situation brightened. Her new job as editor of the *Lady's Book* freed her from the financial worries she had at the *Ladies' Magazine*. Horatio was about to graduate and take up his job with the U.S. Exploring Expedition at a salary that would allow him to help with his siblings' school expenses.[30] Fanny and Josepha were still in Troy, and Willie would enter Harvard in the fall.

In 1838, David, by now a lieutenant assigned to an army artillery unit, was fighting the Seminole in Florida. In early 1839, he was transferred to Plattsburgh in upper New York State to defend the American border with Canada. War was looming over the disputed Aroostook area of Maine and the Canadian province of New Brunswick.

Then, on April 30, 1839, the nightmare of every military parent became real. David died. The official explanation for the cause of his death was "a sudden and unexpected effusion of the lungs." David suffered from an illness that was later explained as a consequence of the extreme change in climate occasioned by his move from hot, humid Florida to the much colder New York. Perhaps, like his father, David caught a cold, which turned to deadly pneumonia.

Hale received a copy of the letter that David's commanding officer, Lieutenant Colonel B.K. Pierce, wrote to Army Adjutant General Roger Jones reporting David's death. The colonel extolled David as "amiable, brave & talented," but the words sounded pro forma, in keeping with the rest of the letter, which appears to have been a stock letter intended for the army's files.[31] Just plug in the name and rank of the deceased and off it goes.

David's death was a crushing blow to the family. As the oldest son, David had replaced his father in the family circle. He bailed out Horatio when he ran short of money at Harvard. Another time he counseled his serious younger brother not to spend all his time on his studies, enclosing a gift of money in a New Year's letter and admonishing Horatio to have a "good frolic."[32]

Hale had an intense attachment to David and relied heavily on him. An excerpt from a letter she wrote when he was still a cadet at West Point indicates the extent of her feelings: "You are yet ignorant of the fervent and engrossing affection which a parent feels for a child. The love of a mother, especially a widowed mother, who enters her thoughts and builds her hopes of future earthly happiness only on the merit and success of her children is of all human feelings perhaps the most intense and exhaustless."[33]

A few weeks before David's death, Hale had written to tell him how happy she was to receive a letter from him and expressing her fears about his safety. She was concerned both about the "warlike" men in Maine who seemed eager to start a shooting war with Canada and about David's general good health. "I was very glad to see your handwriting once more," she wrote. "You do not know how these long intervals of silence trouble me. I imagine you are sick—and suffer a thousand inquietudes." She closed her letter with the words: "I shall think of you every time I lay my head on my pillow. May God guide and bless you." Now her worst fears were realized.[34]

Hale sent Godey a poignant letter, parts of which he reprinted in the *Lady's Book*, informing readers of David's death: "It is not a common loss that I mourn," Hale wrote to Godey. "I depended on him as a friend . . . and as the protector of my daughters and young son—His death has destroyed all my plans of life. . . . I cannot, at once, summon fortitude to enter on the occupations of a world so dark and desolate as this now appears."[35] Godey announced that Hale would be taking a leave of absence from her duties as editor for several months.

By 1841, William was in his final stretch at Harvard, where he went on to graduate in 1842, earning both bachelor's and master's degrees. After nearly five years of editing her magazine from afar, in the fall of 1841 Hale decided that Willie—the one she called the "youngling of the flock"—was old enough to get along without her. It was time for her to take up her duties in Philadelphia.

Hale and Fanny moved to Philadelphia after the ladies' fair for the Bunker Hill Monument concluded in September. Fanny and Josy had finished their studies at the Troy Female Seminary. Josy accepted a teaching job in the South.

"My regret at leaving Boston was great," Hale later wrote, "for my residence there had been a happy one: but it was necessary for me to be nearer the publication office of the *'Lady's Book,'* and my health had suffered in the cold climate of New England."[36]

As she departed the city that had been her home for more than a dozen years, she may have recalled a line in a letter that David wrote to her in 1831, when he was a cadet at West Point. David's youthful letters were usually lighthearted. But in this particular one, he allowed himself to turn serious for a moment: "Your children will *never* forget the education and support you have given them," he wrote his mother.[37] Now, ten years later, David was dead, Horatio was somewhere in the South Pacific

with the Exploring Expedition, Willie was soon to seek his for-
tune after his graduation from Harvard, and Josepha was teaching in Georgia. With her children so scattered, Hale was ready
to move on.

CHAPTER SEVEN

Literary Ladies

F ROM A LITERARY STANDPOINT, Hale's first twenty years
as editor of *Godey's Lady's Book* were the magazine's glory years. She was on the money when she told readers in 1838
that "thanks to the wise liberality of the Publisher, we have a
larger list of contributors."[1]

The *Lady's Book*, with its growing national circulation, generous payments to authors, and celebrity editor, was the magazine
in which every writer, male or female, wanted to appear. These
were the years when many of the great, now-familiar, names of
the country's emerging literature wrote for the *Lady's Book*: Edgar Allan Poe, Nathaniel Hawthorne, Washington Irving, Henry
Wadsworth Longfellow, John Greenleaf Whittier, James Russell
Lowell, Dr. Oliver Wendell Holmes, William Cullen Bryant. Two
men whose work was immensely popular in the nineteenth century but who are little remembered today appeared frequently:
T.S. Arthur and N.P. Willis.

Hale had worked with or written about many of these authors

at the *Ladies' Magazine*. Now, at the *Lady's Book*, she wrote approvingly of Hawthorne's books in her reviews, published two of his short stories, and invited Poe to write a lengthy, positive critique of Hawthorne's work. She greatly admired Longfellow, "our American poet," publishing several of his poems as well as praising and quoting him frequently in editorials and reviews. In one article, she took the opportunity to attack unnamed Transcendental poets, noting approvingly that Longfellow was "perfectly free from the nasal whine of the transcendental school, which is so much in vogue these days and which is destined to be universally regarded with a feeling of nausea at no very distant future day."[2] Hale's opinion of the Transcendentalists stemmed less from her literary taste than from her Christian faith, which made her question their subjective definition of God. Her judgment didn't hold up with the years. History does not see Ralph Waldo Emerson, Henry David Thoreau, and other notables of the Transcendental school of poetry as whiners. It is worth noting that her disapproval of Transcendentalism didn't stop her from printing several lovely poems by Emerson.

Whittier contributed poems to the *Lady's Book* as well as a charming, flight-of-fancy essay about fairies that inhabited a ramshackle tavern in New England. Lowell provided a sonnet. Holmes, Hale's old friend from her Boston boardinghouse, contributed a half dozen poems. Washington Irving wrote travel essays from England for the *Lady's Book*, including one decrying the literary animosity growing between England and America over the comments by British writers such as Frances Trollope and Charles Dickens, who wrote unfavorably about their trips to this country. Irving urged readers to cherish the "land of our forefathers."[3]

Poe was a special favorite of Hale, who had praised his earliest work when the poet was still at West Point. At the *Lady's*

Book, she continued to follow his career until his early death in 1849. In her review of *Tales of the Grotesque and Arabesque*, Hale called him a "writer of rare and various abilities" with an "unusually active imagination" who had produced "some of the most vivid scenes . . . in English literature."[4] Poe, in turn, wrote forthrightly about his admiration of Hale, describing her in one instance as "a woman of great force of thought and remarkable purity of style. She writes invariably well."[5]

Hale's interest in Poe was personal as well as literary, spurred by her son David's acquaintanceship with the writer at West Point. After Poe was court-martialed and discharged from West Point in 1829, the cadets took up a collection to finance publication of a book of Poe's poems. The book's dedication reads, "To the U.S. Corps of Cadets this volume is respectfully dedicated." Years later, in Philadelphia, Hale's kindness to Poe extended to Mrs. Maria Poe Clemm, Poe's impoverished aunt and mother-in-law. (Poe married his cousin.) Hale befriended Clemm, who benefited from the editor's personal charity. When Clemm dropped by Hale's house, she would depart with a basket full of food.[6]

Poe wrote frequently for the *Lady's Book* in the 1840s. His famous stories "The Cask of Amontillado" and "The Oblong Box," among others, first appeared there. These horror tales—the first a revenge story about a man trapped alive behind a brick wall and the second about a man who is buried alive—weren't the typical sort of fare for readers of the *Lady's Book*. Hale, however, perceived their literary value and their popular appeal. Poe, who was always famously short of cash, appreciated the fees that Godey paid, as well the status that came with writing for the *Lady's Book*.

In addition to being a poet and author of short stories, Poe was a literary critic. In 1846, Hale published Poe's incendiary series of articles skewering famous members of New York City's literary elite, such as N.P. Willis, Margaret Fuller, and Thomas Dunn English. The full title hints at the explosive personal nature of Poe's critiques of his fellow writers: "The Literati of New York City— Some Honest Opinions at Random Respecting Their Authorial Merits with Occasional Words of Personality." After the first entry in the series, which sold out the issue of the *Lady's Book* in which it appeared, a firestorm of protest ensued, with readers threatening to cancel their subscriptions. Friends of Godey and Hale wrote to express their disapproval. Publisher and editor stood firm in support of Poe, however, telling readers that they would not cancel his series. They printed a stern note in the following issue of the *Lady's Book*: "Whether we agree with Mr. Poe or not is another matter. We are not to be intimidated by a threat of the loss of friends or turned from our purpose with honeyed words."[7] They published the rest of the series.

HALE'S LITERARY JUDGMENT and publication decisions helped advance the careers of the men whose work she published, but they had an even larger impact on the women whose reputations she helped build. At the *Ladies' Magazine* she had encouraged women to sign their articles rather than using initials or coy designations such as "A Lady of Hartford," thereby helping them to make names for themselves. At the *Lady's Book*, she took a chance in encouraging little-known female authors to write serious works of fiction with American settings and true-to-life characters. The popularity of the *Lady's Book* demonstrated that there was a market for literature aimed at the growing number of middle-class women readers who were both literate and interested in reading a different kind of story—one that mirrored their own experiences and acquaintances.

When she took over the editorship of the *Lady's Book*, Hale announced her intention to seek out women writers, saying that she wished to promote American authors, especially women, and to use the *Lady's Book* to address issues concerning women. As the scholar Elaine Showalter has pointed out, the 1820s and 1830s saw the emergence of gifted women writers who, like Hale, were motivated by a wish to celebrate their native land and contribute toward the creation of a distinctly American literature.[8] At the *Ladies' Magazine*, Hale built up a strong list of distinguished literary ladies. She took those authors with her to the *Lady's Book* and recruited more women. Most of the writers will be unfamiliar today, but they were the great names of the female literary awakening of the three decades before the Civil War.

Foremost among her stable of writers was Lydia Huntley Sigourney. The "Sweet Singer of Hartford" was among the most prolific writers of the early and mid-nineteenth century and one of the first women to establish a successful literary career. Born in 1791 and 1788 respectively, Sigourney and Hale were near-contemporaries, and the two women became close friends. Like Hale, Sigourney needed the money, which provided motivation to work hard. Hale dedicated one of her early books to "My Friend Mrs. L.H. Sigourney as a token of the esteem and affection cherished for her by the Author."[9]

Sigourney's poetry and essays appeared in both of Hale's magazines as well as in countless other publications. Frank Luther Mott, a historian of American magazines, reckons that she made more than 2,000 contributions to more than 300 periodicals.[10] Sigourney wrote about public issues such as Native Americans, slavery, female education, and patriotism, along with highly personal and emotional topics such as death and grief. One of her notable poems, "The Execution," about a condemned man who goes unrepentant to the gallows, appeared in the *Ladies' Magazine* in 1833. Her contributions for Hale at the *Lady's Book* numbered in the dozens, beginning with the poem "The Indian Girl's Funeral," which ran in 1838. Hale, like Sigourney and other female writers of New England, was highly critical of what they saw as the white man's mistreatment of the first Americans.

Sigourney was so popular with readers that between 1839 and 1842, Godey reportedly paid her five hundred dollars a year for the prestige of listing her name on the title page of the *Lady's Book*, just under Hale's, as an assistant editor. Sigourney didn't do any editing, but she boosted the number of contributions she made the magazine to roughly one poem and one article monthly. In 1839, Godey and Hale sent her to Europe to write her "impressions of foreign scenery and manners" and to seek contributions from notable women abroad. The trip resulted in a number of pleasant, educational essays by Sigourney about the places she saw and the people she met on her travels. One of her few successes at the latter objective was persuading the Anglo-Irish novelist Maria Edgeworth to contribute a poem to the *Lady's Book*.[11]

ELIZA LESLIE was another frequent contributor whose name appeared on the title page for a few years as a regular contributor. Leslie, a Philadelphian, was a versatile writer who was best known for her cookbooks, etiquette books, and writing for juveniles. (She has gone down in culinary history for publishing in 1847 the first recipe for chocolate cake.) She contributed short stories, essays, and household advice to the *Lady's Book*.

In 1845, Hale dispatched Leslie on a journey to Niagara Falls, a three-day journey from New York City by steamboat and railroad. Leslie's two-part series described the travel arrangements in detail, with the underlying message that rail travel was a safe means of transportation for genteel women. There was no la- dies' car on part of the journey, she noted—a lack that made Leslie apprehensive at first—and "gentlemen and ladies and men and women were seated promiscuously" throughout the train. When Leslie raised the issue with the conductor, he informed her that "all the cars were equally polite"—and he was right, she concluded. Leslie was so pleased with her journey that she imagined a distant time when trains would transport travelers from the Atlantic to the Pacific, where they could transfer to a steamboat and sail to the Sandwich Islands.[12]

By the 1840s, Americans were on the move as railroads and steamboats made travel easier. Hale often published travel es- says, which she saw as a means of educating readers about their native land. She had a particular fondness for essays about the how-tos of travel, especially when they featured women trav- eling without a male "protector." In 1846, she penned a com- ic account of her own mishap-laden journey by stagecoach in New Hampshire on her way home to Philadelphia from New- port, where she had been an honored guest at the Fourth of July festivities commemorating the eightieth anniversary of the set- tlement of the town. "Stage-Coach Adventures" was the title of her essay, and "adventure" is how she seemed to think of travel overall.[13] She certainly didn't approve of women being confined to home and denied the pleasures of travel because they lacked a male escort.

Long before she penned *Uncle Tom's Cabin*, the young Harri- ett Beecher Stowe wrote for Hale at the *Lady's Book*. Among her articles was an essay examining the quiet virtues of journeying by canal boat—where "there is no power, no mystery, no danger; one can't blow up, one can't be drowned unless by some special effort."[14] Stowe also contributed short stories and poetry.

Hale's promise that the *Lady's Book* would cover issues of special interest to women was borne out in the fiction she published, including the dozens of short stories and novellas by Eliza Leslie that were set in the domestic arena inhabited by women. Leslie's short story "The Centre-Table" is one example.[15] The setting is the home of an affluent widow in Philadelphia, where a group of ladies are debating the appropriate responses to unwanted questions about how much something cost them. A tale within the tale recounts the comic reverberations following a woman's boast about the low price she paid for a particular item of clothing. "The Centre-Table" is an amusing story that addresses both Godey's stricture that the *Lady's Book* be entertaining and Hale's desire that fiction carry a moral—in this case about the evils of consumerism. For the modern reader, Leslie's stories and novellas are a window on life as it was lived by middle-class women of the mid-nineteenth century—how they dressed, ate, shopped, furnished their homes, entertained their guests, treated their servants, talked to their husbands. The same can be said of many stories by other writers whom Hale published.

CATHARINE SEDGWICK and Caroline M. Kirkland were two other skilled authors who wrote trenchant short stories about social and domestic matters for the *Lady's Book*. Like Leslie and Sigourney, Sedgwick was a regular contributor whose name appeared on the title page for a few years.

Sedgwick was probably the most talented female writer Hale published. Her stories are little gems about human foibles and frailties that read well today. They feature believable characters, usually women, who are so well depicted that they could step off the pages of the *Lady's Book* into real life. Showalter praises Sedg-wick's "outstanding gifts as a writer: wit, intelligence, warmth, a sense of structure and coherence, an ear for believable dialogue, and an eye for accurate detail."[16] One of the recurring themes of her stories has to do with the kindness and generosity of older women who care for younger women who have fallen on hard times. The settings are realistic, as is the subject matter. Readers learn about the ugly anti-Irish bigotry of the day, the lack of op-tions open to women without families to support them, and more. Sedgwick's multipart tale "Wilton Harvey," serialized in the *La-dy's Book* in 1842, was one of the first magazine articles to carry a copyright notice. It appeared three years before Godey made the decision to copyright the contents of the *Lady's Book*.

Like Sedgwick, Kirkland was also a master at presenting realistic stories of domestic life—often with a dollop of gentle humor. Hale praised her work as "piquant and lively."[17] Unlike many of Hale's writers, who were from New England, Kirkland hailed from the West, which is to say that she wrote from the frontier town of Detroit, where she had moved in 1837. Part of the charm of her stories came from their Western settings and Kirkland's droll depictions of Western customs, which were less formal than in the established East.

Other writers for the *Lady's Book* in the 1840s and 1850s included the New York poet and socialite Emma Embury, who followed Hale from the *Ladies' Magazine* to the *Lady's Book* in Philadelphia. Caroline Lee Hentz, Hannah Flagg Gould, Eliza-beth Ellett, and Fanny Fern—all well known in their day—are other writers who graced the pages of the *Lady's Book* during that period.

Hale's encouragement of female writers was on copious dis-play in the January 1841 issue, one of three issues written en-

tirely by women—including Sigourney, Leslie, Embury, and Ellett. The issue concluded with an editorial essay by Hale on the
subject of philanthropy in which she struck her familiar themes:
Take an active role in your local philanthropies. Don't dispense
alms indiscriminately. Help the poor find jobs at fair wages. Finally, she entreated readers to pay fair wages to the women who
worked for them, remembering that seamstresses and washer-
women have families to feed.

The last word of the all-women issue was given to a man,
namely Godey, who took the opportunity to boast: "The publisher's interest will render it necessary to make the *Lady's Book*
superior to what it has been in former years, *if such a thing is
possible*. At least, this number shows that he commences well."
From the publisher's perspective, it would seem, Hale's commitment to publishing women writing on women's issues was a
profitable commercial undertaking.

THE CONCEPT OF authorship as a profession for women or men
was relatively new in 1828, when Hale began her editorial career. Scholar Patricia Okker points out that in the 1820s most
writers, editors, and publishers "accepted the eighteenth-century idea of the scholar gentleman, thus equating literary pursuits
with leisure activities."[18] Few authors were able to earn money from their work. If they wrote books, they either paid the
printing costs themselves or they sought out a patron to finance
them—as Hale did when the Freemasons of Newport supported
the publication of her first book, *The Genius of Oblivion*, in 1823.

For Hale, however, writing was not a leisure activity; it was
her means of making a living. Okker credits Hale with redefining
authorship as a vocational pursuit appropriate for women and
with creating the idea of a professional female author. Hale did

so by her own example and also by her support of the women who wrote for her.

Her first principle was that writers deserved to be paid for their work. In this, she agreed with N.P. Willis, who once counseled her that "every line you write is saleable, so do not send it to those who do not pay for poetry."[19] Hale's financial arrangements with Godey are unknown. But her correspondence with her book publishers indicates that she had become a good negotiator about the terms under which her books were published. The woman who had dreaded talking business with men when she first took up the editorship of the *Ladies' Magazine* had grown more confident about money matters and able to speak up for herself without a male intermediary. (One of her standard contractual demands was that she receive six copies: one for herself and each of her children.)

The no-reprint policy that Hale took with her from the *Ladies' Magazine* to the *Lady's Book* grew out of belief that reprinting articles without credit or payment was a form of theft. Godey was praised for having the courage to buck tradition and copyright his magazine, but it is impossible to imagine that he made such a decision without consulting Hale and securing her support. She may well have been the driving force behind his decision.

Hale warned would-be authors that a successful literary career was not for dilettantes. It was a professional undertaking that required training, talent, time, and hard work. Hale often made this point in her "Editor's Table" column when she listed the submissions she had accepted and those she had rejected. She identified the submissions by their titles, never revealing the names of the authors. This was a kindness, as her notices frequently included biting critiques of the rejected articles.

She chided one writer that his submission was so lengthy that if accepted it would fill the magazine, going on to lecture that overwriting "is a serious fault" that would-be authors should avoid. "We want short, racy, spirited essays," she instructed.[20] In another case, she offered consolation of a sort to a disappointed author, telling him that one day he would thank her for sparing him the embarrassment of publishing his submission. In another column Hale—apparently fed up with the execrable quality of submissions—let loose, describing three categories of authors whose work she had rejected: promising, mediocre, and hopeless.[21] Promising authors had a chance at success provided they worked diligently to develop their talent. Literary success was unlikely for authors in the mediocre category. As for those writers whom she classified as hopeless, well, they ought to resign themselves to writing for their own pleasure, because they weren't capable of writing to please others.

Frances Hodgson Burnett, who went on to write the classic children's books *The Secret Garden* and *The Little Princess*, avidly read Hale's rejection notices for tips on how to improve her writing. Her first published short story appeared in the *Lady's Book* in October 1868,[22] and she went on to write a steady stream of pieces for the magazine.[23]

THE 1840s AND 1850s were a productive time not just for the *Lady's Book* but also for Hale's own literary output. Her writing for the magazine focused on poetry, literary reviews, and editorial essays, where she reported on the same women's issues she had covered in the *Ladies' Magazine*: education, achievements by notable women, property rights for married women, philanthropic work. She began a new focus on two topics that would occupy her for the rest of her editorship—employment for women and the business of homemaking. She kept up the editorial drumbeat on the country's pressing need for female teachers and the establishment of normal schools to educate them. She continued her advocacy on behalf of children and lobbied for Philadelphia to lift its ban on children playing on the grass in its parks. She launched spirited campaigns for a national Thanksgiving Day and for female doctors.

In style, her monthly column read much like a modern-day blog. The monthly edition of "Editors' Table" usually carried a long list of items, short and long, important and mundane, serious and lighthearted—not to mention highly opinionated. She addressed readers directly in a voice of authority. She used a firm tone that occasionally crossed a line to moralizing or lecturing. Most of the time, though, her style was conversational and friendly, as if she were addressing readers from a seat in her front parlor.

Her literary reviews, which appeared in a separate column titled "Editors' Book Table" or "Literary Notices," were more numerous and generally shorter than they had been at the *Ladies' Magazine*, probably due to the increase in the number of books being published. She still favored books written by women. Authors who wrote for the *Lady's Book*—female or male—could be sure of receiving favorable mentions. Promotion of their books was another way she helped build the careers of the women who wrote for her and another reason writers of both sexes liked being published in the *Lady's Book*.

Another source of income for writers of the day was the annual gift book, published by numerous book publishers and typically aimed at female readers. These were illustrated collections of poetry and short stories by American authors that were intended as Christmas or New Year's gifts. They bore such titles as *The Token, The Atlantic Souvenir, The Boston Book,* and *Youth's Keepsake*. Hale had been contributing to gift books since the mid-1820s, when she was still living in Newport. By the 1840s, she contributed poems to several gifts books every year, often at the invitation of colleagues who were editing them and wanted to oblige their friends by giving them a paid commission. Hale herself was a star attraction; featuring a poem with her name on it helped sell books.

N.P. Willis, Eliza Leslie, and Lydia Sigourney—all closely associated with the *Lady's Book*—called on Hale to write for the gift books they edited: *The Opal, The Violet,* and *The Religious Souvenir*, respectively. In 1844, Hale took on the editorship of a gift book, succeeding Willis as editor of *The Opal*. She also edited a bridal gift book titled *The White Veil* and provided a poem to *The Sons of Temperance*, a collection of anti-alcohol works edited by T.S. Arthur. Arthur, a frequent *Lady's Book* contributor, was well known for his 1854 best seller *Ten Nights in a Bar-Room and What I Saw There*.

Hale wrote, too, for numerous Christian publications, including a volume titled *The Women of the Scriptures*, for which she contributed an essay on Queen Esther. She edited collections of the letters of Madame de Sevigne, an iconic seventeenth-century French wit, and those of Lady Mary Wortley Montagu, an English traveler to Turkey. She wrote cookbooks, edited poetry anthologies, penned two plays (one in blank verse), and wrote the lyrics to several hymns and songs. She edited poetry anthologies, including a six-hundred-page collection of quotations from four hundred British and American poets.

Her output of fiction during this period included short novels that carried moral messages in support of opinions she expressed in her "Editors' Table" essays. *My Cousin Mary: Or the*

Inebriate advocated for temperance. *Keeping House and House-keeping* and *Boarding Out*, both novels of domestic life, depicted the many challenges of running a household and the value a dedicated wife and mother brought to the job.

The 1850s saw publication of Hale's two novels on slavery. The first was a revised and expanded edition of *Northwood*, which came out in 1852, on the heels of the success of Harriet Beecher Stowe's *Uncle Tom's Cabin*. Hale was deeply against slavery, which she saw as anti-Christian and a profound moral wrong. One of *Northwood*'s themes was that slavery dehumanizes masters as well as slaves. The *Lady's Book* had a strong circulation in the South, and Hale may have hoped that her views had some influence among readers there.

The revised edition of *Northwood* carried a new subtitle. *Life North and South: Showing the True Character of Both* replaced the original subtitle, *A Tale of New England*. The preface to the revised version made it plain that she was both pro-Union and antiwar. "The great error of those who would sever the Union rather than see a slave within its borders," she wrote, "is, that they forget the master is their brother, as well as the servant; and that the spirit which seeks to do good to all and evil to none is the only true Christian philanthropy." She added a section calling for a national Thanksgiving, in the belief that civil war might be averted if all Americans celebrated their nation's shared blessings on a common day.

Unlike many, perhaps most, of her friends and colleagues, including Stowe, Sigourney, and Lydia Maria Child, Hale was not an abolitionist. Believing that emancipated slaves would not be welcomed or accepted by white Americans, she supported the American Colonization Society, which had been established in 1817 for the purpose of sending freed slaves to Africa. In 1822, the society founded a colony on the west coast of that continent that in 1847 became the republic of Liberia. Hale supported Liberia as a place where former slaves could live and prosper free from the racial discrimination they would face in the United States.

These views form the backdrop for her novel *Liberia: Or Mr. Peyton's Experiments*, published in 1853. The book recounts the story of slaveholder Mr. Peyton, who wants to free the slaves on his plantation in Virginia. He feels a responsibility to ensure that they will be happy with their newfound freedom and able to work to support themselves. The "experiments" of the novel's title refer to Mr. Peyton's investigations about the most desirable place to send them—a farm in the South, a city in the North, and Canada. In every location, Mr. Peyton's former slaves end up being worse off and unhappier than they were on the plantation, having been bullied, belittled, and mistreated by whites. Finally, Mr. Peyton and his former slaves conclude that they would be better off in Liberia, where they would not suffer the abuse of bigoted whites.

In making the case for colonization, Hale didn't provide an answer to critics who rightly pointed out the impracticality of relocating four million American freed slaves to Liberia, nor did she discuss white Americans' moral obligation to protect them and integrate them into society. As a practical matter, colonization was a preposterous idea. The costs alone were prohibitive. Plus, as her friend Lydia Child pointed out, the Colonization Society would have to send 70,000 former slaves a year to Liberia just to keep up with the expected birth rate.

Mr. Peyton's Experiments was prescient in describing the prejudice and abuse that African Americans encountered after the Civil War as well as the trouble that emancipated slaves experienced in adjusting to freedom. The author was right on both counts. Hale was a strong voice condemning slavery, but she never used her position and status, before, during, or after the Civil War, to call for African Americans to be accorded their full rights as citizens or to condemn racism by whites. We can't be sure why Hale never took up this mantle as she did for women, who also were denied the freedoms guaranteed by America's founding documents. We know she feared the dissolution of the Union, and it possible that she believed that by leaving the emancipation of the slaves to a future day, as the founders had done, a peaceful solution might be arranged.

BY HALE'S OWN estimation, the most important book she wrote was *Woman's Record, or Sketches of All Distinguished Women*, first published in 1853. It was a nine-hundred-page opus containing the biographies of 2,500 women since the beginning of recorded history—or, in Hale's immodest subtitle, *From the Creation to A.D. 1853*.

In 1853, Hale was sixty-five years old. Yet she was still at the top of her game. *Woman's Record* was her most ambitious book. It was an immense undertaking, requiring three years of research into biblical studies, world history, classical literature, and much more. She corresponded with some of the living women she included in the book, asking for information or clarification of their bios. The English poet Mary Howitt helped her gather information in Britain.

Dr. Elizabeth Blackwell, the first woman to obtain a medical degree, was aghast at the prospect of being included in Hale's book. She replied to Hale's letter asking for biographical details that it would be "a source of deep mortification" to find her name associated with illustrious women of history and pleading that she not be included.[24] Hale disregarded Blackwell's wishes, including her in the book. In contrast to Dr. Blackwell, Harriet Beecher Stowe answered Hale's letter by replying she "was quite amused" and "innocent of any pretensions to rank among 'Distinguished Women.'" She read Hale's letter to her children and asked them what they thought about the "unexpected honor [that] had befallen Mamma."[25]

Hale had two objectives in writing *Woman's Record*. One was to ensure that the names and deeds of celebrated women were not lost to history. The other was to advance her views on the moral superiority of women, which was the book's guiding theme. In *Woman's Record*, she called woman "God's appointed agent of morality."[26]

Hale sent copies of *Woman's Record* to many eminent women, including First Lady Sarah Polk, the queens of Spain and Portugal, and England's Queen Victoria. She reached Victoria through future president James Buchanan, then ambassador to the Court of St. James's. It is a measure of Hale's self-confidence that she requested such a favor. And it is a measure of the high esteem in which Hale was held that Buchanan quickly acceded to her request and carried the book with him to London. Perhaps most amazing of all, the queen replied, through her secretary, that she was "very much gratified by these marks of personal good will, which are so frequently shown Her Majesty by the citizens of the United States."[27]

Woman's Record holds the distinction of being the first volume of history to put women at the center of its research. As such, it is a distinguished forerunner of a school of academic discipline, women's studies, that didn't emerge until the middle of the twentieth century.

CHAPTER EIGHT

The Dignity of Housekeeping

N OT LONG AFTER Hale's death in 1879, a friend from
Newport, writing a remembrance of the late editor for
a New Hampshire magazine, related an anecdote told her by a
mutual acquaintance. Hale, then a young matron, was sweeping
the front hall of her house overlooking the village green when
someone dropped off a book for her to read. Several hours later,
when the mutual acquaintance paid a call, she found Hale still
standing in the front hall—leaning on the broomstick, engrossed
in her new book.[1]

The writer of the article cited this anecdote for the purpose
of illustrating Hale's intellectual curiosity and her lifelong love
of reading. But the image of Hale with broom in hand suggests
another aspect of her life as well: her expertise in the job held by
most women of her day—that of housewife.

As a farmer's daughter, Hale was intimately familiar with the
daily workaday routine of the American housewife and profi-
cient in the essential domestic arts of the late eighteenth and

early nineteenth centuries. She grew up at a time when house-holds grew or hunted the bulk of the food they ate and made most of the products they used. Hale knew how to pluck a chicken, churn butter, roast meat on a spit in a fireplace, dry apples, cut out and sew a shirt, and launder clothes in a tub of boiling water mixed with lye, along with dozens of other necessary skills that a farmer's daughter would have acquired in the course of her everyday life. As she noted in the preface to her 1839 book, *The Good Housekeeper*, she had overseen households in both rural and urban settings. She knew whereof she wrote.

One of the truths Hale had absorbed about housekeeping was that it could be a ruinously hard life. A letter she received from a farmer's wife in Pennsylvania struck a familiar chord, and she published it in her "Editors' Table" column under the heading "A Cry for Help." The farmer's wife describes her daily routine:

> Getting up in the morning at five o'clock, milking my share of the cows, getting breakfast, baking, scrubbing, skimming milk, lugging it out of the cellar, washing milk-pans, washing dishes, sewing, making beds, cooking for three or four hungry harvest hands three times a day . . . churning (butter) by hand; picking and canning berries and cherries . . . children to wash, dress and feed; baby to tend, butter to make—all this and more is a good day's work. Then there is garden to tend, washing, ironing, and a multitude of lesser duties.[2]

Is it any wonder, the overworked wife asks Hale, that a woman's thoughts grow bitter and that "her heart aches sometimes as badly as her head and back?"

Hale's comments on her correspondent's woes were characteristically kind and encouraging. But she also notes that the woman's complaints will ring true to exhausted, overworked wives in all parts of the country. The unnamed woman in Pennsylvania was not alone in her unhappiness.

At the *Ladies' Magazine* Hale seldom published articles about household management except as fillers—short, often quirky, items to fill out the white space on a page. "Coffee," a two-paragraph article that she published in 1833, is one such example. We are informed that the beverage "will remove the sense of fatigue and exhaustion and give vigor and hilarity to the mind." Who knew?

Godey's Lady's Book was another matter. Godey rightly saw a market for his magazine among the homemakers who belonged to the country's rapidly expanding middle class. It was Hale's job to help him figure out how to appeal to these women. In the words of John Spaulding, coeditor of a charming volume of Hale's recipes, readers of the *Lady's Book* "were the wives not only of doctors, lawyers, ministers, bankers, newspaper editors, teachers, merchants, prosperous farmers, and storekeepers, but also of master craftsmen such as carpenters, blacksmiths, and ironmongers, middle managers in factories and large stores, and even skilled craftsmen such as journeyman machinists and pattern makers."[3] By the time the Civil War began, when the circulation of the *Lady's Book* was at its peak, the middle class constituted about 40 percent of the population. Middle-class families typically owned their own homes and employed one servant.

At the *Lady's Book*, Hale introduced an innovative editorial approach that struck a balance among three categories of content—intellectual, entertainment, and practical advice. If that sounds familiar, it should. Hale's winning approach to editing a periodical for women persists today. Virtually every women's magazine uses a variation on the formula she created.

The intellectual content in the *Lady's Book* would have been familiar to readers of the *Ladies' Magazine*: essays, profiles, travelogues, literary reviews. One of the reasons Godey hired Hale was that he wanted to bring a higher tone to his magazine. As in the *Ladies' Magazine*, many of the articles examined women's roles. There was a special focus on education for girls and women, as Hale kept readers up to date on schools and, eventually, colleges that admitted women. She also kept on top of developments on property rights for married women, job opportunities for women, and philanthropic endeavors to help impoverished women and children.

A second category of subject matter was entertainment. Poetry was hugely popular in the mid-nineteenth century, and Hale published a half dozen or more offerings in every issue, some of which were written by her. Popular topics included love, death, grief, and nature. Hale wasn't a first-rate poet but she was a good one, and her poetry spoke to the concerns and emotions of her female readers. Fiction was also popular, and there was at least one original short story in every issue; occasionally she would serialize a short novel over the course of several issues.

The third element of Hale's editorial formula consisted of practical, how-to articles that provided guidance to readers about how to manage their homes and take care of their families. It is unclear whether she or Godey came up with the ideas for specific sections, but there is no question that Godey left Hale to implement them. In promotional materials, he once described the content as "under the control" of Hale. In her valedictory column in 1877, Hale described Godey as the "sole proprietor and business manager."

These new features—or "departments" as they were called—

were a product of her belief that learning was as "necessary for [woman] in her household life as it is for man in his public life." Society undervalued household skills, she firmly believed, thereby demeaning women. Hale aimed both to improve life for housewives and to elevate their status. She created the idea of a professional housewife just as she had created the concept of a professional female author.

Women's work, like men's work, was worthy of scientific study and analysis, she wrote. To prove her point, she posed a telling question: "Is not science as necessary in perfecting the art of making good bread as it is in raising good wheat?"[4] The farmer's wife had as great a need for education as did the farmer.

UNDER HALE'S editorship, the *Lady's Book* established many new sections of the magazine pertaining to commonplace household activities. Among them were patterns for sewing, embroidery, and crocheting, lumped together in a section known as the "Work Department"; etiquette tips; health and beauty; and children's activities such as games and paper dolls. "Godey's Model Homes" debuted in 1846, providing blueprints for houses that, once built, earned the sobriquet Lady's Book Houses. "Godey's Model Homes" was followed in 1849 by a related section, "Cottage Furniture," which provided do-it-yourself patterns for chests, dressers, desks, and other pieces of household furniture. If you built yourself a Lady's Book House, you could furnish it with Lady's Book Furniture.

Hale's biggest innovation was the introduction of the "Receipts, &c" column—that is, recipes. The *Lady's Book* appears to have been the first American periodical to feature a regular recipes column. Today, we take for granted the presence and availability of recipes in magazines, especially those aimed at women. It is hard to imagine that there was a time when a home cook couldn't open a magazine or Sunday newspaper and turn to the food section. The idea of collecting, editing, and publishing recipes as a dedicated feature of a periodical seems to have originated with Hale.

The concept of a written recipe that provides methodical instructions for how to prepare a dish was relatively new in the first half of the nineteenth century. The first American cookbook, *American Cookery* by Amelia Simmons, was published in 1796, less than a half century before Hale became editor of the *Lady's Book*. It wasn't until 1896 that Fannie Farmer's *Boston Cooking-School Cook Book* introduced standardized measurement cups and spoons, replacing ambiguous measurements such as "a pinch of salt" or "handful of nuts."

In Hale's own day, Catharine Beecher, Eliza Leslie, and Lydia Maria Child—writers Hale admired, worked with, and wrote about—published cookbooks. Child, whom Hale had succeeded as editor of *Juvenile Miscellany* in 1834, was the author of the best-selling *Frugal Housewife*, published in Boston in 1829. It went into more than thirty-five printings. Hale called Child "a lady of the first literary attainments"[5] and praised *The Frugal Housewife* as a useful manual for young housekeepers—though she expressed a concern that the book's focus on saving money could encourage stinginess or avarice in readers. Beecher's 1841 book, *Treatise on Domestic Economy*, went into fifteen editions and made its author famous. Hale reviewed it favorably, later praising Beecher, a sister of Harriet Beecher Stowe, as "one of the most vigorous thinkers of our day."[6]

For the "Receipts, &c" section in the *Lady's Book*, Hale relied on her personal knowledge and experience as a housekeeper as well as on a wide circle of friends and readers who submitted recipes that had been tested in their own family kitchens. Hale edited the submissions to provide instructions in what she termed a "concise, straight-forward manner" so that they could be easily implemented by any housekeeper in any kitchen.[7] "Receipts, &c" proved so popular that Hale edited several book-long collections of recipes that had appeared in the *Lady's Book*. Her celebrity status in mid-nineteenth-century America was such that one of her cookbooks was titled simply *Mrs. Hale's New Cook Book*. No full name necessary. Book buyers knew who Mrs. Hale was.

One reason for the popularity of the recipes published in the *Lady's Book* and in Hale's cookbooks was that most were intended for at-home family dinners, not for fancy occasions. As she explained to readers: "Our *Lady's Book* receipts deal less with grand dishes for high-company occasions, and more with the common dishes of every day. . . . The dinner may be of scraps, but those scraps must be savory. . . . No one can read the *Lady's Book* receipts without being struck by the good sense that pervades them as a general rule."[8] She also published menus. The December 1860 issue featured menus for "Christmas and New Year's Dinner" as well as "Very Nice Winter Dinners for Families."

Reading Hale's cookbooks and "Receipts, &c" columns, the modern reader will be struck by the heavy emphasis on meat, including parts of cows, pigs, sheep, and wild animals that most Americans wouldn't dream of consuming today. Think feet, tongues, brains. Or even ears. A recipe for pig's ears directs the cook to boil them for three hours, or "till tender." She recommends serving the ears covered with bread crumbs and tomato sauce or melted butter thinned with mustard and vinegar.[9] Yum.

The country was largely rural during the first half of the nineteenth century, and many if not most of Hale's readers would have lived on farms, where the meat put on the family's table was slaughtered on site or hunted in neighboring woods. Before a farm wife could grill, roast, boil, stew, or fry a cut of meat, she first had to prepare it for cooking using processes that Hale's recipes describe in detail and which may seem a bit grisly to modern readers, who lack close personal acquaintanceship with the animals that provide the food. Hale's background on the family farm in Newport, New Hampshire, came in handy here. She explains how to remove the hair of a calf's head, for example, and the best way to take out a chicken's gallbladder. A brain sauce for roast suckling pig calls for the cook to "cut off the head, and cut the pig down the middle into two parts; then cut off the ears, and cut the head in two, take out the brains, chop them very fine."[10]

Hale's cookbooks were novel in that they reflected the growing ethnic diversity of the nation. Before the Civil War, the majority of Americans came from British stock, and most of the recipes she published reflected that shared heritage. But she also selected recipes that new arrivals brought with them from other parts of Europe and, occasionally, from places even farther distant. Readers learned how to make Dutch fish, macaroni Milanese, French currant wine, and Indian curry powder. Germany, Ireland, Norway, Scotland, and Westphalia are also represented in recipe titles. Hale is sometimes credited with introducing the French word *canapés* to America.

Another innovation in her culinary journalism was the inclusion in her cookbooks of recipes for invalids and children. Women had always been cooking for the sick and the very young, of course, but it wasn't the sort of specialized information that usually was written down. As part of her effort to professionalize the job of housekeeper, she wanted her books to be educational.

Safety was another concern. Her articles and books on culinary topics are filled with information about handling, storing, and preserving food. Readers learn the best methods for handling poultry, how to tell whether an egg is fresh, how long cream can be stored, and the importance of avoiding the consumption of eels in April and May. Water is the healthiest beverage, she advised, but it is not always possible to find wholesome spring water, and she cautions readers not to take chances. It is safer to imbibe beer or another beverage rather than drink water that might be contaminated. If reliable water is not available, she provides elaborate instructions on how to filter water using charcoal and sand. Her overall exhortation to readers about "living well and being well while we live" could be the slogan of a modern-day celebrity chef or the subtitle of any number of self-help books.

Hale was an early supporter of the temperance movement, often noting in her fiction and nonfiction the suffering imposed by alcoholic husbands on their wives and children. She advised the readers of one of her early cookbooks, "I have not allowed a drop [of alcohol] to enter into any of the recipes contained in this book."[11] (She apparently excluded beer from her definition of alcoholic beverages, for in the same book she published a recipe for it.) Unlike the purists who banned wine and brandy from everything they cooked though, Hale published several cake recipes that contained alcohol as an ingredient, knowing that the alcohol would have dissipated during the baking.[12]

As HALE'S recipes reveal, the amount of time and effort necessary for preparing meals in the mid-nineteenth century was enormous by modern standards. Consider her recipe for "Christening Cake," which the *Lady's Book* published in 1860. Whisking and beating alone took close to one hour. The cook is instructed to separate sixteen eggs, whisk the whites to a froth, beat the yolks by hand for ten minutes, and then beat the batter for thirty minutes. That doesn't include the time spent drying five pounds of currants by the fire, chopping up nutmegs, mace, and cloves, blanching and pounding almonds, and cutting up candied orange and lemon peel.[13]

The "Receipts, &c" column was part of Hale's broader effort to professionalize women's work inside the home. She was always on the lookout for timesaving devices that could ease the burden of women's housework.

Take the sewing machine. Invented in 1846 by Elias Howe, it was developed by Isaac Singer into something that could be mass-produced for general domestic use, becoming widely affordable for middle-class households in the 1850s. Hale perceived its revolutionary potential early on.

Before the sewing machine was invented, a man's shirt sewn by hand took fourteen hours and sixteen minutes, according to a table she published in the *Lady's Book*. Making a calico dress took six and a half hours. With the invention of the sewing machine, those commonplace tasks were reduced to an hour or two. The most accomplished seamstress had the ability to make only 30 stitches a minute compared with the 7,000 or so made by machine.[14]

Hale wrote passionately about what she termed this "Queen of Inventions" and its potential for transforming women's lives by freeing them from the drudgery of hand sewing. The poor, especially, would benefit. The sewing machine will "banish ragged and unclad humanity," since clothes will now be readily available, she wrote. Poor working women—"whose sad destiny it was to earn a scanty livelihood by sewing" will be able to labor in comfort, producing a garment in two or three hours instead of twenty. A professional seamstress's earnings will increase, and she will be able to clothe her children "neatly, even fashionably."[15]

She urged women who couldn't afford to buy their own sewing machine to seek neighbors with whom to pool their money and purchase a shared machine. And she recommended that philanthropists consider donating sewing machines to women who relied on needlework to make their living. The suggestion that benefactors help the poor not by handouts but by helping them learn a skill by which they could provide for themselves and their families was a familiar theme in Hale's writing and the basis for her earlier work in Boston with the indigent wives of seamen.

Hale pointed out that more prosperous women—those who don't have to work for a living—would also benefit from this new "treasure." Thanks to the sewing machine, the time that women once spent stitching in "everlasting toil," will now be available for reading and studying. "Instead of busy fingers and vacant minds, young ladies throughout all the country can have the opportunity of improving their minds."[16] In her enthusiasm for the sewing machine, she apparently didn't consider the possibility that young ladies might have ideas about what to do with their new free time that didn't include expanding their knowledge.

There was another aspect of the sewing machine that excited Hale. She expected that the sewing machine would help women become more adept at "mechanics"—or "technology," in today's parlance. Writing in 1860, she quoted approvingly an unnamed writer who spoke of how the sewing machine could broaden women's knowledge of "mechanical powers," helping them "become enlightened upon a subject now dark to them."[17] The country was undergoing an Industrial Revolution, and Hale foresaw a time when more occupations would be open to women with the knowledge and confidence to operate machinery.

Reformer Amelia Bloomer shared Hale's enthusiasm about the transformational potential of the sewing machine. It will free woman from "toilsome, ill-paid labor," she wrote, and "send her forth into more active and more lucrative pursuits." Bloomer predicted that soon there would be more "women merchants, women bookkeepers, women shoemakers, women jewelers, women booksellers, typesetters, editors, publishers, farmers, physicians, preachers, lawyers."[18] Hale would have been largely in accord with Bloomer's statement—though she would have been uncomfortable with women entering a couple of the professions Bloomer mentioned.

Hale's interest in the emerging technology of mid-century America was fostered by her interest in science overall. It was a subject area to which she believed women ought to pay more attention. A woman couldn't be considered fully educated unless she studied biology, chemistry, botany, and other scientific subjects, she wrote. In both of her magazines, she published articles by and about female scientists such as Almira Phelps, botanist and sister of educator Emma Willard, and Maria Mitchell, the astronomer who in 1847 discovered a new comet that was named after her. Mitchell and Phelps became, respectively, the first and second women to be elected to membership in the American Association for the Advancement of Science.

In the 1850s, the *Lady's Book* ran a series of illustrated essays titled "Everyday Actualities." A contemporary commentator has described the series as a nineteenth-century version of *The Way Things Work*.[19] Written and illustrated by C.T. Hinckley, a professional wood engraver in Philadelphia, the articles delivered detailed looks at the manufacturing processes behind the creation of ordinary objects with which every reader would have

Sarah Josepha Hale was sixty-two when this portrait was painted in 1850.

The farmhouse where Hale grew up in Newport, New Hampshire.

The schoolhouse in Newport where Hale taught before her marriage.

The Rising Sun Tavern, where Sarah Buell met and married David Hale in 1813.

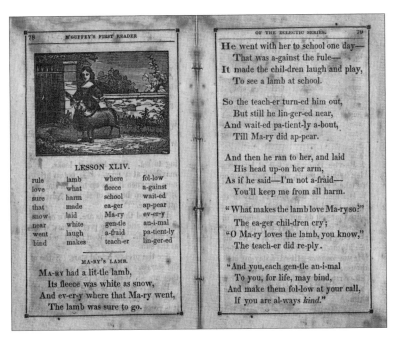

Millions of first-graders learned Hale's poem "Mary Had a Little Lamb"
in *McGuffey's First Reader*.

New Goods,
AND NEW FASHIONS.

MRS. & MISS HALE,

HAVE just received, by their order from *Boston* and *New-York*, and now offer for sale, at the building formerly occupied as an Attorney's office, opposite Nettleton's Hotel, a variety of

Fashionable Goods,

Such as Black, green and white Gros de Naples; Sinchaws; Sarsnetts; Crapes; Camlet; plain and figured Muslin Dresses; figured and Velvet Gauze, for Turbans; Velvets; Garniture, Crape, Gauze, Satin, and Lutestring Ribbons; Madrass, Zelia and Gauze Handkerchiefs, some with elegant painted borders; Piping Cords; Gimps; Frill; Mecklin and Silk Lace; Thread Laces and Edgings; Wreath and Bunch Flowers; Pink, white and buff Lisse Crape; Scarfs; Kid, Silk and Beaver Gloves; Kid, Morocco and Satinette Shoes; Braids; Sewing Silks; Beads; Muslin Prints, Calicos and Ginghams, in new style; Crape Shawls; Imitation, Ivory and Shell Combs; Insertings; Muslins; Irish Linens; Ladies Pocket Handkerchiefs; Fans; Buttons; Tapes; Needles; Pins; Scissors; Thread, &c. &c.

Mrs. & Miss H. have likewise obtained the latest and most approved fashions for Gowns, Spencers, Bonnets and Turbans, and intend keeping constantly for sale

Fashionable Millinary;

Such as Leghorn, buff and white Willow, figured Satin, and plain Silk BONNETS; Calashes and Mourning ditto; Caps and Turbans.

Miss H. and a young lady who is an experienced Milliner, will devote all their time and attention to satisfy all who may favour them with patronage. *Newport, June 5th*, 1824.

WANTED IMMEDIATELY,
A STOUT, healthy boy, from 15 to 17 years of

TOP LEFT: Louis A. Godey, publisher of *Godey's Lady's Book*.

TOP RIGHT: Lydia Maria Child, whom Hale succeeded as editor of *Juvenile Miscellany*.

—

LEFT: An advertisement for the millinery shop Hale opened with her sister-in-law after her husband's death.

LEFT: Lydia Huntley Sigourney, poet, wrote for both of Hale's magazines.

RIGHT: Edgar Allan Poe, 1846.

THE EVENING STAR.

BY HENRY W. LONGFELLOW.

Just above you sandy bar,
   As the day grows fainter and dimmer,
Lonely and lovely, a single star
   Lights the air with a dusky glimmer.

Into the ocean, faint and far,
   Falls the trail of its golden splendor;
And the gleam of that single star
   Is ever refulgent, soft, and tender.

Chrysaor, rising out of the sea,
   Showed thus glorious and thus emulous,
Leaving the arms of Callirrhoë,
   For ever tender, soft, and tremulous.

Thus, o'er the ocean, faint and far,
   Trailed the gleam of his falchion brightly:
Is it a god, or is it a star,
   That, entranced, I gaze on nightly!

One of the poems by Henry Wadsworth Longfellow
published in *Godey's Lady's Book*, 1850.

TOP LEFT: Dr. Elizabeth Blackwell, the first woman to receive a medical degree.

TOP RIGHT: Oliver Wendell Holmes, poet and physician.

—

LEFT: Hale published the work of the young Harriett Beecher Stowe.

BELOW: A "Dinner Cap" from *Godey's Lady's Book*, 1861.

OPPOSITE: The white wedding gown caught on in America in the 1840s after Hale introduced it in *Godey's Lady's Book*.

THE CHRISTMAS TREE.

Hale published this illustration in 1849, launching
Americans' devotion to the Christmas tree.

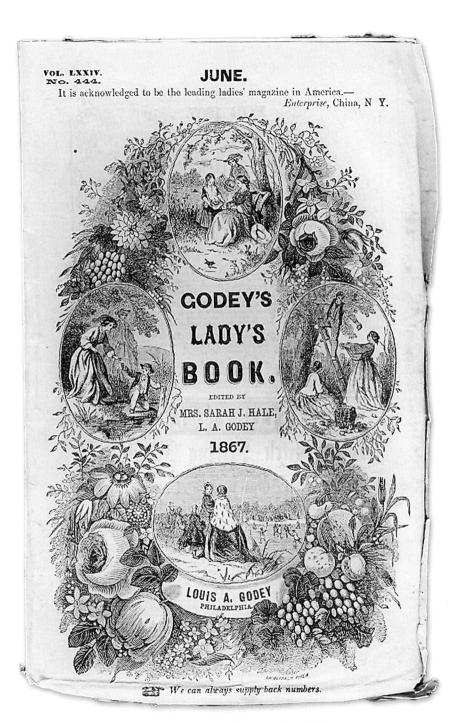

Cover of *Godey's Lady's Book*, June 1867.

A fashionable dinner dress from *Godey's Lady's Book*, 1862.

Abraham Lincoln's secretary of state, William Seward.

Matthew Vassar, founder
of Vassar College.

Thomas Edison recorded
"Mary Had a Little Lamb" on
his new phonograph
invention in 1878.

Sarah Josepha Hale at eighty-five.

been familiar, such as calico, paper, gas fixtures, and artificial flowers. Hinckley also devoted columns to behind-the-scenes tours of local Philadelphia businesses, including T.K. and P.G. Collins, the firm that printed *Godey's Lady's Book*, and he traveled to Albany, New York, to visit and report on a piano factory.

HALE INTRODUCED the term "domestic science" into the English language via an item published in 1833 in the *Ladies' Magazine*. She intended "domestic science"—and the variants "household science" and "domestic economy"—as complimentary terms with positive connotations about women's work in the home. Her objective was to raise the level of respect for housework and homemaking. The term caught on, and the Beecher sisters—Catharine Beecher and Harriet Beecher Stowe—used it in the title of their 1869 book, *The American Home: Or Principles of Domestic Science*. The sisters wrote that the aim of their volume was to elevate the honor and remuneration of domestic employment. By the beginning of the twentieth century, the term "domestic science" had grown out of fashion, replaced by "home economics."

Hale also turned her efforts toward encouraging the acceptance of domestic science as a field of academic study. She called for the establishment of female seminaries for the instruction of household work. She wanted public high schools to instruct girls in basic homemaking skills such as sewing and cooking. She encouraged colleges to add courses in domestic science to the curriculum.

Hale supported the passage in 1862 of the Morrill Act, also known as the Land-Grant College Act. Under the legislation, which President Lincoln signed into law, Congress appropriated money to states in the Union to finance the establishment of colleges specializing in agriculture and the "mechanical arts," or engineering. A second Morrill Act, enacted in 1890, extended the legislation to the Southern states. The Morrill Acts ultimately led to the founding of 109 colleges, including many state universities.

Hale called the first Morrill Act "magnificent" and praised Congress for its wisdom in helping states create agricultural colleges for young men. But she was angry that the Morrill Act did not specify that the land-grant colleges be coeducational. It was deplorable, she wrote, that "one-half of the community should be shut out from the benefits of this grant."[20] She was upset, too, that the legislation did not extend to the establishment of schools of domestic science for young women. In an editorial published in January 1868, she reprinted the memorial she sent to Congress in 1853–54: "Does not the lady who presides over the duties and destinies of family life require the aid of a thorough education . . . in order to be capable of using her faculties to the best advantage?"[21] She called on Congress to correct this injustice and "offer education, the best gift of the Republic, to its daughters as to its sons."[22] Congress did not oblige, but individual states eventually did.

Meanwhile, land-grant colleges began to admit women and offer courses in domestic science. Kansas State Agricultural College, founded in 1863, became the first land-grant school to welcome women. Not only that. The college—now known as Kansas State University—soon established a domestic economy department and appointed a woman professor.

Iowa State University began to teach domestic science in 1871. In 1872, the wife of the university president gave lectures to support what may have been the first laboratory classes in cooking, laundry, and other household arts. The University of Nebraska admitted women in 1869, and Colorado State University went coeducational in 1879, the year of Hale's death. By 1890, eleven years after Hale's death, the state charter of every land-grant college required the admission of women.

HALE APPLIED the same serious approach to her writing on domestic matters as she did to her writing on education, books, and other issues. She paid her readers the compliment of taking them seriously, never talking down to them or making light of the subject matter. Yours is an important and difficult job, she seemed to say. I know because I've been there. Here's how you can do it better. Her attitude is apparent in the dedication to her 1845 novel, *Keeping House and House Keeping*: "To all young married people, who aspire to the dignity of House Keeping; Who wish to do good in the world, to live in comfort and with honour, and to be happy at home, This little Work is Inscribed."[23]

Hale's belief in the enabling power of education extended to the middle-class homemakers who made up the majority of her readers at the *Lady's Book*. Just as she wanted women to have the opportunity of furthering their education by going to college, where they could study philosophy, chemistry, and other subjects traditionally off-limits to them, she wanted women to have the opportunity of learning how to excel in the domain where most of them worked—the home. Young men undergo professional or vocational training for their work, she pointed out, yet young women are denied a systematic education for their future important duties running a household.

In support of her argument that managing a household ought to be considered a professional occupation, Hale liked to say that every wife had to be prepared to perform the duties of five professions. She needed to know how to cook healthy meals, teach her children, sew the family's clothes, care for sick relatives, and run a household budget. She was, in Hale's view, housekeeper, teacher, dressmaker, physician, and accountant.[24] It was an empowering message. Hale was telling readers that what they did was valuable and worthy of study.

Many of Hale's contemporaries believed that woman's place was in the home, that women's work should be confined to the domestic sphere. Hale took a broader view of the place of women in American society. She saw women as individuals who were defined not just as wives and mothers but also as beings independent of their fathers, husbands, or brothers. They were as capable as men in succeeding at work outside the home, providing they received the proper education.

At the same time, she believed that women were better suited by nature to some kinds of work than others. Hale, who rarely was at a loss for an opinion, expressed strong views about women's work. But she wasn't consistent on the subject, and she often contradicted herself. As we shall see, there were professions she deemed inappropriate for women and others she thought ought to be reserved exclusively for their sex.

CHAPTER NINE

A Suitable Job for a Woman

L ET THEM be sea-captains."

That was the clarion call with which Margaret Fuller—scholar, critic, feminist—launched her appeal for legal equality for women in her 1845 book *Woman in the Nineteenth Century*, arguing that every occupation ought to be open to women. The full quotation reads: "But if you ask me what offices they may fill, I reply, any. I do not care what case you put. Let them be sea-captains, if you will."[1]

Like Hale, Fuller, who was twenty-two years Hale's junior, had been homeschooled by a parent intent on giving his daughter the kind of rigorous education usually reserved for sons. Fuller's course of study was classical—Latin, ancient Greek, philosophy—supervised by her learned father. When she was in her thirties, her scholarly abilities were such that she managed to accomplish a feat no woman before her had done: She secured permission from Harvard College to use its library to research a book she was writing on the American West. A male student at Harvard at the time later recalled the extraordinary sight of the female scholar invading the "sacred precincts" of the college's reading room. As the leading female figure in the New England–born philosophy known as Transcendentalism, Fuller was closely associated with the more famous men in the movement—Emerson, Thoreau, Hawthorne. Emerson recruited her to be editor of the Transcendentalist journal *The Dial*.[2]

Hale had a high opinion of Fuller, who reportedly did not return the favor when she declined to write for the *Lady's Book*. She admired the younger woman's erudition, saying that "probably no American woman was ever before so fully educated." At the same time, Hale was troubled by Fuller's lack of orthodox religious faith. *Woman in the Nineteenth Century* contained many "useful hints and noble sentiments," Hale wrote in *Woman's Record*, and she noted approvingly that Fuller clearly "wanted a wider field of usefulness for her sex." But the search for truth wasn't purely intellectual, Hale cautioned. To find true happiness, women also need the kind of "moral strength" that can only come from God. For that reason, Hale concluded that Fuller's works weren't destined to hold a high place in the canon of literature by women. "There is no moral life in them."[3]

While both women shared a commitment to equal educational opportunities for their sex, they did not see eye to eye on the subject of work. Captaining a ship was not Hale's idea of women's work. She did not believe that every path should be laid open to women as freely as to men.

At the *Ladies' Magazine*, Hale had declared, in a memorable phrase, that "there is no sex in talents, in genius."[4] Throughout her career, she never deviated from her view that women were the intellectual equals of men. Men exceeded them in physical strength, but women were capable of doing almost anything else that men could do so long as they were well educated in how to do the job. Women, she believed, had the intellectual capacity to carry out almost any task. She had little patience for men who believed women were intellectually or emotionally incapable of certain kinds of work. "Give women some pursuit which men esteem important, and see if their work is not well done, provided they are suitably trained," she wrote.[5]

But capability and advisability were different matters. As she repeatedly stated, Hale believed that women's paramount responsibility lay in the home, where her superior moral authority would enable her to counsel her husband wisely and raise their children to be good citizens. Because of their higher moral character, women were better suited than men to be in charge of the family. At the same time, Hale was a child of the Enlightenment, raised to believe that individuals had a duty to use their abilities to make the world a better place. That included women.

She differed from many of her contemporaries who believed that women's activities should be confined to the domestic space. Rather, as the scholar Patricia Okker has observed in her analysis of Hale's editorship, Hale had a far more flexible interpretation of what constituted the appropriate sphere for women. Hale expanded the standard definition beyond the realm of the home to include separate spaces for women in many public activities—both in philanthropy and in paid work.[6] In her advocacy for women to be allowed to work in many areas that hitherto had been closed to them, she preferred that they operate separately from men, but she reluctantly recognized that wasn't always practical.

She fought for women's entry into a range of jobs, especially in helping professions such as teaching and medicine, where she thought women's inherent compassionate nature gave them an advantage over men. It also encompassed philanthropy, where Hale encouraged women to play leadership roles in providing social services to the poor, the sick, and other members of society in need. She went so far as to argue that all charities that served women and children should be managed by women. Women could, and should, be active in public life, but on tracks that were separate, or as separate as possible, from men. She disliked the idea of women competing with men in the workplace. If she had her druthers, certain professions would be set aside for women; no men allowed.

WHEN WRITING about women's work, Hale was always keenly aware of the financial demands on women with no men on whom to rely. Having been there herself, she understood the ignominy of financial distress and the practical necessity for many women to earn an independent living.

This was a persistent theme in her writing. She wanted women to have the education and opportunities to obtain work that would pay enough to provide for themselves and their families if they were left adrift. The alternative, which she deplored, was for women and children to rely on charity. This was true whether they were the widows of seamen lost at sea or women whose husbands, fathers, or sweethearts had died in battle. The same sympathy and determination to help women help themselves that had prompted Hale to found the Seaman's Aid Society in Boston in the 1830s spurred her to action in the 1860s in support of Civil War widows.

Early on in her editorship, in an essay for the Ladies' Magazine, she lamented the few options available to women who needed to support themselves: "'What can she do?' is a question frequently propounded when a woman is left . . . to struggle for herself," she wrote. "What can she do? There are but very few avenues of business in which women are privileged to walk. The wages paid for female labor [are] very trifling; and when she has others besides herself to provide for, it seems almost impossible that a woman can succeed."[7] More than three decades later, she praised the benefactor of what would become Simmons College in Boston for specifying that the women's college he endowed was to teach subjects that would enable the scholars to acquire independent livelihoods.[8]

She understood, too, that marriage wasn't a blissful state for all women—and she wasn't bashful about saying so. While marriage usually was presented in a positive light in the pages of her magazines, she also published stories—true and fictional—in which husbands abused, deserted, or deceived their wives. An early supporter of the temperance movement, Hale showed special compassion for the wives of alcoholics. Her novella, *My Cousin Mary: Or the Inebriate*, tells of a young woman who is blithely confident that the drunk she is about to marry will reform. She ignores the warning of her grandfather, who tells her: "Mary, you have sealed your fate! So sure as you marry that man, misery will be your portion." And so it was. The novel predictably ends in tragedy. Hale described the book as a warning to young women of the "evils of intemperance." Many girls marry, she warns, and "have found their dreams of bliss rudely dissipated, while awakening to the reality of wretchedness which the wife of an intemperate man, in any station in life, must endure."[9]

In contrast to her frequent paeans to the joys of motherhood, Hale had little to say about women seeking self-fulfillment in work outside the home. Moreover, she found the idea of professional ambition unwomanly. Men seek distinction, she wrote;

they aspire to "eminence, glory, wealth, and power." But "it is not so with women." Rather, she explained, women want to do good. She wrote these words in an essay extolling women who became famous through work that benefited humanity. Among them were Dorothea Dix, who transformed the treatment of the mentally ill and went on to oversee the women's nursing corps for the Union during the Civil War; Mrs. Cornelius Du Bois, who founded and oversaw a children's hospital in New York City; and the English nurse Florence Nightingale.[10] She frequently provided readers with such examples of female success in the workaday world. The message was: Look at what women are capable of accomplishing. That said, the modern idea of "having it all" never came up in her writing. Her underlying assumption was always that working women would put their families first to the extent that their circumstances allowed.

IF HALE'S philosophy about the proper sphere of activity for women sounds inconsistent and confusing, that's because it was. She sometimes seemed to be making up her mind on the go about the proper role for women in the workforce, taking readers along with her as she discussed and developed her views. But even when she fumbled or backtracked or contradicted herself, she was influential in helping to shape her readers' attitudes toward acceptance of women who worked.

The printing trade, accountancy, bookkeeping, waiting tables at restaurants, clerkships in the federal government—none of these occupations qualify as helping professions, yet Hale wrote favorably of women's employment in these areas and more. The astronomer Maria Mitchell excelled in a scientific domain dominated by men. Yet when Mitchell discovered a comet that was named after her Hale was full of praise for the star scientist (pardon the pun). She viewed certain factory jobs and positions requiring artistic skill as falling into the feminine domain, arguing that women's smaller hands meant that their manual dexterity was superior to that of men. She praised women's managerial and business skills. And of course she identified, coached, published, and paid dozens of female writers over the course her career. Interestingly, she had little to say on the subject of domestic workers, who made up more than half of the female workforce, other than to challenge her readers to pay their servants fair wages.

The inconsistencies and contradictions in Hale's view of women's work were present in her own life. Her standard explanation for why she accepted the editorship of the *Ladies' Magazine* and moved to Boston was that she needed to provide for the education of her five children. But that doesn't explain why she continued to edit and write for decades after her children finished their schooling and were well launched in the world. It is hard not to believe that self-fulfillment and even, perhaps, a touch of that dreaded trait, "unwomanly" ambition, played a role in the decisions she made about her own career.

Another inconsistency can be seen in her treatment of Hannah Murray, an Irish immigrant who worked as a domestic for Hale for decades and was a much-loved member of the family. One of Hale's granddaughters quoted her grandmother as saying that if Hannah had had an education as a girl "she could have been almost anything."[11] Hannah was illiterate, and it is curious that Hale apparently never helped Hannah learn to read or write. Hannah witnessed Hale's will by marking an *X* on the document.

Over the course of her career, Hale gave her stamp of approval for the entry of women into many different jobs outside the home. The two professions for which she campaigned the most vigorously and to which she devoted the most attention throughout her half century in journalism were teaching and medicine. Neither profession was open to women when Hale began her career. Two other occupations whose opening she pressed hard for—but with less success—were those of post-mistress and bank director.

Surprising as it might seem today, when women have long accounted for a majority of schoolteachers, two hundred years ago the prevailing view was that women were unsuited for the teaching profession. Consider the words of Oliver Johnson, reminiscing about his schooldays in Indiana in the 1820s: "There was no such thing as a woman teacher," he noted in a memoir. "It wasn't a woman's job, any more than milkin' a cow was a man's job."[12]

During colonial days and into the early part of the nineteenth century, women were thought to lack the intelligence and moral stature to be successful teachers. So, too, their inferior physical strength was viewed as a liability when it came to controlling unruly boys in a classroom. While women often taught small children their ABCs—as the young Sarah Buell did back in New Hampshire—the job of instructing older youths was left to men, who typically taught for a few years before moving on to more lucrative opportunities.

At the *Ladies' Magazine,* Hale editorialized repeatedly about the suitability of women as teachers of all ages of schoolchildren, not just the very young. In an unsigned essay in 1829, the writer, almost certainly Hale, called for women to "direct their talents and energies" toward the teaching profession. "There is no branch of learning taught in our common schools, which females would not be capable of teaching."[13] This was a radical idea in the 1820s.

By the 1840s, public attitudes about female teachers had changed—thanks in good measure to Hale's editorial campaigns. Young women were beginning to enter the teaching profession in unprecedented numbers. By the 1850s, most teachers were women, and attitudes about female teachers had done an about-face. Hale had long argued that women made better teachers than men, and now many Americans seemed to agree. The feminization of the teaching profession was under way.

Hale then turned her attention to teacher training colleges, or normal schools. Ever since her years in Boston, where she had admired the work of Horace Mann, the innovative secretary of the Massachusetts state board of education, Hale had advocated for the establishment of normal schools. As always, Hale's focus was on education as the key to women's success in the workplace or at home. If young women were to become effective teachers in public schools—or common schools, as they were usually called—she insisted that they needed a professional education in pedagogy and curriculum. She supported Mann's establishment of the first government-supported normal school in Lexington, Massachusetts, in 1839. Other states went on to adopt Mann's model for training professional educators.

In 1850, she turned to her old comrade-in-arms Mann, by then a member of Congress, for help gathering statistical information about female teachers in Massachusetts. He responded with specific numbers: In 1849, the total number of public school teachers in Massachusetts was 8,163. Of these, 2,426 were men and 5,737 were women. "You will see by this," he continued, "that considerably more than half of all the teachers in our *public* schools are females. They teach not only small children but large boys—men grown; & if they have knowledge and . . . character, they manage young men not only *like* a charm but *with* a charm." He closed his letter by reminding his old friend that he had long supported employing female teachers.[14]

Not long after her correspondence with Horace Mann, Hale began to petition Congress to grant land to individual states for the establishment of free normal schools for women. Sixty thousand teachers are needed to educate two million children who now lack the opportunity to go to school, she wrote to Congress in 1853. Normal schools are the most efficient way to prepare young women to become teachers.

As in her campaign for a national Thanksgiving Day, Hale's campaign for normal schools had both a public face and a private face. She kept up the drumbeat in the *Lady's Book*, where she reprinted her petitions to Congress and editorialized on the excellence of female teachers and the need for professional schools of education. The following line, from an 1853 column quoting her petition to Congress, was typical: "That young women are the *best teachers* has been proved and acknowledged by those men who have made trial of the gentle sex in schools of the most difficult description . . . because of the superior tact and moral power natural to the female character."[15]

In making the case to the all-male Congress for educating young women to be teachers, she tailored her appeal to address possible concerns about educated, independent women forgoing marriage, taking care not to appear to be promoting spinsterhood. "That it is not designed to make a class of *celibates*," she assured the senators and representatives. Rather, "these maiden school-teachers will be better prepared to enter the marriage state after the term of three or four years in their office."[16]

At the same time that she was promoting land grants for normal schools in the pages of the *Lady's Book*, Hale privately wrote to individual members of Congress urging them to enact legislation granting federal land to every state for the purpose of building free normal schools. The only way to meet the pressing need for public school teachers in the expanding country, she argued, was to train and hire young unmarried women. Not only did women make better teachers than men, but they cost less. Single women could be paid half the salary of married men.

She had made the same points in the 1820s, arguing that the only way the country could afford to offer universal education was to hire women, who would work for lower wages than men. She reprised the argument in the 1840s when she supported Catharine Beecher's proposal to send educated young women from the East to the West and South to fill the pressing need for teachers in frontier towns. Unlike women, men had other career options, Hale rightly noted. Teaching wasn't at the top of the list of men's preferred work. "The Great West, the mines of California, and the open ocean laying China and the East, are inviting them to adventure and activity."[17]

In another petition to Congress, in the 1860s, she added an argument that was a sad commentary on the lives of many young married women of Hale's era: The young female teachers, she said, would be so committed to their work that they would be inclined to delay marriage by a few years—by which she meant until they reached their mid-twenties. This would be a blessing for them, as "there can be no doubt" that women who marry young are apt to face much unhappiness—"many sorrows, sickness, and premature decay and death." Hale herself married the day before she turned twenty-five.[18]

In 1863, she wrote her acquaintance Secretary of State William Seward urging him to seek President Lincoln's support of land grants for normal schools. She accurately foresaw a time once the Civil War ended when thousands of single and widowed women would need employment. She wrote: "What a host of fatherless girls and widows in their youth this sorrowful war has already made. Many of these are left in poverty and must depend on public sympathy and their own exertions."[19] Ultimately, Congress never enacted legislation providing land grants for normal schools.

ANOTHER public-sector job Hale wanted to see open for women was at post offices. She wrote in 1852, "We are glad to find that women are now frequently appointed to take charge of post-offices." She noted approvingly that there were 128 women holding that position in the nation.[20]

Hale championed women working as postmistresses—and yes, she meant "postmistress." "Postmaster" was—and is—the official government designation of the job, whether it is held by a man or a woman, but Hale despised the word when used for women. The term "female postmaster" was "monstrous," she said, and she insisted on using the word "postmistress" in her own writing in the hope that her favored word would catch on.[21] (It did. You still hear the word misused today for a woman who runs a post office.)

The history of female postmasters dates to the day when Benjamin Franklin served as the nation's first postmaster general. Mary Katherine Goddard, a printer in Baltimore, was the only female postmaster in office at the time. A half century later, Sarah Black, also of Maryland, became the first female letter carrier in 1845. Before that, in 1814, a dispute arose over the interpretation of the federal law pertaining to the appointment of postmasters. While the law didn't bar the appointment of women, it used only masculine pronouns, leading some to argue that women were ineligible to considered for appointments as postmasters. The dispute was resolved in favor of women.

During the Civil War, Hale intensified her call for female post-masters, keeping readers up to date on their progress at the post office. In 1862, she reported that the number of postmistresses had grown to 411 spread across twenty-four states.[22] The largest number was found in Pennsylvania, home to 98 postmistresses. The fact that Hale lived in Pennsylvania, where she might have encountered a woman working as a postmistress, may have been the reason this trend had been called to her attention.

Hale conceded that 411 postmistresses amounted to just a tiny percentage of the estimated 40,000 postmasters nationwide, but she had high expectations for expanding that number. In 1864, with the number of female postmasters still at 411, she called for the appointment of at least 4,000 more women by the end of the year. Women have proved themselves to be capable managers of post offices, she wrote, and deserved to hold more such places.

She also saw a moral imperative for the government to assist the widows and other female relatives of Civil War soldiers who had died in the service of their country. The deaths of these women's husbands, fathers, or sweethearts had left many of them with the sole responsibility for taking care of themselves and their families. In any case, "men are wanted for duties and in professions where women cannot act," she wrote—a veiled reference to soldiering—"but in this duty [women] could become efficient agents in public service. Let them have this branch of government beneficence open for their needs. It would be a blessing, to many a sorrowing woman beyond expression in mere words."[23]

Her campaign for the appointment of female postmasters is an example of her preference for women to work separately from men. At one point, she proposed that seven-eighths of postmaster positions be awarded to women.[24] Seven-eighths seems an arbitrary number. But it reflected her view that the job of postmaster belonged in the female sphere.

As it happened, following the Civil War many women were named postmasters—but not in a manner that Hale had foreseen. In the South, prospective postmasters were required to swear that they had not voluntarily aided the Confederacy or Confederate soldiers. Few Southern men could take that oath. So women stepped forward.

HALE'S SUPPORT for women as directors and managers of banks was an offshoot of her regard for Priscilla Wakefield, the eighteenth-century English Quaker and social activist who founded the first savings bank. Women deserved to be directors of an institution that had been created by a woman.

When Wakefield established her bank in 1798, she used the term "frugality bank" rather than "savings bank." The designation reflected her objective, which was to serve the poor by enabling them to save money one small sum at a time. Workers would make monthly contributions to their bank accounts, which would accrue toward pensions for their old age. If they became sick before they retired, they could withdraw money to help pay the bills. Today Wakefield is sometimes referred to as the Mother of Microsavings.

Hale wasn't stretching her definition of a helping profession by including banking in that category. In her view, women's caring nature qualified them to be prudent managers of banks, especially when it came to safeguarding the money of the non-wealthy. There are many experienced businesswomen "known for the prudence, probity and success" with which they had managed their affairs, she wrote.[25] Such women were as capable as men as managing banks or serving as directors. She went so far as to assert that if women served on bank boards, fewer banks would fail.

She was outraged at a newspaper report in 1866 that the comptroller of the currency, Freeman Clarke, had expressed the opinion that women could not serve as directors of banks with national charters because they didn't have the same rights as male citizens.[26] Not true, she thundered in an editorial titled "The Rights of American Women as Citizens." The newspaper must have got it wrong, she said. The comptroller of the currency would not have made such an uninformed statement without having taken legal advice, and no lawyer would make "so gross an error."[27] Since the law doesn't specifically exclude women from directorships of banks, she said, they have every right to be appointed and to serve. She took the opportunity to praise women who worked in other positions for the federal government. "Many clerkships in the public offices at Washington are held by ladies," she wrote, "who, it is generally understood, are exemplary in the regular and efficient performance of their duties."[28]

IN THE LATE 1840s and early 1850s, Hale took up the subject of female doctors. It was a focus of her close attention for the rest of her career.

At the *Ladies' Magazine*, Hale had supported the entry of women into the field of nursing, such as it was. Nursing didn't become an organized profession until the Civil War created an urgent need for nurses to care for wounded soldiers. Before then, patients were cared for mostly at home, with hospitals reserved for the indigent and mentally ill. While women took on the responsibilities of caring for the sick at home, nurses who worked for hire were usually men.

Female nurses were one thing, but female physicians were another. In mid-nineteenth-century America, the notion of women attending medical school and qualifying as licensed, practicing doctors was unimaginable to most people. Not to Hale, who believed women, if allowed to be trained, would make superior doctors. Women are the *preservers*," she wrote. They are by nature better qualified to take charge of the sick and suffering. "They should be instructed in medical science and become physicians for their own sex and for children."[29]

Not only did Hale want women to qualify as doctors for women and children, she went a step further. She wanted the job to be theirs exclusively. That is, beyond approving of women entering a professional field hitherto open only to men, Hale proposed cordoning off a huge section of it for women only. In the medical profession envisioned by Hale, female physicians would not treat men, and male physicians would leave the care of women and children to female physicians. This no-man-allowed medical domain was the purest example of Hale's ideology of expanding women's role into all-female public spaces.

Hale held up the model of Elizabeth Blackwell, the first woman to earn a medical degree. Blackwell graduated in 1849 from Geneva Medical College in central New York State. Her admission to the college was a fluke. Assuming that the all-male student body wouldn't want a woman in their midst, the faculty allowed the young men to vote on her admission. After the students voted "yes" as a joke, the faculty, believing that it would be dishonorable to go back on its promise, admitted Blackwell. For Hale, Dr. Blackwell was a pioneer. Thanks to her, Hale wrote, "the propriety of admitting young women to the study of medicine and qualifying them to become physicians" is now generally acknowledged.[30]

For the rest of her editorship of the *Lady's Book*, Hale closely followed the advancement of women in the medical field in
her "Editors' Table" column, noting progress and setbacks and
encouraging women to consider entering medicine. Blackwell
managed to get into medical school, but other women who wanted to be doctors were not so lucky. Hale pushed for the establishment of medical schools for women only, tracking the opening of ones in Boston, Philadelphia, Richmond, and elsewhere
and protesting Harvard's reversal of its initial decision in 1850
to admit women to its medical school. She was present at the
Female Medical College of Pennsylvania for the laying of the
cornerstone, which included a letter from Hale along with an
issue of the *Lady's Book*. She kept readers abreast of the activities of the Ladies' Medical Missionary Society of Philadelphia,
which financed the medical studies of women who were then
dispatched to Christian missions abroad to work as doctors.

She lauded Dr. Blackwell for founding, in 1857, the New York
Infirmary for Indigent Women and Children in New York City—
not least because the hospital would provide an opportunity for
the practical training of female doctors. Teaching hospitals, which
provided essential hands-on experience for male doctors, refused
to hire women with medical degrees, thereby setting up an effective barrier to entry to women who wanted to practice medicine.

Hale employed her most vehement editorial voice to condemn
the intrusion of men into the practice of midwifery, a time-hon-
ored way for women to earn a living. She was reacting to laws
passed in the 1820s in many states limiting the practice of midwifery to doctors with medical degrees. Since medical schools at
that time did not admit women, that meant—in Hale's view—that
men were pushing women out of one of the few jobs that had been
their domain. She published Lydia Sigourney's opinion that "the

word *midwife* proves that this profession has been filched from the woman, and the sooner it is restored to her the better for society."[31] She did not publish Dr. Blackwell's alternative view in favor of trained doctors caring for women who were giving birth. Blackwell wrote Hale that midwifery "was an idea of the Past quite incompatible with the spirit of the Present," noting noted approvingly that it was "dying out in every country of Europe."[32]

THE DAY AFTER Hale's death in 1879, the opening line of the obituary in the *Philadelphia Inquirer* identified her as the "venerable authoress and editress." Heaven's new arrival must have been smiling to see the newspaper's use of two of her favorite "-ess" words.

Feminine versions of nouns denoting a woman by the position she holds are on a long, slow journey to extinction in our century. "Authoress" and "editress" long ago fell out of use, and has any English-speaking person alive today used the words "huntress" or "poetess" or "sculptress" except in quotation? Even once-commonplace designations in recent memory such as "hostess," "waitress," "stewardess," and "actress" are losing ground to the gender-neutral substitutes "host," "server," "flight attendant," and "actor." These and other nouns with feminine terminations are being hastened to obsolescence by rights activists who think their use demeans women. The few "-ess" words still in wide use today mostly refer to royalty or female animals. The language police haven't yet caught up with "princess" and "countess," "tigress" and "lioness."

Hale began her literary career as "editor," not "editress." In her introductory essay for the first issue of the *Ladies' Magazine* in 1828, she called herself "the Editor." At some point along the way, as more women entered the profession, she began to refer to herself as "editress" to distinguish herself from male editors. Her letter to President Lincoln requesting him to call a national Thanksgiving Day began with the words, "Permit me, as Editress of the 'Lady's Book,' to request a few minutes of your precious time." An exception to her insistence on "editress" was the title of her monthly column, which curiously remained "Editor's Table" and then "Editors' Table." Perhaps she found the sibilant sound of "Editress's Table" too jarring.

Hale was much taken with the work of an English philologist, the Reverend Richard Chenevix Trench, dean of Westminster Cathedral and later archbishop of Dublin. In his book *English, Past and Present*, Trench traces the history of words with feminine terminations, citing many that had been used by Chaucer, Spenser, Shakespeare, Milton, and other towering literary figures of the English language. Hale provided a partial listing in a *Lady's Book* column: teacheress, singeress, servantess, neighboress, sinneress, victoress, ministress, flatteress, discipless, auditress, cateress, detractress, husteress, tutoress, and the delightful farmeress. Most of these words had fallen out of use before even Hale's day.[33]

No matter. Hale deployed her pen to do battle with the English language. She pushed for the revival of words with feminine designations especially when both sexes were engaged in the same occupation. Now that so many women were employed as teachers, she favored the use of "teacheress" for women and "teacher" for men, using the analogy of "actor" and "actress." She published a long list of male/female designations then in current use. To that list, she added a few that did not yet appear in dictionaries and that she hoped to add to the lexicon.

The new words were appropriate, she explained, because before the nineteenth century the professions or offices had never been filled by women. Her creations included *postmistress,* *scholaress, presidentess,* and one she especially liked, *professoress.* Now that women were entering the field of medicine, she favored the revival of an obsolete word—*doctoress*—which she used repeatedly in print. She praised a female attorney for advertising her services as a "lawyeress" even though she considered the law a profession better left to men.

Modern-day proponents of jettisoning gendered classifications say it is about justice. In their view, the use of separate words for women diminishes them and their work. Hale took the opposite point of view. The use of the "-ess" words separated men and women in a positive way, she argued. Since women weren't widely represented in the workplace, she wanted to acknowledge those who were. Singling them out gave women a dignity that their separate identity deserved. So declared the editress of *Godey's Lady's Book.*

CHAPTER TEN

Mrs. Hale's Magazine

⊸⚬⚬═☉─▪─☉═⚬⚬⊷

THE ENORMOUS POPULARITY of *Godey's Lady's Book* was such that it acquired a bevy of nicknames. When addressing readers in his monthly "Arm-Chair" column, Godey referred to his magazine by his personal shorthand, "The Book of the Nation" or, simply, "The Book"—a designation he inevitably wrote with capital *T* and *B* and sometimes in all capital letters. Among his colleagues in the magazine publishing industry, "The Book" was sometimes jokingly called "Godey's Bible" or even, derisively, "God-ey's Bible." Another nickname—one in which the publisher expressed special delight—was "The Bouquet of the Boudoir."[1]

Ordinary readers, however, had a more telling nickname for the *Lady's Book*. They called it "Mrs. Hale's Magazine." The title of their favorite magazine may have carried the name of the owner and publisher, but for the magazine's devoted readers, it was Mrs. Hale, not Mr. Godey, who mattered most. She was the voice of the *Lady's Book*, the one who spoke with knowledge and authority on the issues they cared about, the one who addressed her readers as "friends." Hers was the trusted voice on matters mundane as well as sublime, whether she was advising readers on what to cook for dinner, telling them where their daughters could get a good education, or making the case for female physicians.

In 1837, the year Hale took over as editor, Godey claimed 10,000 subscribers for his *Book*. By June 1849, the subscriber list had ballooned to 40,000. In April 1850 he boasted that 62,500 readers subscribed to the *Lady's Book*. "There is perhaps no work published in the world that has so large a list of subscribers," he claimed.[2] By 1860, circulation peaked at 150,000 subscribers. It was an astounding achievement in an era when the average number of subscribers for American magazines was 7,000.[3] By way of comparison, the Transcendentalist journal *The Dial*, edited by Margaret Fuller, counted the number of its subscribers in the hundreds.

Because subscribers to the *Lady's Book* shared their copies with family, neighbors, and friends, the pass-along rate made the magazine's actual readership far higher. Many readers had their issues bound in six-month segments to put on their bookshelves and preserve for future reading. Godey's decision to recruit Hale to edit his magazine was well rewarded, surpassing even his highest expectations. Her editing genius was responsible for carrying his name into almost every middle-class home in America.

As the *Lady's Book*'s circulation numbers rose in the 1840s and 1850s, so too did Hale's influence and celebrity. The phrase "Mrs. Hale says" became a kind of gold-medal guarantee. If Hale recommended something—a new book, a school for girls, a recipe, a health tip—the reader could be assured of its quality. She was so well known that newspapers sometimes didn't feel the need to identify her by her full name. "Mrs. Hale" was sufficient identification. In the two decades before the Civil War began in 1861, no woman was better known or more influential.

AT THE *Ladies' Magazine*, Hale had succeeded in her twin objectives of promoting education for women and encouraging the development of an American literary culture. She carried those priorities with her to the *Lady's Book*, where she developed them more fully. She impressed upon her new readers the need for continuous self-reflection and self-improvement, along with the concept that women could take responsibility for bettering their families' lives and the lives of their communities. And she set out to help them do so.

The *Lady's Book* brought a challenge that she hadn't anticipated and which took on added importance as the years passed. As the magazine's circulation expanded, Hale became instrumental in shaping a shared popular culture—attitudes, mindsets, taste—for the emerging middle class. Women in every pocket of the nation turned to Hale's magazine for advice on many everyday matters: what to wear, what to read, what to eat, how to behave. In that sense, Hale became America's first taste-maker. Under her direction, the *Lady's Book* set the standards for what was popular, what was fashionable. As one of the nation's first national publications, it did so not just for the elites of Philadelphia, Boston, and New York City—but for women throughout the country. Mark Twain, writing in *Life on the Mississippi*, put a copy of *Godey's Lady's Book* on parlor tables in every town and village along the river from Cincinnati to New Orleans.[4]

THERE IS no better example of Hale's sway as the preeminent cultural influencer of the mid-nineteenth century than two traditions she introduced in the 1840s that continue to flourish in the twenty-first century: the white wedding gown and the Christmas tree.

Both stories begin with Queen Victoria. Hale greatly admired the young queen, who was eighteen years old when she succeeded to the British throne in 1837. A year later, at the time of Victoria's coronation, Hale wrote, rather wistfully, that she would have given half the yearly profits of the *Lady's Book* to have witnessed that magnificent royal pageant.

Hale and the queen had several things in common. Both women were petite. Both were deeply in love with their husbands, with whom they had many children. Both were proponents of exercise for women and fond of dancing. Both were strong-minded, opinionated, and highly moralistic. Geraldine Ellis, author of an unpublished biography of Hale, wrote: "While Victoria was England's Queen, Sarah might be likened to America's godmother. She was present at its birth. She influenced its tastes, morals and conscience for fifty years. She corrected its rough manners and instructed it in the way to live, to learn, and, by example, to revere God. She did more than most to transform American women and raise them to a less humble place in society."[5]

For an editor who worked to create a distinctly American culture separate from that of the English motherland, Hale's admiration for the English queen was surprising. Hale saw the queen as an exemplar of moral leadership and a role model for American women. Victoria, she wrote, may have been of the physically weaker sex—the sex whose intellect was usually belittled and who more often than not was denied a suitable education. But the queen rose above any such disadvantages because of the superiority of her "moral endowments." Heaven had raised her to the throne to "show the beauty of virtue and the strength of moral principle."[6] Like Victoria, in Hale's view, many ordinary

American women set a moral example for their families and communities. The moral superiority of women was a central aspect of Hale's view of womanhood.

When Victoria married her cousin Prince Albert of Saxe-Coburg and Gotha in 1840, Hale took the unusual step of providing a detailed description of the monarch's wedding gown in her own "Editors' Table" column, where she usually eschewed fashion. When she did write about fashion, it was to warn of the dangers of vanity and make a plea for readers not just to copy European fashions willy-nilly but to adapt them for practical American use. In this case, though, she made an exception to her usual harangues. She described, without a hint of censure, Victoria's dress "of rich white satin" trimmed with expensive lace. (She did, however, take the opportunity to inveigh against the poor wages that the female lace makers received—though she softened that criticism by praising Victoria for giving the women an opportunity to earn even paltry sums.)

Victoria's selection of white for her wedding gown was unusual for the day. Wedding gowns in the early nineteenth century were of a variety of hues, but seldom white. Royal wedding garb tended to be more about the tiaras, brooches, necklaces, and bracelets than about the dress. Victoria's choice set off a craze in Britain for white wedding gowns. Bridal white became associated with purity and modesty, and the bride, robed in white, became a literary icon. Think of *Great Expectations*, by Charles Dickens, and the character of Miss Havisham, the jilted bride who refuses to change out of the now-tattered white gown in which she was supposed to have been married.

In the United States, the positive reference to Victoria's gown in the *Lady's Book* introduced the white wedding dress to Americans, who enthusiastically adopted the style. Less than a decade later Hale wrote that the white wedding gown was "an emblem of the innocence and purity of girlhood, and the unsullied heart which she [the bride] now yields to the keeping of the chosen one."[7] In 1858 she observed that "white satin is just now the principal material for full bridal costume."[8]

AT CHRISTMAS 1848, the trend-setting queen, now the mother of six, set off another craze in Britain that crossed the Atlantic and took hold in American homes after the *Lady's Book* took note. It started when the *London Illustrated News* published a woodcut engraving in a sixteen-page Christmas supplement on December 23, 1848. The engraving pictured Victoria and Albert, along with five of their children and a governess. The family was standing around a table that held a fir tree gaudily decorated with candies, ornaments, and small toys and illuminated by candles. An angel stood watch from its perch atop the tree. Dolls, toy soldiers, and other gifts that were too big or too bulky for hanging were displayed under on the tabletop under the tree. The caption read, simply, "Christmas Tree at Windsor Castle." There was no accompanying commentary.

The British royal family had taken a fancy to Christmas trees ever since Victoria's grandmother, Queen Charlotte, wife of George III, brought the custom with her from her native Germany in the 1800s. A small Christmas tree had decorated Victoria's chambers since her childhood. When she was thirteen years old, the future queen wrote in her diary: "After dinner . . . we then went into the drawing-room near the dining room. . . . There were two large round tables on which were placed two trees hung with lights and sugar ornaments."[9] Albert, too, grew up with Christmas trees, and he wanted to share the German tradition with his children. He wrote a correspondent, "I must now seek in the children an echo of what Ernest [his brother] and I were in the old-time, of what we felt and thought; and their delight in the Christmas-trees is not less than ours used to be."[10]

When Hale was growing up at the end of the eighteenth century, Christmas was not widely celebrated in the United States. That was especially so in New England, where, a century and a half earlier, the original Puritan settlers had banned the celebration of the holiday. Christmas was associated with the Church of England, from which the Puritans had broken. By the 1820s, attitudes about Christmas were beginning to change, thanks in part to the publication of Washington Irving's *Sketchbook*, in which he described the convivial Christmas traditions he had observed on a visit to London—caroling, gift-giving, and other festivities. Until 1870, when Christmas became a federal holiday, December 25 was just another workday in the United States. The first Christmas tree didn't appear in the White House until 1889, during Benjamin Harrison's administration.[11]

Hale's interest in the holiday may have been encouraged by her conversion from Congregationalism, the faith in which she had grown up, to the Episcopal Church after her move to Philadelphia. As an offshoot of the Church of England, the Episcopal Church marked Christmas as the day of the birth of Christ. Another possible influence on Hale could have been the Pennsylvania Dutch—German and Swiss immigrants who put up Christmas trees. Hale could have come across one when she traveled outside Philadelphia.

Whatever the reason for her interest—Queen Victoria, the Episcopal Church, or the Pennsylvania Dutch—Hale was touched by the engraving of the royal family with their Christmas tree and decided to publish it in the *Lady's Book* in December 1849. There was no accompanying commentary, no mention even of Queen Victoria. The caption read, simply, "The Christmas Tree."

She made an unexplained decision to Americanize the engraving. Gone were the prince's mustache (Hale hated whiskers) along with his royal sash. The queen's tiara disappeared. Hale's changes turned the picture into a cheerful, domestic scene of an anonymous family gathered together to celebrate the holiday. It could just as easily have been set in America as in England.

Americans, it turned out, loved the Christmas tree as much as their cousins across the pond. Thanks in part to the publicity in *Godey's Lady's Book*, the custom quickly took hold in the United States. Other magazines followed the example of the *Lady's Book* and started publishing pictures of Christmas trees during the holiday season. *Harper's Weekly* printed an engraving by Winslow Homer depicting a boisterous family party around the tree.[12]

Hale continued to publish engravings of Christmas trees in subsequent December issues. Among them were a family "dressing"—that is, decorating—a tree, Father Christmas delivering a small tree along with his bag of toys, and two children returning from the snowy woods dragging a freshly cut tree behind them. In 1860 she reprinted the expurgated plate of Victoria and Albert's Christmas tree at Windsor Castle. It accompanied a short story set on Christmas Eve in America in which the happy denouement at the end of the tale takes place around a Christmas tree. By then the Christmas tree was a familiar feature in American homes.

HALE'S INFLUENCE could be seen when it came to many more cultural topics too.

The polka is one example. Dancing was controversial in the nineteenth century. Unlike some of her religiously conservative readers, Hale didn't believe that dancing was a sinful indulgence.

Just the opposite. She approved of it because she saw it as healthy exercise. It fit with her long-held view that girls and women needed exercise. She argued, too, that dancing was an innocent amusement, a "means of imparting happiness to our friends and promoting cheerfulness in our intercourse with society."[13]

When the polka became fashionable in Europe in the 1840s and immigrants brought it with them to the United States, she began to write about it. In November 1846, she devoted an entire "Editors' Table" column to the dance, publishing detailed how-to instructions provided by an unnamed professor. She also ran a colorful plate depicting couples dancing the polka. She promised her readers that they "will be enabled to accomplish with ease and grace this exquisite dance without the aid of a master."[14] Dozens of references to the polka followed in subsequent issues, in the "New Music" department and other sections of the magazine. Meanwhile—probably not unrelatedly—Americans' love affair with the polka kept growing.

Another example of the *Lady's Book*'s cultural influence under Hale's editorship is the word "lingerie." The Oxford English Dictionary puts its first appearance in the English language in *Court* magazine in London in 1835. "Lingerie" was an elegant-sounding euphemism for intimate items in a woman's wardrobe, and the *Lady's Book* took up the word when it began to write about ladies' undergarments in its fashion columns. It quickly entered the American lexicon.

Speaking of underwear, the corset was one of Hale's bugaboos. She voiced her disapproval of corsets even as they were discussed approvingly in the *Lady's Book*'s fashion columns. The magazine's "Health Department," written by physicians whom she had invited to contribute, railed against them. "Let [women] unloosen their corsets," exhorted one of Hale's health columnists, "and give the great important organs of the interior of the body a chance to perform their functions free and unfettered."[15]

In one of her own essays, Hale reprinted an amusing anti-corset anecdote told by Lady Mary Wortley Montagu, the eighteenth-century English writer whose vivid letters about her travels in the Ottoman Empire Hale later collected and published:

> One of the highest entertainments in Turkey is having you go to their baths. When I was first introduced to one, the lady of the house came to undress me—another compliment they pay to strangers. After she had slipped off my gown and saw my stays, she was very much struck at the sight of them, and cried out to the ladies in the bath, "Come hither, and see how cruelly the poor English ladies are used by their husbands. You need not boast, indeed, of the superior liberties allowed you when they lock you up thus in a box!"[16]

Hale had taken her first shots at corsets during her *Ladies' Magazine* days, when she also campaigned against the fashion for exposed necks and chests that left women vulnerable to the cold; tight, thin-soled shoes; and other wearables that imprisoned women for the sake of vanity. She was an early advocate of clothing that that was comfortable, seasonally appropriate, and allowed freedom of movement. Hale didn't win her battle against corsets, which remained popular until the beginning of the twentieth century as women continued to manipulate their natural shapes with whalebone, steel ribs, and tight lacing. But she effectively made the case against them, laying the groundwork for eventual reform.

Another cultural battle that Hale lost had to do with the fashion for whiskers. She disliked them, and she advanced the unsubstantiated opinion that other women shared her view. Most women don't like them, she proclaimed. "They so effectively conceal the countenances of the wearers that young ladies are sometimes unable to distinguish their own brothers and cousins."[17] What's more, she said—again without offering evidence—men with whiskers are shifty. "Persons who carry their faces behind a mask of this sort cannot be supposed to possess clear consciences, for honesty and fair dealing have no motives for any such concealment."[18] Needless to say, history shows that Hale lost her war against whiskers. Two of the men to whom she was closest—her son Horatio and her employer Louis Godey—wore impressive beards later in their lives. Perhaps she found some small consolation in removing Prince Albert's mustache from the Christmas Tree engraving.

HALE'S IMPACT as a taste-maker carried over into the short stories and essays she selected for publication. The fiction that appeared in the *Lady's Book* usually took place in contemporaneous American settings. The literary quality of the short stories and novellas varied greatly—for every Hawthorne or Poe there were dozens of lesser writers. Taken as a whole, the fiction published in the *Lady's Book* provides a vivid picture of everyday life in the mid-nineteenth century. A modern-day reader who wants to learn how Americans of that era interacted with one another, what they wore, what they ate, their biases and prejudices, and what they thought about relations between the sexes would do well to spend some hours with the fiction found in the *Lady's Book*. For readers of the day, the stories reflected and reinforced emerging cultural norms, especially as they pertained to women's roles.

Godey often boasted that readers could trust the moral integrity of his *Book*. Mrs. Hale, he proclaimed, would never allow anything improper to darken its pages. Just as Hale's children's poems and books contained moral messages, the stories she selected for publication in *Godey's* usually did as well. Three short stories that ran in the January 1845 issue are representative of this point. Each of the authors was a frequent contributor.

"Engaged at Sixteen," by T.S. Arthur, opens with the parents of a fifteen-year-old girl debating the pros and cons of early marriage. The mother, who favors early marriage, wins the day and within a year the daughter marries a ne'er-do-well who has won her heart. Arthur's description of the daughter—longing for romance but lacking the life experience to make wise judgments about herself or her suitors—is especially fine. After her marriage, her husband demands that his father-in-law bail out his failing business. When the father-in-law refuses, the husband sends his wife, not yet eighteen, and their baby back to her parents. Hale disapproved of early marriages, and this story supports her point of view.

The second short story in the January 1845 issue, "The Convict's Daughter" by Emma C. Embury, recounts a tale of filial duty. A young woman learns that the father she thought had died when she was a child is actually serving a long sentence for bank robbery. When the father is released from prison, he is unrepentant, but the daughter nevertheless decides to devote her life to caring for him. It is a preposterous tale—the story ends with the daughter becoming a Moravian nun—but it provokes serious thoughts about the limits, if any, of a woman's responsibility to family.

Finally, there is Catharine Sedgwick's "Fanny McDermot," a two-part story of which the first ran in the January 1845 issue. It relates the story of a gullible young woman who falls prey to the charms of a rich, handsome man, who deserts her and their child when he tires of her. This is an age-old story, and the moral is obvious. The interesting twist here concerns the women to whom the fallen heroine turns for help. The young mother seeks respectable employment so that she can provide for herself and her child without having to rely on charity. Will the women help her? Sedgwick thus examines women's empathy for and responsibility to their fellow women.

HALE'S INFLUENCE extended, too, into the realm of philanthropy. Her leadership of the campaign for the Bunker Hill Monument was well known, and more than a decade after she left Boston, it had an influence on the woman leading the effort to memorialize another important piece of American history—George Washington's house and burial site at Mount Vernon, Virginia.

While sailing on the Potomac River in 1853, Louisa Cunningham, a South Carolina matron, traveled past Mount Vernon. Dismayed at seeing the ruin and desolation of the estate of the nation's revered first president, Cunningham wrote to her daughter, Ann Pamela Cunningham. She asked, "Why was it that the women of [Washington's] country did not try to keep it in repair if the men could not do it? It does seem such a blot on our country!"[19]

Why, indeed. Miss Cunningham took up her mother's challenge over the restoration of Mount Vernon, establishing a Ladies' Committee that mirrored Hale's organizing structure of her Bunker Hill campaign. The younger Cunningham was living in Philadelphia when she received her mother's letter about the disrepair of Mount Vernon. The city was a second home to Miss Cunningham, who spent several months of the year there. She stayed on Spruce Street, not far from where Hale lived, and was among Hale's circle of acquaintances, moving in the same social set.

Letters from Hale to Cunningham show that the editor offered advice to Cunningham about the restoration of Mount Vernon. "I shall do all I can," she wrote Cunningham's secretary after receiving an update on the project.[20] Hale also provided publicity for the cause in the *Lady's Book*. In an 1857 letter she assured her friend, "You will see in the Feby. and March nos. of the 'Lady's Book' that I have kept the matter before our friends."[21] Hale remained in the background, but she encouraged and counseled Cunningham all along the way.

The restoration of Mount Vernon is often cited as the first major philanthropy founded, led, and run by women. But clearly it wasn't the first such endeavor. More than a decade before Ann Pamela Cunningham led the rescue of the home of the nation's first president, Sarah Josepha Hale set the precedent by leading the rescue of the monument honoring the men who fought in the first major battle of the Revolutionary War.

BECAUSE OF ITS LARGE pass-along rate, even the *Lady's Book*'s strong circulation numbers don't demonstrate the full extent of the magazine's impact on popular culture. It is possible to get a glimpse of it through other media's numerous references to the *Lady's Book* and to Hale. Local newspapers frequently printed snippets from the magazine, quoted Hale's poetry, reproduced her recipes, and asked her opinion on matters of public interest.

A few examples, taken from several different decades: Pittsburgh's *Daily Morning Post* ran an excerpt from one of Hale's essays in support of female physicians in 1854.[22] The *North-Carolina Standard* quoted Hale in 1837 on female happiness.[23] The *Cincinnati Daily Star* asked Hale's opinion in 1877 on women's views on law and order.[24] The *Washington Evening Star* reprinted a few lines of a poem by Hale in 1855.[25] Her recipe for gingerbread made it into the *Rutland (Vermont) Weekly Herald* in 1871.[26] And so on.

Godey extended the influence of the *Lady's Book* by repurposing its content in the books and engravings sold by his publishing empire. An advertisement in the October 1857 issue of the *Lady's Book* listed fourteen Godey's publications for sale, including two books by Hale. Readers could order volumes on such subjects as how to make your own shoes, recipes for summer beverages, embroidery patterns, and advice for young mothers. Godey even sold needles, as a service, the magazine said, to "ladies living in the country . . . [who] cannot procure good needles."

Hale's astonishing literary output helped cement her reputation. From the time she became editor of the *Lady's Book* in 1837 until 1860, she wrote, edited, or made contributions to more than six dozen books. She penned poetry, novels, plays, children's books, etiquette manuals, and cookbooks. Her byline was everywhere—variously Sarah Josepha Hale, Mrs. Sarah J. Hale, Mrs. S.J. Hale, and sometimes simply Mrs. Hale.[27]

OVER THE COURSE of her half century as an editor, few issues pertaining to women escaped Hale's notice. Large or small, important or trivial, Hale reflected on the issue and had a point of view. She wrote about women's education, work, financial independence, civic responsibilities, and philanthropic leadership. Women's duty to their families was a recurrent topic, including household management, raising children, manners, recreation, religion, and more.

It is not always possible to tell whether Hale ignited a trend or helped popularize it. But given her national platform as editor of the *Lady's Book*, and the widespread esteem for her opinions, it is fair to say that she was an important force in forging a shared popular culture for the new country. Just as readers absorbed Hale's views on serious topics regarding the advancement of women, they also relished her magazine's opinions on less weighty matters.

Laura Ingalls Wilder, author of the *Little House* books for children, wrote about the impact the *Lady's Book* had on a quasi-fictional family living on a remote homestead in South Dakota. *Little Town on the Prairie* is the seventh in her series of autobiographical novels drawing on her experience growing up on the prairie in the 1860s.[28]

In *Little Town*, Laura's older sister Mary is about to leave home for college, and Ma is sewing her a new best winter dress. When it comes time to make the dress's skirt, Ma and Laura encounter a problem. The last time the family had made the long trip into town, a friend told them that hoop skirts might be coming back into style. What's more, they learned that in anticipation of the fashion trend, Mr. Clancy at the general store was thinking of stocking some hoops. What to do? Should they make Mary's skirt full enough to accommodate a hoop? It would be awful for her to arrive at college with a dress that was out of style.

They quickly came up with an answer to their problem: They needed to get their hands on a copy of *Godey's Lady's Book*.[29] Even on the frontier, in a ramshackle cabin surrounded by cornfields and situated miles away from its nearest neighbor, the ladies of the house knew whom to consult on this and other matters of importance to women. Their oracle was the Book of the Nation, the Victorian Bible of the Parlor, the Bouquet of the Boudoir—*Godey's Lady's Book*, also known as Mrs. Hale's Magazine.

CHAPTER ELEVEN

Our Glorious Thanksgiving Day

O N OCTOBER 3, 1789, George Washington, responding to a request from the First Congress of the new United States, issued the first-ever presidential proclamation. He named the last Thursday of November of that year as a "day of public thanks-giving," a time for Americans to express gratitude to God for "the civil and religious liberty with which we are bless-ed" and for the recent establishment of a "form of government for their safety and happiness." Eight weeks later, on Thursday, November 29, Americans throughout the thirteen states came together for the first time to give thanks as a nation.

Sarah Buell was one year old on that first national Thanks-giving Day, too young to remember the celebrations that took place throughout the land. Newspapers published Washington's proclamation, states held public functions in honor of the day, houses of worship opened their doors for religious services, cit-izens—including Washington himself—made donations to help the poor, and families gathered for festive meals. Hale gave a tip of the hat to Washington and the first national Thanksgiving in her 1827 novel *Northwood* by placing a portrait of the first president in the room where her fictional Yankee family was celebrating the holiday.

Seventy-four years and fifteen presidents later, Abraham Lincoln became the second president to ask all Americans to come together to celebrate a day of national Thanksgiving.[1] The thread between Washington's Thanksgiving Day and Lincoln's was Sarah Josepha Hale.

Hale didn't invent the American festival of Thanksgiving. But it was thanks to her that the holiday became a permanent fixture on the American calendar. Without Hale, we might still be stuck at the point at which she began her campaign for a common Thanksgiving Day in 1847—with individual states celebrating the holiday on separate dates that had been designated by their governors and some states not bothering to celebrate at all. Hale used her influence to encourage the celebration of Thanksgiving in every state and territory and to advocate for a common Thanksgiving Day.

New Englanders have been celebrating Thanksgiving since the early seventeenth century and the arrival of the English settlers known as the Pilgrims. The holiday began as a local festival, proclaimed by a single church or community. The first thanksgivings in America were religious occasions, designated to express gratitude to God for specific beneficences such as the end of a drought or a military victory in a skirmish with Native Americans. Worship services were often followed by a communal meal.

Connecticut in 1639 became the first to name a colony-wide day of Thanksgiving, and it wasn't long before the rest of New England followed suit. By the turn of the eighteenth century,

Thanksgiving was a well-established and much-loved custom in New England. It was a day off from work characterized by religious worship, charity to the poor, family reunions, and an enormous feast.

Hale's interest in creating a national Thanksgiving holiday dated back to when she was a young widow in New Hampshire, and her early writings carry references to the holiday. She first wrote about Thanksgiving in 1827 in *Northwood,* the novel whose success led to her being offered the editorship of the *Ladies' Magazine.* She devoted a chapter to the subject, describing in rich detail a classic Yankee Thanksgiving that a visitor from England celebrates with a family in New Hampshire. It remains the finest account in American literature of the mood, spirit, and emotion that generations of Americans have brought with them to the holiday. You can almost smell the roast turkey at its "lordly station" at the head of the table.

For a later edition of *Northwood,* published in 1852, she inserted a piece of dialogue plugging her proposal for a national Thanksgiving Day:

> "Is Thanksgiving Day universally observed in America?" inquired Mr. Frankford [an Englishman on a visit to New Hampshire].
>
> "Not yet, but I trust it will become so. We have too few holidays. Thanksgiving, like the Fourth of July, should be considered a national festival, and observed by all our people."[2]

Hale turned to the holiday in another early piece of writing. "The Thanksgiving of the Heart" appeared first in the *Ladies' Magazine* in 1829 and was later published in a collection of her short stories. The tale is highly autobiographical—a poignant reimagining of how different her life might have been had she not lost her husband. In the story, a husband goes missing, leaving his young wife to support herself and their children, one of whom—as in Hale's case—was born after the husband's disappearance. Like Hale, the woman turns to needlework as a way of earning a small living. Also like Hale, the woman in the story has to grapple with the painful issue of whether to parcel her children off to live with relatives who will be able to care for them. As Thanksgiving approaches—a season "associated with mirth and rejoicing"—the wife's grief intensifies. Unlike Hale's situation, however, the story has a happy ending, with the surprise return of the husband on Thanksgiving Day. And so, Hale writes, "the funeral faced month of November is thus made to wear a garland of joy."[3]

"The Thanksgiving of the Heart" contains intimations of her later campaign for a national Thanksgiving, notably the idea that a celebration of Thanksgiving will bring together families and communities. "There is a deep moral influence in these periodical seasons of rejoicing in which a whole community participates," she wrote.[4]

BY THE TIME Hale became editor of the *Lady's Book* in 1837, the Thanksgiving tradition had spread beyond New England to other states and territories, often carried there by migrating New Englanders. If a state celebrated Thanksgiving—some did not—selection of the date was left to the governor. The president sometimes named a Thanksgiving Day in federal territories. But there was no uniform date for the holiday.

By tradition, Thanksgiving Day fell in the fall. Depending on the date decreed by their governor, Americans celebrated the holiday anytime between late September and early December.

In 1837, Hale was a resident of Massachusetts, which marked the holiday on November 30. In her home state of New Hampshire, Thanksgiving fell a week later, on December 7. Pennsylvania, where the *Lady's Book* was published, did not celebrate Thanksgiving that year.

Hale loved Thanksgiving with a passion that other mothers feel for their favorite child. She wanted every American, in her day and forever more, to share her ardor. She accurately forecast that the time would come when all American citizens across the country, and no matter where in the world they might find themselves at the end of November, would pause to give thanks on a common Thanksgiving Day.

As a homegrown holiday, Thanksgiving was dear to Hale on several counts. It fit into her journalistic mission of helping the new country develop a common culture, something that would differentiate Americans from their former colonial masters. Today Thanksgiving is linked inextricably with the Pilgrims and the Wampanoag Indians and their now-famous feast of 1621. But if you had mentioned them to Hale, she would have looked at you blankly. The story of the harvest feast of 1621 was lost to history until the middle of the nineteenth century, when Pilgrim documents that had gone missing for two centuries came to light.

As a religious matter, Hale saw Thanksgiving as embodying a founding principle of the United States—freedom of worship. Protestantism was the dominant religion of the period and Hale sometimes referred to Thanksgiving as a Christian tradition. But she recognized that, like America itself, the holiday was open to people of all faiths, a point Washington stressed in his Thanksgiving proclamations. In 1795, he called on "all Religious societies and Denominations . . . to set apart and observe . . . a Day of Public Thanksgiving and Praise."

Hale was intrigued by the Jewish holiday of Shavuot, or the Feast of Weeks, and often cited it as one of the roots of the American holiday. She pointed to God's command to the Jews in the Old Testament book of Nehemiah to celebrate a harvest festival—and she believed that His command applied just as much in times of war as in times of peace. "In a time of national darkness and sore troubles," she wrote in 1863, "shall we not recognize that the goodness of God never faileth, and to our Father in heaven we should always bring the Thanksgiving offering at the ingathering of the harvest?"[5] Her words have added meaning when it is realized that she wrote them shortly after the bloody Battle of Gettysburg.

She also saw Thanksgiving as a time for expressions of patriotism, on a plane with the Fourth of July and Washington's birthday, the only other national holidays born of the American experience. The fact that Washington, whom she admired above all other men, saw the value of a national Thanksgiving Day, elevated its status in her mind. An additional selling point was that while Thanksgiving took place in the autumn, Independence Day fell in the summer and Washington's Birthday—February 22—was a winter holiday. This was a trivial consideration, to be sure, but Hale cited it to build support for her proposal. She also applauded the fact that a late-November Thanksgiving meant that the "war of politics"—that is, elections—"will be over for the year."[6]

THE PUBLIC PART of her Thanksgiving campaign unfolded in the pages of the *Lady's Book* in a series of articles published over the course of seventeen years. The *Lady's Book*, with its tens of thousands of readers, was a powerful platform, and she used its pages to carefully build a consensus for a common nationwide Thanksgiving Day. Hale saw Thanksgiving, with its emphasis on gratitude to God, family reunions, and a special meal, as falling into the feminine sphere. Her readers were located in every state and territory. Hale understood that if they got behind her call for a national Thanksgiving, politicians would likely pay heed.

SEPARATE FROM her *Lady's Book* campaign, Hale privately sought the support of elected officials and other public figures. Tapping into what would today be called her personal network, she wrote hundreds of individual letters to statesmen and other opinion makers urging them to lend their prestige and clout to her idea for a common Thanksgiving Day. Considering that each letter was written by hand and personalized for the recipient, it was an enormous task.[7]

Her initial goal was to persuade every governor to agree on a date for Thanksgiving. As the years went by, she came to believe this that wasn't a practical solution. It would require a permanent campaign to make sure that every governor cooperated every year on the date for that year's Thanksgiving Day. Politics or personal preference inevitably would interfere, leading one or more governors to go his own way, choosing a separate date for his state's celebration. As Hale diplomatically put it in her letter to Secretary of State Seward making the case for a presidential proclamation naming a national Thanksgiving, a governor might "have special purposes to answer or will forget the importance of cooperation."[8] Her preferred path to a national Thanksgiving was to find a president willing to do what Washington did: issue a proclamation designating a date for the holiday to be marked nationwide.

HALE LAUNCHED her Thanksgiving campaign in her "Editors' Table" column of January 1847. She had traveled to her hometown of Newport, New Hampshire, the previous summer, and that visit seems to have stimulated childhood memories of the joyful Thanksgivings she experienced as a child.

The "good old puritan custom" of Thanksgiving was becoming popular throughout the country, she wrote. By her count, twenty-one or twenty-two of the twenty-nine states celebrated Thanksgiving in 1846. Seventeen celebrated on the same day, Thursday, November 26. She closed her column with an exhortation to her readers:

> Would that the next Thanksgiving might be observed in all the states on the same day. Then, though the members of the same family might be too far separated to meet around one festive board, they would have the gratification of knowing that all were enjoying the blessings of the day. From the St. John's to the Rio Grande, from the Atlantic to the Pacific border, the telegraph of human happiness would move every heart to rejoice simultaneously, and render grateful thanks to God for the blessings showered on our favored country.[9]

As the year progressed, Hale kept the subject alive for her readers. In March, she reported that her proposal had been well received and called on other publications to lend editorial support. The "month of gloom," she wrote, referring to November, "would then become the gladdest in the year." In October, she praised the governor of New Hampshire for naming the last Thursday of November as Thanksgiving, which she favored as the annual date since that was what Washington had chosen.

Hale's work continued in much the same vein over the following seventeen years as she promoted a national Thanksgiving in the *Lady's Book*. She kept track of where and when the holiday was celebrated, she lauded governors who coordinated with other governors on a common date, and she reported cheerful anecdotes on how various American regions celebrated.

In the 1850s, after observing the variations in the dates that governors had chosen for their state Thanksgivings, she flirted with the idea of holding Thanksgiving on the third Thursday of the month. That might be more suitable, she wrote, since it was the approximate middle point between the dates selected by governors the previous year. The third-Thursday notion didn't take flight, however, and she soon went back to pushing for Thanksgiving to be held on the last Thursday of November. Godey weighed in in his own column, "Godey's Arm-Chair," characteristically using the opportunity to enthuse about "the ladies of the nation" and how they could help.[10]

HALE USED every feature of the *Lady's Book*—editorials, recipes, poetry, short stories, sermons, book reviews—to consolidate support for a national celebration of Thanksgiving.

In the fiction and poetry she published, the holiday was portrayed as a time of joyful family reunions and bountiful tables. One such offering, by an author identified only as "S.G.B.," tells the story of a wartime Thanksgiving, when a mother who has just sat down to Thanksgiving dinner is surprised by the arrival of the son she believed had been killed in battle.[11] S. Annie Frost, a mid-century writer of household affairs and manners, contributed four short stories with Thanksgiving settings. In one, a little orphan girl invites a reclusive hunchback to Thanksgiving dinner at her adoptive home, an event that leads to the happy discovery that they are father and daughter.

Hale used the illustrated "Receipts, &c" column to indirectly promote Thanksgiving by publishing recipes for traditional Thanksgiving dishes such as pumpkin pie and roast turkey.

Since many of her readers lived on farms and raised their own Thanksgiving turkeys, her instructions began with elementary information that would be of use to farmers' wives. Modern-day cooks don't have to know how to handle the bird's crop skin or that a crooked wire is the most efficient method of removing the turkey's gizzard.

A holiday dinner menu published by the *Lady's Book* included New England classics as well as sweet potato pudding, a Southern standard. Hale's drive for a national Thanksgiving wasn't based on a desire to see Americans feast on the same foods on the same day, but she was shrewd enough to realize that the culinary appeal of Thanksgiving was another selling point for her vision of a shared celebration.

THE MORAL INFLUENCE of a communal holiday was a theme to which she often returned, especially as the country moved toward civil war. Hale hoped that a national celebration of Thanksgiving would help preserve the Union. "Such social rejoicings," she editorialized in 1857, "tend greatly to expand the generous feelings of our nature, and strengthen the bond of union that finds us brothers and sisters in that true sympathy of American patriotism."[12]

In 1859, she again stressed her belief in the unifying impact of a national Thanksgiving: "If every State should join in union thanksgiving on the 24th of this month," she wrote, "would it not be a renewed pledge of love and loyalty to the Constitution of the United States, which guarantees peace, prosperity, progress and perpetuity to our great Republic?"[13]

Even as war loomed, Hale renewed her argument, writing that a national Thanksgiving could help keep together the divided country. "This year the *last Thursday in November* falls on the

29th," she wrote in 1860. "If all the States and Territories hold their Thanksgiving on that day, there will be a complete moral and social reunion of the people of America. Would not this be a good omen for the perpetual political union of the States?"[14] There was a note of desperation in her plea. By the time the next autumn rolled around, the United States was engulfed in civil war. In 1861, Hale sought a Thanksgiving Day of Peace, pleading that "we lay aside our enmities and strifes . . . on this one day." Her entreaty went unheeded.[15]

By 1860, Hale was close to achieving her goal of seeing Thanksgiving celebrated in every state on the same day. In 1859, thirty of the thirty-three states had celebrated on November 24, the last Thursday of the month. Two of the ten territories—Nebraska and Kansas—also celebrated on that date. Success was near at hand. Thanksgiving was celebrated, too, by an increasing number of Americans living abroad, and Hale published accounts about Thanksgiving celebrations in India, China, Switzerland, and elsewhere.

The American ambassador to Prussia sent the *Lady's Book* a detailed description of Thanksgiving in Berlin, written by an American woman who was residing there. Sixty-five Americans came together for dinner at a large hotel after having worshipped in the small chapel where Sunday services were usually held. The Americans were a heterogenous group, the American in Berlin wrote, hailing from Connecticut, Ohio, Illinois, and other states. Many, including fifteen women, were students of law, medicine, or theology. Also present at the dinner were clergymen, diplomats, musicians, and their wives. The Prussian chefs, unfamiliar with American fare, were instructed in how to prepare baked beans and roast turkey. A local American lady contributed pumpkin pies, an accomplishment for which she was warmly toasted by the assembly. In keeping with Thanksgiving's charitable tradition, the Americans took up a collection for the poor of the city. In short, Thanksgiving in Berlin, wrote Hale's correspondent, was "something of a thrill, as if it suddenly allowed a glimpse of home."[16]

Even farther away from home, Townsend Harris, the first American envoy to Japan, wrote Hale in 1860 that he had asked Americans living in Yokohama and Yedo (the ancient name of Tokyo) to mark this "honoured Festival in Japan."[17]

HALE DIDN'T INFORM her readers that concurrent with her *Lady's Book* campaign to make Thanksgiving a national holiday, she also was promoting her proposal in private communications with the governors of every state, members of Congress, military officers, American diplomats abroad, and other public figures. Every year—usually in the late summer or early September—she would write personal letters to a long list of well-placed men in the hope that they would advance her cause. There was no trace of the shyness she had experienced in her early years in Boston about approaching men she didn't know. Her personal fame coupled with years of operating successfully in the all-male world of publishing gave her the confidence she needed.

She wrote every governor—some of whom she knew from previous causes she had championed—and encouraged them to name Thanksgiving Day in their state for the last Thursday of November. Clips from the *Lady's Book* featuring her articles on Thanksgiving would flutter out of the envelopes they opened.

In their replies, governors were generally obliging and often enthusiastic about the prospect of celebrating the holiday on a uniform date. An 1859 letter from New York governor E.D. Morgan was typical of the responses she received. "The propriety of designating a common day in each of the States," Morgan wrote from Albany, "must be obvious to all and will, I trust, be regarded by all."[18] The governor of Michigan, Kingsley Bingham, wrote, "I concur entirely with your suggestion."[19] A number of the governors sent Hale copies of the Thanksgiving proclamations they had issued in their own states.

An exception was Virginia, where Governor Henry Wise, a slaveholder, refused to have any part of Thanksgiving, which, because of its New England roots, had gained a reputation in the South as a Yankee abolitionist holiday. Writing to Hale in 1856, an irate Wise railed against churches that "profess to be Christian" and castigated the "thousands of pulpits" where ministers were preaching "Christian politics," which is to say, inveighing against slavery. He heatedly informed Hale that the Commonwealth of Virginia would not be signing on to this "theatrical national claptrap of Thanksgiving." Wise concluded by telling Hale she was welcome to publish his letter. She did not take him up on his suggestion.[20]

In fact, Hale never mentioned this private correspondence in print. The omission was in keeping with her view that women should not involve themselves directly in political affairs but instead exercise their influence behind the scenes.

AT THE SAME TIME Hale was working with governors to orchestrate a de facto national Thanksgiving Day, she was quietly pursuing another path—one that, if successful, would relieve her of the task of seeking the annual approval of every governor. She hoped to persuade the president of the United States to follow Washington's example and issue a proclamation declaring a national Thanksgiving Day.

As she quickly learned, there was a potential stumbling block to this course of action: the Constitution. Washington's 1789 proclamation had been controversial. Members of Congress objected that under the Constitution's separation of powers doctrine, the president didn't have the authority to proclaim days of thanksgiving. That was among the unenumerated powers left to individual state governments. A second objection had to do with the religious aspect of Thanksgiving. In the view of some members, proclaiming a day of thanksgiving was a religious matter and therefore outside the authority of Congress or the president. Washington skirted these objections by requesting—not ordering—governors to agree to the date he named.

The nation's third president, Thomas Jefferson, renewed the objections that had been raised in the First Congress. In 1808, when he was asked his view on the constitutionality of a presidential proclamation of Thanksgiving, his reply was emphatic: "It must rest with the states."[21] Jefferson, who had issued a thanksgiving proclamation when he was governor of Virginia, refused to issue one as president.

The presidents of Hale's day agreed with Jefferson, as Hale discovered to her dismay. In 1849, a letter from Zachary Taylor appeared on the front pages of newspapers in New York City and Washington in which he explained why he would not proclaim a national Thanksgiving. "I have yet thought it most proper to leave the subject of a thanksgiving proclamation where custom has so long consigned it—in the hands of the Governors of the several States," he wrote.[22]

President Taylor's letter, clearly intended for public consumption, was addressed to an unnamed male friend, who submitted it to the press. There is no evidence that Hale had a role in soliciting Taylor's view on the subject, but given that she wrote to other presidents asking them to name a Thanksgiving Day, it is possible that she wrote to Taylor or asked a friend who knew the president to do so on her behalf.

Millard Fillmore and Franklin Pierce, who followed Taylor into the White House, both declined Hale's request to name a day of Thanksgiving. In a detailed response to her letter, Fillmore courteously rejected her suggestion that he recommend to Congress that it legislate a national Thanksgiving holiday. Since Thanksgiving is usually regarded as a religious festival, it is not an appropriate subject for legislation, he told her. He went on to reject her second suggestion that he issue a presidential proclamation for the same purpose, repeating President Taylor's point that custom has left Thanksgiving proclamations to governors, not the president. Otherwise, "I should unhesitatingly assume the authority of issuing a proclamation appointing a day of thanksgiving for the whole nation."[23]

Four years later, President Pierce's response to Hale's letter was polite but terse. "I perceive serious objections," he wrote, without elaboration.[24] It was a brush-off to his fellow New Hampshirite. Pierce's successor in the White House was James Buchanan, with whom Hale became well acquainted when he was secretary of state in the administration of President James Polk. Buchanan also declined to proclaim a Thanksgiving Day.

DESPITE HALE'S string of failures with Lincoln's immediate predecessors in the White House, Hale was nothing if not indefatigable, and in 1863, she resolved to approach the president about Thanksgiving.

Hale family lore has it that their famous ancestor traveled to Washington in 1863 for a personal interview with Lincoln on

Thanksgiving. Years after her death, a grandson, Charles Hale, son of Horatio Hale, told an interviewer, "I remember my father saying that his mother had visited President Lincoln and had found him a very kindly and interested gentleman."[25] He added no details about the meeting.

Lincoln was famously approachable, and the well-known editor of the *Lady's Book* surely could have secured an interview with the president on the basis of her professional standing alone. She also had a family connection that she could have used to facilitate a request. Major General David Hunter, a longtime friend of Lincoln and an honorary pallbearer at his funeral, was the older brother of Hale's son-in-law. Dr. John Hunter married Hale's daughter Frances in 1844. An introduction from Major General Hunter would have opened doors at the White House.

While a meeting between Hale and Lincoln is entirely plausible, there is no evidence to support it other than the secondhand recollection of her grandson years after the presumed meeting took place. Hale never wrote about it, and there is no mention of it in the papers of Lincoln's presidency.

Rather, the evidence shows that, as she had done with other presidents, Hale made her case to Lincoln for a national Thanksgiving in a letter. Her first step was to write Secretary of State William Seward. They had met in Philadelphia some years previously and she regarded him as a friend.

Writing Seward was a strategic move. Hale correctly surmised that he would be receptive to her proposal for a national Thanksgiving. As governor of New York from 1839 to 1842, Seward had issued four Thanksgiving proclamations. Each was a beautiful piece of prose, lyrical in its descriptions of American abundance and American liberty. According to his son Frederick, Seward always found this aspect of his gubernatorial duties a particular pleasure. His Thanksgiving proclamations were "no mere form," Frederick recalled, but heartfelt expressions of Seward's belief that the American people have, in all the world, the greatest grounds for giving thanks.[26] Seward was second to none, too, in his enjoyment of the day itself. He recorded in his memoirs the "fine roasted turkey and . . . venison-steak" that he and his law clerks enjoyed on Thanksgiving Day 1836.[27]

His memoirs show that as governor, Seward was well aware of the disparity in the dates on which states celebrated Thanksgiving. In 1841, he designated Thursday, December 9, as the date for the holiday in New York. That same year the governor of Ohio designated December 21 and the governor of Rhode Island named November 25—giving truth to the witticism that a traveler with a well-planned itinerary could enjoy a Thanksgiving dinner on each Thursday between Election Day and Christmas Day.

In Hale's lengthy letter to Seward, dated September 26, 1863, Hale reviewed the history of her campaign for a national Thanksgiving and made a case for why a presidential proclamation would be the best way to achieve that goal. Waiting for every state to legislate a fixed date would take too long, she explained, and it was unrealistic to expect that every governor would agree on a common date every year.

Taking a cue from Washington, she recommended that Lincoln "invite and recommend" the governors to unite in approving a date chosen by the president, thereby skirting constitutional objections. She concluded by urging the president to move quickly. The presidential proclamation should be issued by the following week. The brashness—effrontery even—of Hale's request to a wartime president was typical of her self-confidence and her devotion to her cause.

Hale was in such a hurry that she didn't wait for Seward's

reply. Two days after she posted her first letter to Seward, she wrote directly to the president, imploring him to declare a day of national thanksgiving. "Thus, by the noble example and action of the President of the United States," she wrote, "the permanency and union of our Great American Festival would be forever secured."[28]

Events moved swiftly after that. Seward's reply to Hale, dated September 29, 1863, informed her that he had received her "interesting" letter and had "commended [it] to the consideration of the President."[29] On October 3—only seven days after Hale's initial letter to Seward—Lincoln issued his Thanksgiving Proclamation naming Thursday, November 26, as Thanksgiving Day.[30]

Not since Washington had a president called on Americans to come together to give thanks for their joint blessings as a nation. Lincoln's proclamation was the first in what has become an unbroken string of Thanksgivings up to the present day.

CHAPTER TWELVE
Hale's Civil War

H ALE'S THANKSGIVING editorials urging preservation of the Union were the closest she came in the *Lady's Book* to expressing a view about the coming Civil War. While Godey gave her full editorial discretion over the content of the *Lady's Book*, he strictly barred discussion of most political topics in all of his magazines, including the one she edited. Consistent with prevailing attitudes, he considered politics an unsuitable subject for his lady readers. He also was mindful of commercial considerations. Before the war, which halted mail delivery between the Union and the Confederacy, one-third of the *Lady's Book*'s circulation was in the South. He had aspirations of rebuilding the magazine's readership there once the conflict ended.

Godey put his no-politics views into action in 1850, when he fired Grace Greenwood, assistant editor of the *Lady's Book*, after Southern readers complained about articles she had written for the *National Era*, a prominent antislavery weekly. Grace

Greenwood was the pen name of Sara Jane Clarke. She was a popular young writer, whom Godey first hired to edit his *Lady's Dollar Newspaper* and then elevated to a masthead position at the *Lady's Book*. It is possible he was grooming Greenwood to succeed Hale, who, in 1850, was sixty-two years old—which is to say that she was old in the context of an era when the average life expectancy was forty.

Godey took heat from Northern readers for his decision to fire Greenwood. No less a literary eminence than John Greenleaf Whittier, poet, prominent abolitionist, and occasional *Lady's Book* contributor, used the occasion to ridicule him in verse. Hale, who stayed silent about the firing, was criticized for not resigning her position in solidarity with Grace Greenwood. To Hale's credit, after Greenwood's dismissal, she mentioned Greenwood's books in her columns and gave them positive reviews.

Given her strong views on women's duty to educate themselves, it is unlikely that Hale fully agreed with Godey that politics was an inappropriate subject for women to follow. Hale saw woman's role as rising above the rough-and-tumble of partisan party politics to a higher moral plane, from which she could advise her husband. But she never recommended that women remain in ignorance about political issues. How is a woman supposed to advise her husband on something she knows nothing about? As a journalist, she kept up a running blaze of commentary on current issues that impacted women and families—with no objection from Godey about straying into forbidden territory. As for the debate about slavery and secession, it was absurd to think that readers of the *Lady's Book* had no views—moral or political—about these pressing issues. Some of the most prominent antislavery voices in antebellum America were women.

Some—most famously Harriett Beecher Stowe—wrote for the *Lady's Book*, though not about slavery.

That said, the mission of the *Lady's Book* was narrowly tailored. It wasn't a general-interest magazine. Its focus was on content of special interest to women. That necessarily included some commentary on political issues—such as Hale's appeals to state legislators to extend property rights to married women and her lobbying of Congress to fund normal schools for the education of female teachers. What Godey really meant by his so-called ban on politics was that he wanted his magazines to stay clear of the two most divisive issues of the day—slavery and secession.

His message sunk in. If Hale wanted to share her antislavery views or her thoughts on the coming war with her readers, she had to find a way to do so without direct reference to them. Her campaign in the *Lady's Book* calling for a national Thanksgiving Day fit into that mold, as did her support of sending freed slaves to Liberia as expressed in her novels *Northwood* and *Mr. Peyton's Experiments*.

But this indirect approach showed her to be living in the past, unwilling to face the reality of the coming Civil War. Her antiwar mindset was fixed in the eighteenth century, when the founders made an ugly compromise on slavery for the purpose of holding together the disparate elements of the new country. For her, preservation of the Union was the supreme priority. She seemed to think—unrealistically—that America's political leaders could again come together for the sake of unity. After the publication of *Liberia: Mr. Peyton's Experiments* and the revised version of *Northwood* in the early 1850s, she didn't write about slavery again.

Godey's no-politics dictum continued during the Civil War.

The *Lady's Book* did not follow the war's progress. There were no battle reports or big-picture analysis. Nor did it report on civilian suffering—food shortages, displaced persons, destruction of private homes and businesses. The Emancipation Proclamation went unnoticed. At the time of Lincoln's assassination, Godey wrote an emotional column focused on the nation's grief without reference to Lincoln's wartime leadership or the reason for his assassin's actions. "The dark stain will linger upon our country's page forever, the stain of blood shed by murder," he wrote, "but the faithful, unselfish heart has gone to meet its reward, while the name that has been the patriot's watchword for four long years, must become now, in the hearts of the people for whom he died, but a memory."[1]

The war didn't go completely unnoticed in the *Lady's Book*, but references were mostly oblique. A series of anonymous articles on widowhood—probably written by Hale—seemed meant to prepare her readers for the all-too-possible wartime fate of being alone in the world without fathers or husbands to support them. As the war took its toll on the men who were fighting, Hale remarked on the large number of women who had lost husbands or beaus, urging the federal government to open more government jobs to women. An item in "Editors' Table" favorably noted the appointment of a woman from Minnesota to a position in the War Department at an annual salary of $1,000.[2]

When Hale mentioned the war directly, it was often in the course of reviewing books on the subject. She compared the anonymous female author of *Notes of Hospital Life*, a record of her service as a nurse in a Union hospital, to Florence Nightingale. Another memoir, *My Days and Nights on the Battle-Field*, is described as "a clear and concise account of the present rebellion." A history of the war's beginnings and a biography of Ulysses S. Grant also won her attention.

She tended to avoid using the word "war" in her columns. She wrote, rather, about unspecified "difficulties and dark shadows" in a "sorrowful year."[3] An editorial titled "Is All War Sinful?" carefully avoided mention of the one that was then raging. In a poignant New Year's greeting to readers in January 1862, she wrote of the war without using the w-word:

This New Year may not—will not, we should say—bring success and earthly enjoyment to us all. The dark clouds of trials and sorrows are over our beloved country, and who can escape the shadow even if sheltered from the bursting storm?[4]

Hale apparently felt she had more leeway to refer to the war when someone other than herself was writing, and the war had a presence in occasional pieces of fiction or poetry that she selected for publication. Wartime settings of short stories didn't specify the precise location, leaving it to the reader to decide whether the story was taking place in the North or the South. A representative example is "A Trip on the Street Cars," which describes the narrator's fellow passengers on a streetcar in an unnamed city. One passenger is a girl on her way to pick up sewing work for her mother, who is the sole support of her family, her soldier-husband having been killed in an unspecified war. Another passenger on the streetcar is a small boy who mistakes a man in uniform for his absent father. The uniform is not identified as gray or blue, Confederate or Union. The exchange between the child and the soldier is sentimental, but it describes an incident that would have resonated with readers.

"Come here, my little man!" the soldier tells the boy. "I am not your papa, but I am fighting in the same army, for the same great cause, and so we are brothers. When is your papa coming home to his little boy?"

The child replies, "When this cruel war is over."[5]

There were other exceptions. She published an elegiac poem, "The Soldier's Wayside Dream," about a soldier who dreams about his Illinois home in the hour before a battle is to begin.[6] The *Lady's Book*'s sole notice of the Battle of Gettysburg appears in a letter from a reader describing the final moments of the life of an unnamed soldier who died holding the photograph of his three children.[7] These were the rare glimpses in *Godey's Lady's Book* of the crushing events disrupting every American's life.

FOR THE COUNTRY'S foremost women's magazine, a striking omission during the war years was the absence of discussion of women's extensive war-relief efforts. Since her years at the *Ladies' Magazine*, Hale had been writing of women's moral duty to participate in charitable work to help the less fortunate. Her work at the Seaman's Aid Society in Boston and the ladies' campaign to build the Bunker Hill Monument provided early examples of philanthropic leadership by women.

Yet when it came to women's efforts in the North to provide wartime assistance to sick and wounded soldiers, the *Lady's Book* was silent. Hale never mentioned the accomplishments of the United States Sanitary Commission, headed by Dorothea Dix, whose work she had previously lauded. During the Civil War Dix enlisted and trained fifteen thousand women as nurses—a profession Hale had long urged be open to women. Other

Northern women organized elaborate Sanitary Fairs around the Union to raise money for the war effort. The first such large-scale ladies' fair was the one Hale organized in Boston in 1841 to benefit the construction of the Bunker Hill Monument. Yet no notice of the wartime, female-led Sanitary Fairs appeared in the *Lady's Book*.

Nor did she inform readers of Dr. Elizabeth Blackwell's efforts to support Union soldiers at the front through the Women's Central Relief Committee, which Dr. Blackwell coordinated. The War Department's appointment of a female physician, Dr. Mary Walker, as an assistant surgeon also went unremarked in the *Lady's Book*. Hale was silent, too, about Clara Barton's call for women to work as nurses at Union Army hospitals. These omissions are hard to countenance in light of Hale's advocacy of medical training for women.

For more than thirty years, women had been turning to Hale and her magazines for information and counsel on how to live productive, useful, moral lives. Yet when her readers might have been seeking guidance on ways to serve their country in its most difficult hour, she had nothing to say. As female nurses and doctors rose to prominence during the war, she was silent. So, too, she was silent as Dix, Blackwell, and other female leaders whose accomplishments she had previously championed were again in the public eye.

Rather, she presented the *Lady's Book* as a place where women could find sanctuary from current affairs. She termed her magazine a "lodge in the wilderness," a haven where readers could escape from the "burning lava" of the war.[8] Forget the war's awful reality, she seemed to be saying. Forget the carnage on the battlefield and the deprivation and suffering among civilians. Retreat to the *Lady's Book*, where the war doesn't reach.

She expressed herself more callously in a letter to a friend. "The whole country is demented on the subject," she wrote. "These *fairs*, and all manner of means to raise money for the soldiers, when the government is spending hundreds of million on the Army and all the women are working or waiting on soldiers!"[9] She wrote these angry words in 1864. It is possible that she was simply war-weary, impatient for the war to end and frustrated that the issues to which she had dedicated her professional work had been put on hold while women devoted themselves to the war effort. Or perhaps she was simply taking the opportunity to pour her heart out to a close confidante without taking careful note of the words she was putting down on paper.

It is possible that she was in a rare mood of personal dejection. Her daughter and namesake, Sarah Josepha, had died suddenly the previous year, at age forty-three. Josepha collapsed over her desk at the successful boarding school she ran in Philadelphia and where mother and daughter resided. A personal health issue also might have been a contributing factor to Hale's uncharacteristically negative mood. Hale was experiencing eye problems that would plague her for the rest of her life, and she had relied on Josepha to assist her with her work.

Regardless, Hale's silence during the war years is hard to comprehend. It may be partly explained by a wish to stand with Godey, a trusted longtime partner, in the expectation that when the war ended they would be in a position to take up their work where they had left off before the fighting began. She had friends in the South, too, which might have been a factor. But there was something else going on—a fury at the very fact of the war and at the men who were fighting it. As she wrote in her "Editors' Table" column a few months before the war began: "Men often push their way into 'the court, the camp, the senate and the mart,' eager for distinction, and not particular about the path, provided it lead them to eminence, glory, wealth, and power. It is not so with women."[10] If anything, the war cemented her beliefs in the essential difference between the two sexes and women's higher moral standing.

The fact nevertheless remains that Hale chose to remain at the *Lady's Book* during the Civil War and accede to Godey's ban on covering it. She was seventy-two years old when the war started. She was financially secure. She could have retired and devoted her energies to the war effort and the preservation of the country she loved. She could have quit the *Lady's Book* and offered to write for another publication, any number of which would have snapped up her services. She might even have stayed at the *Lady's Book* and written a book addressed to women North and South about how they could support their men during the war. Godey never objected to anything she wrote outside of the *Lady's Book*. In the words of Geraldine Ellis, author of an unpublished biography, "Any of these choices would have been more admirable than forgetting that she had always, until now, been a patriot first and an editor second."[11]

IN 1860, on the eve of the Civil War, the *Lady's Book*'s circulation had reached the hitherto-unheard-of figure of 150,000, with an estimated readership of one million. Hale's influence was at its peak. Writers were still clamoring to see their work published in the *Lady's Book*, which had more submissions than it could use. In early 1861, she sent a rejection letter to a contributor, saying: "I am very sorry to say that I cannot accept your poetry, beautiful as it is, because we cannot publish it. We have no room. . . . It is simply the result of too much wealth, too many good things on hand."[12]

The strong circulation numbers belied the fact that the *Lady's Book* was facing serious competition from energetic competitors. Readers with a taste for literature were turning to *The Atlantic*, founded in 1857, and *Harper's Monthly*, which debuted in 1850. *Peterson's Magazine* was giving the *Lady's Book* a run for its money in the market for periodicals targeting women. By the end of the 1860s, it overtook the *Lady's Book* in circulation.[13]

The quality of the fiction published by the *Lady's Book* in the postwar period was uneven. American settings and themes still dominated, but there was an overabundance of sentimental love stories. These stories were popular with readers—perhaps because they were a fleeting diversion from the war's aftermath. But the literary quality was such that Godey himself complained in 1868 about the plethora of short stories in which a wartime nurse discovers her wounded lover in a hospital. "Are there no incidents of which to compose a story but love and marriage?" he inquired. "This is the eternal story drug; and if our subscribers are not tired of them, we are."[14] Hale, who once remarked that every story she published, even the lightest ones, carried a moral, would have been hard-pressed to find a message in some of the tales published during this period.[15] The ever-popular sections on recipes, fashion, and needlework patterns all received more space than they had in the past. Health and hygiene also got more attention.

That said, Hale's ideals still animated the magazine and she continued to report and comment on women's issues. Throughout the war, "Editors' Table" remained a bulletin board for developments in education, with information about new schools for girls and young women, updates on teaching opportunities, and reports on Hale's efforts to persuade Congress to fund normal schools. Given the number and diversity of books she re-viewed, it would appear that the editor's table was groaning with volumes, especially ones written by women.

She kept on top of the topic of Thanksgiving too—both in articles in the *Lady's Book* and in correspondence with pres-idents. She felt the need to defend herself from criticism that her Thanksgiving campaign was an inappropriate plunge into politics. In an editorial essay in 1864, she declared, "We are conscious of not having in any manner gone beyond the proper limits of the sphere in which we have prescribed for the *Lady's Book*."[16] In the same essay, she called for a Thanksgiving Day truce for combatants. Her suggestion went nowhere.

ONE OF THE CAUSES to which Hale devoted herself during and immediately following the war years was the formation of Vas-sar College—that is to say, Vassar *Female* College, as it was orig-inally styled.

Matthew Vassar was a British-born philanthropist who had come to the United States at an early age and made his for-tune in the ale-brewing business in Poughkeepsie, New York. In 1861, a widower with no children, he announced his plan to donate $400,000—about $12.5 million today—and an es-tate of four hundred acres for the establishment of a women's college in that city. Vassar envisioned a highly selective col-lege whose academic offerings would mirror those of Harvard, Yale, and other top-notch schools for young men. Milo P. Jew-ett, first president of Vassar College and a close friend of Mat-thew Vassar, recalled a conversation with Vassar before the founding: "There is not an *endowed* College for Young Women in the world," Jewett wrote. "We have plenty of Female Col-leges (so called) in this country, but they are Colleges only in name—they have no funds, no libraries, cabinets, museum, or apparatus worth mentioning."[17]

When Hale learned of Vassar's intention to found an endowed college for women that would compete with the country's first-rate schools for men, she wrote him, requesting more information and offering to publicize the new school in the *Lady's Book*. "I am much interested, in what I have heard respecting your plan for a new Institution on a very liberal scale, for the Young Ladies of America."[18] Vassar wrote back immediately with a favorable response: "I am honored in finding my own view so much in harmony with Sentiments found in [your] Editorials."[19]

Thus began an intense six-year correspondence between the businessman who was passionate about his vision for a superior college for women and the editor who saw the proposed school as a fulfillment of the cause for which she had dedicated her professional life and a model for more superior women's colleges. It was an unlikely partnership. Hale was a well-educated, articulate professional who had been thinking about the subject of higher education for women for many years and held strong views. For his part, Vassar had a grand idea but was unsure about its practical application. He possessed a sharp business mind, but he had been poorly educated. His letters contained misspellings and grammatical errors.

Yet Vassar recognized in Hale a kindred spirit as well as a source of thoughtful advice, and he jumped at the opportunity to sound her out on issues that he and his advisors were mulling over. He was shrewd enough to recognize, too, that Hale's imprimatur would be invaluable in ensuring the success of his college. There was no better way to attract qualified students to the new school than favorable articles in *Godey's Lady's Book*.

Vassar was overflowing with ideas for his new college and eager to share them with Hale. One was whether to require students to wear a uniform. He favored a college uniform, arguing that it would be democratizing. In his view, since all the young women would be wearing the same outfits, they wouldn't be able to distinguish between rich and poor students. It would also prevent jealousy about dress. He thought a variation on the comfortable bloomer dress—pantaloons worn under a short skirt— would be appropriate attire.

Hale was aghast at the suggestion of the unladylike bloomer costume, but she restrained herself in her return letter, saying only, "Any hint approaching the Bloomer standard would, I greatly fear, be a serious injury to the College."[20] She also disagreed with the idea of a college uniform, arguing that young women should not be shielded from the real-world experience of having to work and live with colleagues of varying backgrounds. "I do not consider sumptuary laws of much use in the service of morality or of economy. Children are not taught to walk well by keeping them in leading strings," she replied. The distinctions between rich and poor "are all around us," and "there will be *richer* and *poorer* in Vassar College. Would it be well to enforce an equality of personal appearance there which cannot be found in Life?—Is not the training in your Institution intended to prepare young ladies for their duties in the world—as it is?"[21] Vassar dropped the uniform idea.

He also solicited Hale's advice on the proposed school calendar, which designated a summer vacation of just one month and a long winter break of three months. Once again, Hale emphatically disagreed. Winter is the best time of the year to stay indoors and study, she argued; in summer, it is healthier for young women to spend more time outdoors. When the school's final calendar was adopted in 1865, it more closely resembled Hale's ideas than Vassar's.

Hale in turn wrote Vassar about her own hopes for the college. She lobbied Vassar and the trustees to hire women for the faculty. Vassar was receptive to the idea from the first, but he reported back to Hale that the trustees were skeptical that they could find qualified female teachers. She had her scholar-son Horatio, now married and living in Ontario, write an anonymous article for the *Lady's Book* making the case for women as faculty members. In the article, Horatio scoffed at the suggestion that there was a lack of women with the intellectual and educational background to teach at Vassar. Just advertise, he advised, and you will have a flood of inquiries from qualified applicants. He put forward the moral argument that an all-male faculty would send a discouraging message to scholarly undergraduates that they would be unfit to teach at their own college after completing their studies.[22] Horatio was his mother's voice here. She was having trouble with her eyes, and she enlisted Horatio, who knew her thinking, to write for her.

Hale's push for women on the faculty was the most important contribution she made to the establishment of the school. When Vassar College opened in 1865, two of the eight professors were women. Maria Mitchell, whom Hale had praised after she discovered a comet, was named professor of astronomy. Alida Avery was professor of physiology and hygiene and the college physician. Of the thirty-five assistant teachers, thirty were women. Another senior woman on the staff was Hannah Lyman, who was appointed Lady Principal, charged with overseeing standards of conduct and morals among the students. The Lady Principal idea had been Hale's.

Hale expressed her opinion on the appropriate salaries for female professors. She was not a proponent of equal pay for equal work as it is interpreted today. In her view, since unmarried women had fewer financial obligations than married men, it was acceptable to pay them less. Widows with children, however, deserved to receive the same salaries as male professors, since they had a "man's duty" to support their families and educate their children. But as a general matter, "it never seemed to me that a lady should claim the same amount of salary as a gentleman professor."[23] She didn't offer an opinion on the appropriate salary for unmarried men.

Another of her academic proposals—that the college offer courses in domestic science—went nowhere despite Hale's vigorous promotion of the idea in the *Lady's Book*. She was disappointed when the trustees decided not to create a professorship of domestic economy, and she called the college remiss for failing to prepare students for their traditional roles as wives and mothers. To make her point, she painted a comic portrait of the neglected husband of a Vassar alumna who arrived at the breakfast table only to find a poor meal and general household chaos. Having for many years encouraged her readers in the benefits of exercise, she was delighted that the college required students take courses in gymnastics, calisthenics, archery, and other sports. A woman was appointed in charge of athletics.

Hale's most zealous campaign was reserved for her peculiar proposal that the word "Female" be removed from the name Vassar Female College. The word was an "animal term" in her view, its usage best left for pigs and other non-human creatures. She variously described it as vulgar, inelegant, absurd, improper, inappropriate, insulting, obnoxious, and degrading. She concluded an editorial on the topic with the query, "Does it seem suitable that the term *female*, which is not a synonym for *woman*, and never signifies *lady*, should have a place in the title of this noble institution?"[24] Hale herself had used the word "female" for decades but somehow had a change of heart in the mid-1850s, when she railed against its use in a column titled "Females—Is the Term Proper to Designate Women?"

From the perspective of the twenty-first century, all this conflict over an everyday word seems a tempest in a teapot, a trivial matter at best. But from Hale's perspective in mid-nineteenth-century America, where educated women had to fight for respect, the name change was a matter of dignity, of conveying the proper status of the young women who would be studying at Vassar. Words matter, and Hale's campaign against the use of the word "female" was part of her push to ensure that Vassar students would be accorded the respect they deserved.

Vassar's stated purpose in founding his college was to elevate the position of women, and Hale saw the school's name in contradiction of Vassar's mission. His initial reaction to Hale's insistence on the name change was indifference. It would be inconvenient to change the name, which had already been registered with New York State, and he didn't at first understand why Hale found "female" offensive. He eventually got on board with Hale's suggestion and fought for it with the board of trustees. After lengthy discussions, the trustees finally voted to change the name, the state legislature approved it, and the word "Female" was removed from the plaque on the college's main building. Vassar wrote immediately to Hale, tongue firmly in cheek: "I hasten to inform you that the great agony is over. . . . Woman stands redeemed, as least so far as Vassar College is concerned from the degrading vulgarization in the associated name of 'female.'"[25]

Over the years, the two comrades in arms became fast

friends through their confidential correspondence, exchanging personal news about health and family matters along with their animated discussions regarding the college. Vassar referred to Hale as his "dear friend," while Hale told him that she spoke to him "as to a brother."[26] Vassar sent her two photographs of himself and, sounding a little like a sweetheart, diffidently requested hers in return. Vassar's biographer, Edward R. Linner, believes that Hale's letters stimulated Vassar to continually assess and reconsider his grand project, helping him refine his goals for the college. In Linner's estimation, Vassar "had become her unconscious and willing student, who in the end went far beyond her."[27]

As fate would have it, the two friends were destined never to meet. Hale declined to accept Vassar's repeated invitations to visit the campus until the removal of "Female" from the school's name. Not long after that took place, Vassar fell ill. In 1867, as his health was failing, he wrote her: "I must see my good friend Mrs. Hale before parting this transitory life."[28] He died in 1868 without ever having met the friend with whom he had accomplished so much.

There was, however, one piece of unfinished business. Several years before his death, Vassar had asked Hale to use the *Lady's Book* to encourage readers to leave bequests in their wills to benefit his college. There is no record of a reply by Hale; she probably thought it would be inappropriate to make a direct appeal for money for Vassar. After his death, perhaps remembering her friend's request, Hale used the opportunity of the tribute to Vassar that she wrote for the *Lady's Book* to pay homage to this idea—one that she had advanced many years previously at the *Ladies' Magazine*, when she excoriated a lady for leaving her money to Harvard rather than for women's education. While not advising readers to give money specifically to Vassar College, she urged women to follow Matthew Vassar's "noble example" and support higher education for women.[29] "His name will live forever in the annals of American educational progress," she wrote, "as the first man who did justice to the mind of woman."[30]

CHAPTER THIRTEEN

Twilight Years

A FTER JOSEPHA'S DEATH in 1863, Hale took up residence with her older daughter, Fanny, and her children at 1413 Locust Street. Fanny's husband, Lewis Boudinot Hunter, a naval surgeon, was away at war. The family's four-story redbrick house was located in a fashionable section of the city just steps from the busy corner that was home to the Academy of Music, the opulent opera house at the epicenter of the Philadelphia arts scene.

One of Hale's few concessions to her advancing age was her decision to work from home, with occasional visits to the *Lady's Book* office on Chestnut Street some blocks away. She relied on her grandson, Richard Hunter, to carry messages, copy, page proofs, and other particulars of her trade to and fro. In later years, as her vision deteriorated, Richard and Fanny functioned as her amanuenses, writing at her dictation.

After departing New Hampshire in 1828, Hale had lived mostly in a succession of boardinghouses in Boston and Philadelphia.

Her residence at Josepha's boarding school represented another variety of communal living. In her novel *Boarding Out*, she describes the cold domestic comforts of life in a modern metropolitan boardinghouse compared with the warmth, security, and contentment of one's own fireside.[1] In a letter to a friend in 1846, as she was contemplating a summer visit to Newport, she reflected on how her hometown carried associations that she had not been able to replace in Boston or Philadelphia: "It is seventeen years since I left the town. I have not a relation there—but still it was my *home* and I have never felt since leaving it that I *had a home of my own*."[2] Now, at the age of seventy-five, living with the Hunter family in Philadelphia, Hale rediscovered the joys of domestic life.

At the Hunter home on Locust Street, her office sat in a large, sunny upstairs room that stretched across the front of the house. The focal point of the room was an enormous work table—always neatly kept—where she spent the day reading and writing. She kept a bowl of grapes near at hand, a habit formed fifty years earlier in New Hampshire when David had cured her tuberculosis with a regimen of grapes and fresh air. Bookshelves lined the walls, and a comfortable sofa accommodated her many visitors, including her grandchildren, who were always welcome to bring a book and settle in for a quiet stay. Her bed and bureau occupied an alcove. She shared the room with four pairs of canaries, whose wicker cages were suspended near the windows and whose cheerful song could be heard throughout the house.

Later in his life, Richard Hunter recalled the stream of visitors who arrived at 1413 Locust Street to see his grandmother. "Everybody who came to Philadelphia must have called on her," he related, "and of course there were always her many local friends and the endless authors and artists who contributed to the magazine."

On Sundays, she spent the morning worshipping at the Church of the Holy Trinity in Rittenhouse Square. She attended to personal correspondence in the afternoon and relaxed with the Hunter family in the parlor in the evening. Hale presided at the piano, and everyone would gather round to sing songs and listen to the stories that Grandmother Hale recounted.[3] On her birthday, October 24, she would recite "Growing Old," the poem she had written the year she turned seventy-one.

One visitor to the house on Locust Street neatly captured two aspects of Hale's persona—the confident, opinionated voice of the *Lady's Book* and the courteous, gracious presence in private life. Vassar College trustee John Raymond described his meeting with Hale in 1864 in a letter to his wife: "Saw Mrs. Sarah J. Hale, who agreeably disappointed me; nothing of the 'strong-minded' in her manner whatever; simple, quiet, ladylike, but bright and sensible, full of conversation and running slightly to enthusiasm on her favorite topics of Woman and the Bible."[4]

A woman from New Hampshire who met Hale at a dinner party in Philadelphia in 1859 was similarly struck upon being introduced to the famous editor: "I expected to see an intellectual old lady who wore glasses and talked books. I did see a charming society lady of middle age, with an undimmed eye, and a clear, broad, high smooth forehead, with never a wrinkle or line or crow's foot on it." When the visitor commented on Hale's youthful demeanor, the editor offered a droll retort: "I'm only seventy-one!"[5]

AS THE POSTWAR ERA began in 1865, Hale, now seventy-seven years old, showed little indication of flagging energy or diminishing commitment to her long-standing causes.

She continued her efforts on behalf of a national Thanksgiving Day, petitioning Presidents Andrew Johnson and Ulysses S. Grant to continue the tradition begun by Lincoln in 1863 and proclaim a national Thanksgiving Day. (They did.) By 1876, though, Hale—perhaps in recognition of the fact that she wasn't going to be around forever to keep up the pressure on future presidents—put forward another idea for securing a permanent date on the American calendar for Thanksgiving. She wrote Grant asking him to urge Congress to legislate a date for a national Thanksgiving Day. "To be preserved," she told him, Thanksgiving "must be made legal—If both Houses of Congress would unite in establishing the last Thursday in November as a Thanksgiving Day, at home and abroad, would it not strengthen the bond of Union between the American people?"[6]

One of the new causes Hale took up was lobbying the City of Philadelphia to hire women as inspectors of prisons.[7] She also revived her interest in urban parks—a topic she had promoted in Boston—as a means of promoting children's health. In the realm of education, she heralded the introduction of coeducation at Cornell University, reporting on the favorable findings of a coeducation committee appointed by the school's board of trustees. The Cornell committee had examined the impact of coeducation at Oberlin College, the University of Michigan, Northwestern University, the State Industrial University of Illinois, and Antioch College. Hale was happy to report that the "evil results prophesied had not been seen."[8]

She also renewed her call, begun in the 1850s, for Protestant churches to allow women to play more active lay roles, specifically as deaconesses. The deaconess movement, launched in Germany in 1833, welcomed women as non-ordained ministers to the sick and the poor. Pointing to Gospel stories, Hale called her campaign for the introduction of deaconesses to America a restoration of privileges that Christ and the apostles accorded to women.[9]

HALE'S READERS were now the daughters and granddaughters of the women whom she had first addressed in the *Ladies' Magazine* forty years earlier. These young women were living in an era that was a world apart from the one in which their foremothers had lived. Some had college degrees; many were teachers; others aspired to be doctors or nurses or other occupations from which their sex had been excluded when Hale began her editorial career. Laws requiring married women to hand over their legal rights and obligations to their husbands had been revoked in many states.

Women, however, still did not have the vote. The issue of women's suffrage, which was gathering steam now that the war had ended, occupied Hale's mind during this period. She had expressed her disapproval years earlier, and there was little indication she was open to reconsidering her view. Even her good friend Matthew Vassar, with whom she shared a zeal for higher education for women, favored the vote for women. "Nothing but men's tyranny & jealousy" has kept women from exercising their right to vote, Vassar wrote.[10]

Hale's cornerstone statement on women's suffrage was an 1867 editorial titled "Ought American Women to Have the Right of Suffrage?" Her reply was an emphatic no. Women were men's intellectual equals, she still insisted, but they were men's moral superiors. In rejecting the vote for women, her essential point was that women operated at a higher moral level than men and would be dragged down if they competed with men in the corrupt world of politics and government affairs, where negotiation and compromise were required. Women's participation in politics, she believed, meant that the family would suffer, as would relations between the sexes. She repeated her old argument that women should exercise their influence through persuasion, not action.

Women are "the moral power of humanity," she wrote, a power that would be degraded if they were enfranchised, held elected office, or participated in the administration of government.

She proposed, instead, that women find ways to elevate men's moral character. She emphasized the need for better educational opportunities for women, so that they could more effectively train their sons to be better men. She recommended legislation to stamp out men's weakness for "drunkenness, gambling, [and] licentiousness," the "blasting sins" that "disgrace the manhood of American culture."[11]

She applauded women's grassroots efforts to reform men—to an extent that is comical by today's standards. In one article, she singled out for praise the protests of the matrons of Clyde, Ohio, and the young ladies of Dover, Indiana. In Ohio, the ladies established the so-called Knitting Machine, whereby a crowd of pro-temperance women walked into a saloon, occupied all the seats, and quietly settled down to knitting. Needless to say, this approach put a damper on the bar's business. The young unmarried women of Indiana took another course of action. They modified the example of the women in Aristophanes's comedy *Lysistrata*, where the women of Greece withheld sexual privileges from their husbands until they negotiated an end to the Peloponnesian War. In Indiana, the young ladies refused to receive the attentions of men who drank, smoked, or swore. Hale concluded—rather preposterously—"If these societies sustain their promise, there will be no need of women suffrage, because men would do their own work so wisely and so well that we women shall have no wrongs to right, and the millennium of family peace and social harmony will be inaugurated."

Hale didn't attack the leaders of the suffrage movement by name, but she made it clear that she disapproved of their work.

The only suffrage leader whom she included in *Woman's Record*, her compilation of biographies of notable women, was Lucretia Mott, whom she praised for her philanthropic and religious work but whose view on the absolute equality of the sexes she rejected because it didn't acknowledge woman's superior moral standing. Susan B. Anthony, Elizabeth Cady Stanton, Lucy Stone, and other suffrage leaders went unmentioned in *Woman's Record*.

In 1852, Lucretia Mott was among three women's rights activists who paid a visit to Hale in Philadelphia, along with Dr. Harriet Hunt of Boston and the writer Frances Dana Barker Gage. Gage described their visit in an article for Amelia Bloomer's magazine, *The Lily*.

> I of course was delighted of an opportunity to look into the face of one who for years had delighted me with her thoughts, so I accompanied them. Mrs. Hale is a very pleasant looking woman, with a very polished manner; and if she receives every one as she did us, I should say kind and cordial. She does not seem to look with favor upon our woman's rights movements, our conventions, &c. Sorry I am for it, for her name and influence would do us much good. Yet while I would be glad to give her a welcome into our ranks, I feel no disposition to find fault with her for not being there.[12]

In her objection to suffrage, Hale reflected the views of the majority of American women at the time.

A half century earlier, Hale's opinions about women's intellectual equality with men and their right to an education were considered radical. But suffrage was simply too big a step for her. That said, Hale's anti-suffrage campaign in the pages of *Lady's Book* was modest, never approaching the aggressiveness of her efforts for a national Thanksgiving Day or any of her exertions on behalf of women's education. She kept readers up to date on the progress of the suffrage movement, reporting on pro- and anti-suffrage measures in state legislatures. And she encouraged readers to sign a petition to Congress protesting the vote for women. She left the impression that she didn't think women's suffrage was anytime in the offing,[13] that it was just too extreme an idea. Hale was right about this; women didn't obtain the right to vote until 1920, forty-one years after her death.

No evidence exists to suggest that Hale ever changed her mind about women's suffrage. But it is interesting to note that by the early 1870s, she was urging that women be permitted to run for election to seats on school boards—a public office. Her proposal came with a twist, in keeping with her view that while it was appropriate for women to operate in the public sphere they should—as much as possible—do so separately from men. In supporting women's service on school boards, she favored the creation of two elected school boards: on one, men of business would handle school finances; on the other, women would oversee the school buildings and the education of the children. By supporting women taking a public role on school boards, she was perhaps taking a tiny step toward approval of women's suffrage.[14]

One women's equity issue on which Hale did modify her position in her old age was equal pay for equal work. Years earlier, when advocating for women to be teachers, one of the advantages she listed was that women were more affordable than men. Schools—especially schools in frontier towns—that couldn't afford to pay the salaries men demanded were able to find young, unmarried women who were willing to work for less. In an 1873 essay titled "Equal Pay for Equal Work," she reversed her position, calling equal pay a "just principle." But she cautioned women not to expect the same pay as men unless they were equally qualified, and she put the burden on women to upgrade their qualifications.[15]

At the women's rights convention in Seneca Falls in 1848, the delegates approved eleven resolutions. Among them were more and better education for women; opening of the professions to women; repeal of laws restricting women's management of their own money and guardianship of her children; and the right to vote. Hale editorialized and campaigned for all of these rights with the exception of the right to vote.

IN HER LATER YEARS, Hale's attention turned more often to religious matters. She had always been devout, but in the last few decades of her life, she spoke more openly about her Christian faith. In a letter to a friend in 1862, she wrote about her grandchildren: "I have thirteen of these dear ones—four of them are with the 'little ones' whom Christ shelters in his bosom—and nine He still trusts to the care of their earthly parents."[16] This wasn't a platitude. Hale's increased outspokenness about her faith was in keeping with the religiosity of the age, which covered every aspect of Americans' lives.

She became deeply interested in expanding women's roles in the Protestant Church at home and abroad. Her belief in women's moral superiority fostered her advocacy of women working in lay positions as medical missionaries, religious teachers, and social workers. The established leadership of the main Protestant denominations—Baptist, Episcopalian, Methodist, Presbyterian—were resistant to allowing women to exercise such authority. It took a decade or more of Hale's signature blend of cordial, behind-the-scenes persuasion coupled with articles in the *Lady's Book* before she saw progress.

By the early 1870s, the Ladies' Medical Missionary Society of Philadelphia, which Hale founded in 1851, was finally having its intended impact. The organization had advanced two of its three objectives—helping women qualify as doctors and giving encouragement to women engaged in medical studies. But it had not made significant progress on the third—supporting medical school graduates who wished to go abroad as missionaries. The Protestant churches that oversaw the missions in China, Burma, and India at first refused to accept unmarried female doctors as missionaries. The mission boards would employ them only if they went overseas as wives. Sending single women abroad as missionaries was an untried experiment, Hale wrote in the *Lady's Book*, and public opinion was not yet ready to support it.

The churches' decision was disappointing to Hale, but rather than dropping the proposal, she set out to persuade the mission leaders to change their minds. She gathered endorsements from clergymen at home and abroad on behalf of sending unmarried female missionaries to Asia and published them at length in the *Lady's Book*. It made for dull reading, but it eventually did the trick. Three unmarried graduates of the Woman's Medical College of Pennsylvania set sail between 1869 and 1872 under the auspices of another missionary society with which Hale was involved.[17]

LIFE WITH the Hunter family remained a source of happiness for Hale. Richard—who as a teenager carried messages for his grandmother between Locust Street and the *Lady's Book* offices on Chestnut Street—graduated from Princeton. Following in the footsteps of his maternal grandfather, David Hale, he became a lawyer and set up practice in Philadelphia. Hale lived to see another Hunter grandson, Charles, follow the path trod by her son, his late uncle David, and take up an appointment at West Point.

Horatio and William lived distant from their mother. Horatio married a Canadian and moved to Clinton, Ontario. William went South after graduating from Harvard—first to Virginia, where he learned the law, then Texas, and finally New Orleans. Horatio made a name for himself as a distinguished ethnologist and philologist, studying the languages and dialects of the native peoples of North America. William became known for his handling of the old Spanish legal claims that flooded the courts of Texas after it separated from Mexico.[18] William died in New Orleans in 1876. Horatio lived until 1896.

SARAH JOSEPHA HALE was eighty-nine years old at the time of her retirement in December 1877. Few would say she looked her age. A portrait painted two years earlier showed a woman whose hair was still mostly brown, arranged in the ringlets that had captivated her late husband when he was courting her in New Hampshire sixty-four years earlier. Failing eyesight and a hand that sometimes shook when she took up her pen proved that she wasn't immune to the passage of years. But her mind had not lost its acuity, and her writing was as incisive as it had ever been.

Shortly before the Thanksgiving holiday, she put to bed the December issue of *Godey's Lady's Book*. For a half century—forty-one years as editor of the *Lady's Book* and nine years at the helm of its predecessor, the *Ladies' Magazine*—the editress never missed a deadline. Now, after editing six hundred issues and writing literally millions of words, she had decided it was time to put down her pen. The December issue of the *Lady's Book* would be her last.

Godey, her partner of forty-one years at the *Lady's Book*, made a coordinated decision to retire at the end of 1877. He was seventy-three years old, in poor health, and he wished to spend the winters in Florida. He noted that he had begun his work "with the pen" when he was fifteen years old. Writing in his familiar, genial way, he conceded that "we may possibly find that idleness is harder to bear than work," but "we intend to give it a trial." In his final column—"the most unpleasant article we have ever written for the *Lady's Book*"—he expressed his gratitude to "our good friend, Mrs. Sarah J. Hale, with whom we have never had, in any one instance, a serious misunderstanding."[19] Hale, in turn, used her valedictory "Editors' Table" column to thank Godey for "his unvarying kindness and consideration during an intercourse extending over forty-one years," which has "deserved and received our entire esteem and gratitude."[20]

In that leave-taking, subtitled "Fifty Years of My Literary Life," Hale reflected on her half century as an editor. She wrote of her difficult decision in 1827 to accept the job in Boston as editor of the *Ladies' Magazine*. "It seemed impossible to me. . . . I must give up [my] precious home, separate for a time from all my children save one, and go out into the world which I so much dreaded." Yet she accepted the offer, determined to make her "first object" at the new magazine "to promote the education of my own sex."

She went on to review the highlights of her working life—the campaign she led to complete the Bunker Hill Monument, her work on behalf of women who wished to teach in an era when "no boy would confess to having been the pupil of a woman," her championship of women doctors, the establishment of a national Thanksgiving Day.

Employing the editorial "we," she summed up her career in a single, pithy line: "It has been our endeavor to devote the influence of the *Lady's Book* particularly to the work of improving the education of women and extending their opportunities of usefulness." And now, the editress declared, "I must bid farewell to my countrywomen."

Sarah Who?

H ALE DIED just sixteen months after retiring. She passed
away in her large office-cum-bedroom overlooking Locust Street at ten o'clock on the evening of April 30, 1879, after
a brief illness. It was a peaceful passing—so peaceful, according
to one account, that the family and friends who were keeping
watch around her bed did not notice when she drew her last
breath. Godey preceded her in death by five months, slipping
away quietly in his favorite armchair at his Philadelphia home
on November 29, 1878.

Hale was alert and engaged until near the end. Four days before her death, in what was probably the final act of her working
life, she dictated a letter to a journalist asserting her authorship
of "Mary Had a Little Lamb," rebutting the allegation of a lady
in Massachusetts who claimed Hale had plagiarized the nursery rhyme.[1]

The positive spirit that had carried Hale through numerous
personal misfortunes did not abandon her in her extreme old

age. The woman who had endured the loss of her husband and struggled to care for and educate her children wrote a friend a few years before her death that "in truth, my life is one continuous thanksgiving."[2] Years earlier, when she was living in Boston, the poet Julia Ward Howe had called Hale an "optimist."[3] And so she was even in her final days.

In keeping with the instructions in her will, Hale's funeral and burial were quiet, private affairs. The only hint of ostentation was the presence of the Episcopal bishop of Philadelphia, who did Hale the honor of officiating at the service of the burial of the dead. The funeral took place at her home on Saturday, May 3, at two-thirty in the afternoon. After the funeral, her body was transported to its final resting place at Laurel Hill Cemetery, a scenic sanctuary along the Schuylkill River. She was laid in a grave next to that of her daughter and namesake, Josepha. The inscription on the plain headstone gives only her name, date of birth, and date of death. She was ninety years old.

After Hale's death, encomiums poured in. *Lady's Book* competitor *Harper's Bazaar* eulogized her as the "pioneer woman-editor" in a lengthy tribute that recounted her long list of accomplishments. In recapitulating the events that the late editor had witnessed during her life and the writers with whom she had worked, *Harper's Bazaar* remarked, "It is like hobnobbing with the last century."[4] Hale was born before George Washington took the oath of office as the first president of the United States, and she died when the nineteenth president was in the White House. As it happened, two years before her passing, that president— Rutherford B. Hayes—had written Hale a letter, addressed in his own hand. He praised her as "a lady who has accomplished so much for the peace and happiness of the American people."[5]

Hale's death was noted extensively in the press. Her long ten-ure at *Godey's Lady's Book* and the numerous books she wrote were mentioned in most of the obituaries; several articles noted the many philanthropies she founded or supported, especially her campaign to save the Bunker Hill Monument. The *Chicago Daily Tribune* said her "name is familiar to lady readers in all parts of the country" and remarked on her "life of usefulness."[6] In Boston, the *New England Farmer* lauded her as "an earnest worker in the cause of woman's advancement."[7] The *Times* of Philadelphia described her "one of the busiest women this country has every produced," saying "a more public-spirited woman never lived."[8] A Maryland newspaper observed that "it would occupy too much space to enumerate all the useful projects to which she gave the assistance of her pen and her personal influence."[9] The *New York Times* said she "did much to benefit the circle she reached in communicating the simple faith and hopefulness of her own life."[10]

But it was the *Philadelphia Inquirer*, a newspaper in the city where she had made her home for nearly forty years, that wrote the words Hale would have appreciated most: "Her pen was always used to elevate and ennoble, as well as to charm, delight and instruct women, and by the force of her writings, aided by her own bright example, she did much to dignify women's work."[11]

A MAGAZINE EDITOR'S work is necessarily ephemeral, and so it was with Hale's. News happens, ideas shift, and readers move on. Just as yesterday's newspaper is used to wrap today's fish dinner, last month's magazine gets thrown away or, as was the case with the *Lady's Book*, issues were disassembled so that the colorful fashion plates could be framed and hung on parlor walls. It is ironic that the editor who raged against fashion lived on in the memory of many through the illustrations that decorated their homes.

Godey's Lady's Book deteriorated rapidly after Hale's retirement. Godey's sons managed the magazine for a few years, followed by a series of owners and editors who failed to restore it to its former glory. Jennie June, the pen name of the well-known journalist Jane Cunningham Croly, had a brief term as editor and part owner in the late 1880s, but even she couldn't revive the magazine.[12] By the 1890s, William Dean Howells was denigrating *Godey's* as "really incredible in [its] insipidity."[13]

The magazine existed until 1898, but it was a pale shadow of what it had been, containing little of literary or intellectual substance and lacking the distinctive editorial voice that had endeared Hale to her readers. As the years went by, the reputation of the late editor suffered by association with the new *Godey's*. She was sometimes unfairly pegged as an antiquated Victorian whose interests turned more toward publishing needlework patterns than fighting for opportunities for women.

By the turn of the twentieth century, the suffrage movement dominated "the woman question," and the memory of Hale's work in expanding opportunities for women faded. Largely forgotten were her accomplishments on behalf of women's education, property rights, employment, and philanthropic leadership, as well as her efforts to increase respect for women's work in the home. Few acknowledged her foundational role on the long road to suffrage, which grew out of the fight by Hale and others for women to be educated.

Hale's letters from presidents, governors, writers, and other famous personages were sold at auction in 1917. Her family destroyed most of the rest of her large correspondence, manuscripts, and personal papers. Thirty-eight years after her death, no library or historical society apparently considered Hale important enough or interesting enough to preserve the record of her life. Her surviving letters are scattered widely, preserved here and there in the collections of numerous libraries and historical institutions.

The list of her publications is immense. The authoritative *Bibliography of American Literature*, published by Yale University Press, counts 129 entries for books written or edited by her and volumes to which she contributed. She wrote hundreds of poems, short stories, and articles for the *Ladies' Magazine* and *Godey's Lady's Book*, in addition to five hundred editions of "Editor's Table" and an even larger number of literary columns featuring her book reviews. In her will, Hale appointed Horatio and Frances as her literary executors in the hope that there would be a collected edition of her work. That never happened.

Several twentieth-century scholars have examined Hale's work. Ruth Finley was the first to write her biography, *The Lady of Godey's*, published in 1931. In the 1930s, Frank Luther Mott, extolled her work in his encyclopedic *A History of American Magazines*. "Mrs. Sarah Josepha Hale was a great woman," he stated. She transformed *Godey's Lady's Book* "from a mediocre miscellany to a literary magazine of importance." He called her "a notable literary figure" in the history of American periodicals.[14] Isabelle Webb Entrikin dived deeply into Hale's editorship of the *Lady's Book* for her 1946 volume, *Sarah Josepha Hale and Godey's Lady's Book*. More recently, Patricia Okker examined Hale's place in the tradition of female editors of the nineteenth century in *Our Sister Editors*, published in 1995.[15] Incredibly, and shamefully, Hale has yet to be elected to the National Women's Hall of Fame in Seneca Falls, New York.

HALE'S MEMORY lives on in her hometown of Newport, New Hampshire. The Rising Sun Tavern, where she met and mar-

ried David, is now a private home. The large frame house overlooking the village green where she and David were so happy
and where Hale developed her prose style still stands, though
it has been moved to a side street. On the outskirts of town sits
the one-room schoolhouse where Miss Buell barred her young
pupils from blabbing their lessons and encouraged them to advance at their own pace. The schoolhouse, enlarged and painted a cheerful shade of pale green, is now a private residence. A
marker on the road near the house informs visitors that this is
the place where Mary's little lamb may once have waited for her
young mistress to be dismissed from school.

The Richards Free Library, housed in a nineteenth-century
mansion, keeps alive the memory of Newport's most famous
daughter. Just outside the library's front entrance is a small
park, where a bronze bust of the editor sits atop a granite pillar;
the granite is black, reflecting Hale's fifty-seven years of widowhood. The library sponsors an annual award in Hale's name to a
distinguished New England literary figure.[16]

Inside the library, hanging in pride of place above the circulation desk, is a portrait of Sarah Josepha Hale, painted in 1831
by James Reid Lambdin. The library scrambled in 1993 to raise
the $3,500 needed to purchase the portrait that no one else ap-
parently wanted. The painting shows a petite woman, dressed in
black, who looks much younger than her forty-three years at the
time she sat for the artist. Her mouth is set in a firm line, and her
large brown eyes gaze forthrightly at the viewer. The pipe curls
that David loved frame and soften her slender face. The pretty
woman in the portrait appears intelligent and strong yet at the
same time approachable.

Sarah Josepha Buell Hale began her life as the bookish daughter of a patriotic New England farmer and ended it as one of the

most influential and celebrated women of the nineteenth century. As a young widow and mother, she transformed herself into a professional author and editor, becoming one of the first women to earn a living through her writing. For more than half a century she deployed her powerful pen in the service of her fellow women, seeking to empower them through education, employment, and philanthropic work while honoring their traditional roles as wives and mothers. She served her country by helping to establish a distinctly American literary culture and by re-inventing Thanksgiving as a national holiday. She lived an extraordinary American life, and she deserves her place in our history.

In Her Own Words

A good and true Yankee Thanksgiving

Northwood: A Tale of New England (1827)

*In Hale's novel, an Englishman experiences his first American
Thanksgiving during a visit to the Romelee home in New Hampshire.*

THE ROASTED TURKEY took precedence on this occasion, being
placed at the head of the table; and well did it become its lordly station, sending forth the rich odour of its savory stuffing, and
finely covered with the frost of the basting. At the foot of the
board, a sirloin of beef, flanked on either side by a leg of pork and
joint of mutton, seemed placed as a bastion to defend innumerable
bowls of gravy and plates of vegetables disposed in that quarter. A
goose and a pair of ducklings occupied side stations on the table,
the middle being graced, as it always is on such occasions, by that
rich burgomaster of the provisions, called a chicken pie. This pie,
which is wholly of the choicest parts of fowls, enriched and sea-
soned with a profusion of butter and pepper, and covered with an

excellent puff paste, is, like the celebrated pumpkin pie, an indispensable part of a good and true Yankee Thanksgiving; the size of the pie usually denoting the gratitude of the party who prepares the feast. The one now displayed could never have had many peers. Frankford [a visitor from England] had seen nothing like it, and recollected nothing in description bearing a comparison, excepting the famous pie served up to the witty King Charles II, and containing, instead of the savory chicken, the simple knight. Plates of pickles, preserves and butter, and all the necessaries for increasing the seasoning of viands to the demand of each palate, filled the interstices on the table, leaving hardly sufficient room for the plates of the company, a wine glass and two tumblers for each, with a slice of wheat bread lying on one of the inverted tumblers. A side table was liberally loaded with the preparations for the second course, placed there to obviate the necessity of leaving the apartment during the repast. Mr. Romelee keeping no domestic, the family were to wait on themselves, or on each other. There was a huge plumb pudding, custards, and pies of every name and description known in Yankee land; yet the pumpkin pie occupied the most distinguished niche. There were also several kinds of rich cake, and a variety of sweetmeats and fruit. On the sideboard was ranged a goodly number of decanters and bottles; the former filled with currant wine and the latter with excellent cider and ginger beer, a beverage Mrs. Romelee prided herself on preparing to perfection....

Such, as I have attempted to describe, the appearance of the apartment and the supper when...the whole family entered and took their stations around the table. The blessing, which "the saint, the father, and the husband" now fervently besought, was not merely a form of words, mechanically mumbled over to comply with an established custom, or perform an irksome duty.

It was the breathings of a good and grateful heart acknowledging the mercies received, and sincerely thanking the Giver of every good gift for the plenteous portion he had bestowed.

I would have them seek some employment

"Sketches of American Character,"
Ladies' Magazine (November 1828)

Should women work?

I DO NOT SAY women have not more learning, that they do not *read* more, but pray tell me what difference this has created in their *pursuits* except to make them less useful—because they now, many of them, think that "to work with their hand" is disgraceful for ladies, and yet there is no employment provided in which they can exercise their talents and learning advantageously—or indeed, at all. I would rouse them from this supineness—I would have them seek some employment, have some *aim* that will, by giving energy to their minds, and the prospect of an honorable independence, should they choose to continue single, make them less dependent on *marriage* as the means of *support*.

We invite every lady in the land to our *Conversazione*

"The *Conversazione*," *Godey's Lady's Book*
(January 1837, Hale's inaugural column as editor)

IT IS OUR AIM to prepare a work which, for our own sex, should be superior to every other periodical.... We shall not affect the learned, logical, or profound style; nor yet permit that air of *bandinage* which usually resolves itself into satire or coarseness. Ours will rather imitate that tone of playful vivacity, intelligent observation, and refined taste. . . . In short, we intend our work as a *"Conversazione"* of the highest order, to which we invite every lady in our land—this "Book" is the ticket of admission, and the first week-day in every month the time of attendance.

Female Colleges, Female Professors, Female Doctors

"Editors' Table," *Godey's Lady's Book* (May 1853)

These excerpts from a typical edition of Hale's monthly column, "Editors' Table," include her thoughts on education, philanthropy, and female physicians.

FEMALE COLLEGES IN THE UNITED STATES.—These are established, chiefly, in the new States of our confederacy, and are promising good results. Among the best is Albion Female College, located at Athens, Michigan, on the Central Railroad. Young ladies in the College pursue a systematic course of study, under the instruction of a large and highly competent faculty, in the natural sciences and kindred studies, they have the advantage of lectures and experiments, conducted after the manner of the best male colleges. There is an optional course for those who prefer it.

A FEMALE COLLEGE IN TEXAS.—It is proposed to establish a Female College at Huntsville, to be under the care of the Texas Conference of the Methodist Church, for which $4000 have already been subscribed towards the buildings.

FEMALE PROFESSOR.—MISS Pennell, niece of the Hon. Horace Mann, has been appointed Professor of the Latin Language and

Literature, in Antioch College, Ohio, of which Mr. Mann was chosen President.

FEMALE EDUCATION IN CEYLON.—Formerly, it was exceedingly difficult to obtain native girls for the boarding-schools; but now the missionaries dare not let it be publicly known when they are about to receive a new class, lest they should be overwhelmed by importunate applicants; and this, although proficiency in a course of preparatory studies is required as a requisite for admission. The number of educated men is also constantly increasing, who employ private tutors for the instruction of their daughters.

FEMALE PHYSICIANS.—A very influential Boston paper submits the following opinions, as those now popular in New England:—That the medical profession is hereafter to consist of women as well as men, is no longer a matter of doubt, judging from the strong setting of public sentiment in this direction. The preference for females in some departments of practice is becoming so general, we understand, that the few who are educated are overtasked with labor, and many incompetent women are prompted to advertise themselves, and, for the want of those better qualified, they are employed. To prevent the evils from this source, it is important that the Female Medical College in this city, designed to accommodate the whole of New England, should be placed in a condition to afford a thorough scientific and practical education to a sufficient number of suitable females.

LIBERAL BEQUESTS.—Mrs. Dorothea Abrahams recently died at Savannah, Georgia, aged seventy-three. She left $1000 towards building a free Episcopal church in Savannah; $1000 to the Savannah Hebrew Benevolent Society, and, after some legacies to friends, the remainder of her estate, valued at from $15,000 to $20,000, is to be expended on a building for the Widow's Society, to be used as a home for indigent widows and single women.

When shall we have the proud satisfaction of announcing bequests from women to build up institutions for the education and employment of their own sex? Funds are now greatly needed for "Female Medical Education" and for the "Schools of Design for Women." Who will give to these noble plans for woman's improvement?

Christening Cake

"Receipts, &c," *Godey's Lady's Book*, April 1860

Beating, beating, and more beating.

RICH BRIDE OR CHRISTENING CAKE.—Take five pounds of the finest flour dried and sifted, three pounds of fresh butter, five pounds of picked and washed currants dried before the fire, two pounds of loaf-sugar, two nutmegs, quarter of an ounce of mace, half a quarter of an ounce of cloves, all finely beaten and sifted, sixteen eggs, whites and yolks kept separate, one pound of blanched almonds pounded with orange-flower water, one round each of candied citron, orange and lemon-peel cut in neat slices. Mix these ingredients in the following manner: Begin working the butter with the hand till it becomes of a creamlike consistency, then beating in the sugar; for at least ten minutes whisk the whites of the eggs to a complete froth, and mix in with the butter and sugar; next, well beat up the yolks for full ten minutes, and, adding them to the flour, nutmegs, mace, and cloves, continue beating the whole together for half an hour, or longer, till wanted for the oven; then mix in lightly the currants, almonds, and candied peels, with the addition of a gill each of mountain wine and brandy; and, having lined a hoop with paper, rub it well with butter, fill in the mixture, and bake it in a tolerably quick oven, taking care, however, not by any means to burn the cake, the top of which may be covered with paper. It is generally iced over on coming out of the ovens but without having any ornament on the top, so as to appear of a delicate plain white.

'Tis a pitiful lot to be poor when it snows
The Ladies' Wreath (1837)

One of Hale's most popular poems, "It Snows" was reprinted in many anthologies during the nineteenth century. It shows how different people respond to the same event. The final stanza is particularly affecting.

It Snows

"It snows!" cries the School-boy—"Hurrah!" and his shout
Is ringing through parlor and hall,
While swift as the wing of a swallow he's out,
And his playmates have answered his call:
It makes the heart warm but to witness their joy—
Proud wealth has no pleasures, I trow,
Like the rapture that burns in the blood of the boy,
As he gathers his treasures of snow;
Then lay not the trappings of gold on thine heirs,
While health and the riches of nature are theirs.

"It snows!" sighs the Imbecile—"Ah!" and his breath
Comes heavy, as clogged with a weight;
While, from the pale aspect of nature in death,

He turns to the blaze of his grate;
And nearer, and nearer, his soft-cushioned chair
Is wheeled tow'rds the life-giving flame;
He dreads a chill puff of the snow-burdened air,
Lest it wither his delicate frame:
Oh, small is the pleasure existence can give,
When the fear we shall die only proves that we live!

"It snows!" shouts the Traveller—"Ho!" and the word
Has quickened his steed's lagging pace,
The wind rushes by, but its howl is unheard,
Unfelt the sharp drift in his face;
For bright through the dark storm his own home appeared;
Though leagues intervened, he can see
The clear, glowing hearth, and the table prepared,
And his wife, with their babes on her knee!
O Love! how it lightens the grief-laden hour—
To know that our dear ones are safe from its power.

"It snows!" says the Belle—"Dear, how lucky!" and turns
From her mirror to watch the flakes fall;
Like the first rose of summer her dimpled cheek burns
While musing on sleigh-ride and ball:
And visions of conquests, of splendor and mirth,
Float over each drear winter's day;
But the tintings of Hope, on this snow-beaten earth,
Will melt like the snow-flakes away:
Turn, turn thee to Heaven, fair maiden, for bliss,
That world has a pure fount ne'er opened in this.

"It snows!" cries the Widow—"O God!" and her sighs

Have stifled the voice of her prayer;

Its burden ye'll read in her tear-swollen eyes,

On her cheek pale with fasting and care.

'Tis night—and her fatherless ask her for bread,

But "He gives the young ravens their food"—

And she hopes, till her dark hearth adds horror to dread,

And she lays on her last chip of wood.

Poor widow! That sorrow thy God only knows:

'Tis a pitiful lot to be poor when it snows.

The Medical Education of Woman

Godey's Lady's Book (July 1864)

Hale makes the case for the use of "doctress" rather than "doctor" in reference to female physicians.

ABOUT FOURTEEN YEARS AGO a Medical College for *Women* was established in Philadelphia, and soon after another was chartered in Boston. Both colleges have now a firm hold on public sympathy. Other colleges have received young ladies, and, probably, there is now as many as three hundred graduates with the full honors of M.D. among the noble womanhood of our Republic.

We hope, for the, honor of our sex, that these gentle *M.D.*'s will insist on retaining their womanhood in their profession, and never assume the style and title of man as *Doctor*, when their own *Doctress* is better and more elegant, being delicate, definite, and dignified. All assumptions are mean because they are false or frivolous. We do not want *female physicians*, that compound term signifying an *animal man*; we want cultivated, refined feminine *physicians*, known as *Doctresses* for their own sex and children, and conservers of domestic health and happiness.

The New England College has wisely adopted the feminine termination in their diplomas; their graduates style themselves *Doctress*, writing the title *Drss.*—so that they will not need an explanation or circumlocution to express their womanhood. One truth is sure; a lady can never elevate herself by becoming manlike or making pretences to be so. She must keep her own place, cultivate her own garden of home. Eve was created in Eden, Adam in the outside world. The daughters of America must guard their Eden name and its equivalents, and make these significant of grace, goodness, and glory, or they will never reach the perfection of their nature as "polished stones" in the grand edifice of Christian Nationalities.

For one woman who desires there are fifty who disapprove

"Woman Suffrage," *Godey's Lady's Book* (May 1871)

From Hale's introduction to a petition to Congress opposing the vote for women.

THERE SEEMS some danger that this question may be forced on Congress before the members have really been informed of the feeling about the *suffrage* among women themselves. To aid in showing how little such a power is desired by the great majority of our sex, we insert the following petition. The editors of the LADY'S BOOK hope that those of their readers who disapprove of the proposed extension of the franchise will take up the matter in earnest. Let ladies copy the petition, and obtain signatures, each in her own neighborhood, sending it then to one of the persons named below; and at the next session of Congress we will be able to show that for one woman who desires there are fifty who disapprove.

Growing old, growing old. Do they say it of me?

Godey's Lady's Book (July 1859)

Hale was seventy years old when "Growing Old" was published. For the next twenty years, she would recite it to her family on her birthday, October 24.

Growing Old

GROWING old, growing old! Do they say it of me?
Do they hint my bright fancies are frozen or fled?
That my garden of life, like the winter-swept tree
Is faded and dying, or fallen and dead?

Is the heart growing old, when each beautiful thing,
Like a landscape at eve, looks more tenderly bright,
And love sweeter seems, as a bird's wandering wing
Draws nearer its nest at the coming of night?

Is the mind growing old, when, with ardor of youth,
Through the flower walks of Wisdom 'tis winning its way,
Or seeking new shells from the ocean of Truth,
And shouting "Eureka!" like childhood at play?

Is the soul growing old? See the planet of even,
When rising at morn, melts in glory above;
Thus turning from earth we creep closer to Heaven,
Like a child to its Father's warm welcoming love.

Does the mortal grow old, as years roll away?
'Tis change, not destruction; kind winter will bring
Fresh life to the germ and perfect it. Decay
Holds the youth bud IMMORTAL, and heralds its spring.

Growing old, growing old! Can it ever be true
While joy for life's blessings is thankful and warm,
And hopes sown for others are blooming anew,
And the rainbow of Peace smiles over the storm?

Growing old, growing old! No, we never grow old,
If, like "little children," we trust in the Word,
And, counting earth's treasures by Heaven's pure gold,
We lay our weak hands on the strength of the LORD.

Acknowledgments

T HE STARTING POINT for my research into the life of Sarah
Josepha Hale was the Richards Free Library in her hometown of Newport, New Hampshire. I am grateful to the library's
director, Andrea Thorpe, now retired, and her colleagues for their
warm welcome. They guided me through the library's holdings on
Hale, put me in touch with local experts, and shared their research
and insights. Andrea introduced me to the amazing Mary Lou Mc-
Guire, historian, archivist, and genealogist, who volunteered her
research services. Mary Lou's assistance and sage counsel were
indispensable as I thought through and wrote *Lady Editor*. I was
fortunate to have her as a researcher and sounding board.

I thank Jayna Huot Hooper, author of a history of Newport,
who pointed me toward Hale's early writings on the nature of
womanhood and offered thought-provoking observations. Also
in New Hampshire, I benefited from the specialized knowledge
of Sharon Wood, a Hale impersonator, who explained how the
widow Hale would have dressed.

My friend Rick Hibberd prepared the book's photographs for production and made creative suggestions about their presentation. I am deeply grateful to Rick, who is a brilliant graphic designer.

The Hudson Institute's Kenneth R. Weinstein and John P. Walters offered encouragement and support for *Lady Editor*. Danielle Balducci provided useful research on education for women in the early nineteenth century and other topics. Jacqueline David spent hours digging up references to Thanksgiving in *Godey's Lady's Book*. Harry Channing helped transcribe Hale's correspondence. Sarah Green, Julia Williams Green, and Grace David guided me on an entertaining tour of Hale-related sites in Philadelphia. The Reverend Rachel Gardner and former church archivist Mike Krasulski supplied information about Hale's membership in the Church of the Holy Trinity, Rittenhouse Square, in Philadelphia. Scott Seligman provided helpful genealogical research. Karl Zinsmeister offered insights on nineteenth-century philanthropy. Claudia Rosett directed me to Laura Ingalls Wilder's reference to *Godey's Lady's Book* in *Little Town on the Prairie*. Kenneth Roman and Amanda Ayers Barnett read sections of the manuscript and offered good suggestions. I warmly thank them all.

I thank my terrific agents, Glen Hartley and Lynn Chu of Writers' Representatives, for their work on my behalf. I am grateful to the virtuoso team at Encounter Books, with whom it was a pleasure to work: Roger Kimball, Nola Tully, Sam Schneider, Lauren Miklos, Amanda DeMatto, Mary Spencer, and Victoria Acevedo. *Lady Editor* benefited from Barbie Halaby's superb copyediting. Katherine Messenger's cover art and overall book design beautifully capture the look and spirit of *Godey's Lady's Book*.

I am indebted to the many skilled librarians who tracked

down Hale's correspondence in the collections of their institutions. The libraries, historical societies, and research institutes with which I worked include: Sarah Josepha Hale Collection, the Athenaeum of Philadelphia; Rare Books & Manuscripts, Boston Public Library; Rauner Special Collections Library, Dartmouth College; Archives of the Episcopal Church; Houghton Library, Harvard University; Historical Society of Pennsylvania; the Huntington Library; Library of Congress; Brooke Russell Astor Reading Room for Rare Books and Manuscripts, New York Public Library; Massachusetts Historical Society; the Fred W. Smith National Library for the Study of George Washington, Mount Vernon Ladies' Association; Pennsylvania State Archives; Princeton University Library Special Collections; Milne Special Collections & Archives, University of New Hampshire; University of Pennsylvania Libraries Special Collections; Rare Books, Special Collections, and Preservation, River Campus Libraries, University of Rochester; Harry Ransom Center, University of Texas; Albert and Shirley Small Special Collections Library, the University of Virginia; Special Collections, Vassar College Libraries; Archives & Special Collections, Madeleine Clark Wallace Library, Wheaton College (Massachusetts); Yale Club of New York City Library; Beinecke Rare Book & Manuscript Library, Yale University.

The website www.accessible-archives.com was indispensable in my research. It is the only online source of which I am aware that has a complete collection of *Godey's Lady's Book*, 1830–1898, fully searchable and available in text and image formats.

I am deeply grateful to my sisters, Holly Kirkpatrick Whiting and Robin Kirkpatrick Koves, and to my friend Gail Buyske, for their enthusiasm, support, and good cheer over the three years I spent researching and writing this book.

Finally, my most heartfelt thanks go to my husband, Jack David, who, as always, was my first reader. He is a tough critic, a demanding editor, and the finest man I know.

—Melanie Kirkpatrick

April 2021

Notes

ABBREVIATIONS

GLB: *Godey's Lady's Book*
LM: *Ladies' Magazine*
LAG: Louis A. Godey
SJH: Sarah Josepha Hale

INTRODUCTION
A Summer Snowstorm

1 Sarah Josepha Hale quoted this line by Goethe in the "Introductory Remarks" to her book *Woman's Record, or, Sketches of All Distinguished Women* (New York: Harper & Brothers, 1853), viii.

2 The full quotation reads, "America is now wholly given over to a d——d mob of scribbling women, and I should have no chance of success while the public taste is occupied with their trash—and should be ashamed of myself if I did succeed." Hawthorne wrote these words to his publisher William Ticknor on January 19, 1855.

3 SJH, "Introduction," LM, January 1828.

4 SJH, "Lady Physicians," GLB, February 1855.

5 Edgar Allan Poe, "New-York," *Columbia (PA) Spy*, June 29, 1844.

6 Oliver Wendell Holmes to SJH, November 20, 1872, mssHM 7193, Huntington Library, San Marino, California.

7 Charles Dickens to SJH, March 11, 1842, mssHM 17557, Huntington Library.

8 SJH to James Buchanan, June 9, 1853, Historical Society of Pennsylvania, James Buchanan Papers (Coll. 91).

9 James Buchanan to SJH, October 3, 1853, Historical Society of Pennsylvania, James Buchanan Papers (Coll. 91).

CHAPTER ONE
Daughter of the Revolution

1 The descriptions of Newport, New Hampshire, in the eighteenth century come from Edmund Wheeler, *The History of Newport, New Hampshire: From 1766 to 1878, with a Genealogical Register* (Concord, NH: Republican Press Association, 1879); and Mary Lou McGuire and Raymond Reid, *Newport, New Hampshire in Time and Place* (Newport, NH: self-pub., 2017).

2 SJH, writing as A Lady of New-Hampshire, "Address to Sugar River," in *The Genius of Oblivion and Other Original Poems* (Concord, NH: Jacob B. Moore, 1823), 110–13; emphasis in original.

3 SJH, *The Ladies' Wreath* (Boston: March, Capen & Lyon, 1837), 386.

4 SJH to Edmund Wheeler, March 26, 1869, Sarah Josepha Hale Collec-

tion, Richards Free Library, Newport, New Hampshire.

5   SJH, writing in Wheeler, *History of Newport*, 127.

6   SJH, writing in Wheeler, *History of Newport*, 127.

7   Wheeler, *History of Newport*, "Genealogy of the Buell Family," 313–21, and "Genealogy of the Whittlesey Family," 571.

8   SJH, *Ladies' Wreath*, 384.

9   SJH, "The Beginning," LM, January 1829. This is one of Hale's most oft-quoted lines.

10 SJH, *Manners: Or, Happy Homes and Good Society All the Year Round* (Boston: J.E. Tilton, 1868).

11 SJH, "Reminiscence," LM, July 1828.

12 SJH, *Ladies' Wreath*, 383.

13 SJH, writing in Wheeler, *History of Newport*, 127.

14 Ernest L. Scott Jr., "Sarah Josepha Hale's New Hampshire Years," *Historical New Hampshire* (1994): 59–96.

15 This is in the collection of the Newport (NH) Historical Society.

16 SJH, "The Village Schoolmistress," LM, Part 1: May 1828, Part 2: November 1828.

CHAPTER TWO
Wife and Widow

1   Horatio Gates Buell to SJH, November 3, 1809, Autograph File, B, Houghton Library, Harvard College Library.

2   Hannah Duston's husband presented the ten scalps to the Massachusetts legislature, which awarded him fifty pounds on his wife's behalf. (Wives had no legal status independent of their husbands.) The unmarried woman and boy who helped her kill the Native Americans each received twenty-five pounds.

3   Charles Henry Bell, *The Bench and Bar of New Hampshire: Including biographical notices of deceased judges of the highest court, and lawyers of the Province and State, and a list of names of those now living* (Boston: Houghton, Mifflin, 1894), 413.

4   SJH, *Ladies' Wreath*, 386.

5   *History of Cheshire and Sullivan Counties, New Hampshire*, ed. D. Hamilton Hurd (Philadelphia: J.W. Lewis, 1886), 267–68.

6   *History of Cheshire and Sullivan Counties*, 267–68.

7   Sarah Hale Hunter, a granddaughter of SJH, as quoted in Ruth E. Finley, *The Lady of Godey's* (Philadelphia: J.B. Lippincott, 1931), 32.

8   Notice published by the Commissioners of Insolvency appointed by Probate Judge Able Parker in the (Concord) *New Hampshire Patriot*, January 20, 1823, 3.

9   SJH, "The Farmer and His Sons," LM, March 1833.

10   SJH, *Ladies' Wreath*, 385.

11   SJH, Dedication, in *Genius of Oblivion*, v–viii.

12   *United States Review and Literary Gazette*, December 1826, 227–28.

13   SJH writing as Cornelia, "Country Literature," *American Monthly Magazine*, April 1824, 303.

14   Scott, "Sarah Josepha Hale's New Hampshire Years."

15   *United States Review and Literary Gazette*, April 1827, 33–39.

16   Mrs. Lucy E. Sanford, "Mrs. Sarah J. Hale," *Granite Monthly*, March 1880, 208–11.

CHAPTER THREE
The Ladies' Magazine

1   See Patricia Okker, *Our Sister Editors: Sarah J. Hale and the Tradition of Nineteenth-Century American Women Editors* (Athens: University of Georgia Press, 1995).

2   Heather A. Haveman, *Magazines and the Making of America: Modernization, Community, and Print Culture 1741–1860* (Princeton, NJ: Princeton University Press, 2015), 26.

3   Bertha M. Stearns, "Early New England Magazines for Ladies," *New England Quarterly* 2, no. 3 (July 1929): 445.

4   Noah Webster, "Acknowledgements," *American Magazine*, February 1788, 130; quoted in Frank Luther Mott, *A History of American Magazines*, vol. 1, *1741–1850* (New York: D. Appleton, 1930), 13.

5   SJH, "Introduction," LM, January 1828.

6   SJH, "Female Education," LM, January 1828.

7   SJH, "Sketches of American Character, No. XI," LM, November 1828.

8   SJH, "Introduction," LM, January 1828.

9   SJH to Catherine Fiske, November 22, 1830, Sarah Josepha Buell Hale Papers, 1830–1855, MS 61, Milne Special Collections and Archives,

University of New Hampshire Library.

10 SJH, "Margery Bethel," LM, April 1828.

11 SJH, "Mrs. Gore's Bequest," LM, June 1834.

12 SJH, "Miss Fiske's School for Young Ladies," LM, December 1833.

13 SJH, "Progress of Society," LM, May 1835.

14 SJH, "Progress of Society," LM, July 1835; emphasis in original.

15 SJH, "Introduction," LM, January 1828.

16 SJH, "Female Education," LM, January 1828.

17 SJH, "What Can Women Do?," LM, May 1834. This story of what Hale calls "female enterprise" appears in a letter from a woman in Tennessee that Hale reprinted in her article.

18 Frank Luther Mott, *Golden Multitudes: The Story of Best Sellers in the United States* (New York: Macmillan, 1947), 317.

19 SJH, "Sketches of American Character: No. I—Walter Wilson," LM, January 1828.

20 SJH, "Sketches of American Character," all published in 1828. They are, in order of mention: "No. II—Ann Ellsworth," February; "No. XI—Prejudices," September; and "No. VI—The Belle and the Bleu," July.

21 SJH, "Sketches of American Character: No. V—The Village Schoolmistress," LM, April 1828.

22 SJH, "Literary Notices," LM, November 1828.

23 SJH, writing as "H***," "To the Editor of the Ladies' Magazine," January 1828.

24 SJH, "Literature for Ladies," LM, March 1834.

25 SJH, "Books and Authors," LM, January 1834.

26 SJH, "Literary Notices," LM, January 1830.

27 Lydia Huntley Sigourney, "Comparative Intellect of the Sexes," LM, June 1830.

28 SJH, "Literary Notices," LM, November 1828.

29 SJH, "Literary Notices," LM, January 1830.

30 David E. Hale to SJH, February 10, 1831, mssHM 7160, Huntington Library.

31 Nathaniel Parker Willis to SJH, December 14, 1829, mssHM 6867-69, Huntington Library.

32 John Greenleaf Whittier, "Metacom," LM, February 1830; James Fenimore Cooper, "No Steamboats—A Vision," LM, January 1834; William Cullen Bryant, "June," LM, April 1832.

33 SJH, "The Token," LM, January 1828.

34 SJH, *Northwood: A Tale of New England* (Boston: Bowles & Dearborn, 1827), 79.

35 SJH, "Fashions," LM, June 1830.

36 SJH, "The Influence of Fashions," LM, January 1832.

37 SJH, "Influence of Fashions."

38 This portrait, by James Reid Lambdin, appears on the cover of this book.

39 Oliver Wendell Holmes, *The Autocrat of the Breakfast Table* (Boston: Phillips, Sampson, 1858).

40 SJH, "Literary Notices," LM, April 1829 (emphasis in original).

41 SJH to David Henshaw, October 26, 1829, Sarah Josepha Hale Papers, Rare Books Department, Boston Public Library.

42 SJH to Henry A.S. Dearborn, March 13, 1830, Boston Public Library.

CHAPTER FOUR

Mary's Lamb

1 Finley, *Lady of Godey's*, 87.

2 Elizabeth Peabody to SJH, May 16, 1878, as quoted in Ida M. Tarbell, "The American Woman," *American Magazine* 69 (November 1909): 665.

3 SJH, "Literary Notices: African Infant School," LM, May 1830.

4 In our own century, the KIPP network of charter schools uses songs and rhymes to teach arithmetic.

5 SJH, ed., "Prefatory Remarks," in *Aunt Mary's New Stories for Young People* (Boston: James Munroe, 1849), iii.

6 Rosalie V. Halsey, *Forgotten Books of the American Nursery: A History of the Development of the American Story-Book* (Boston: Charles E. Goodspeed, 1911), 193.

7 SJH, "Literary Notices: Juvenile Miscellany," LM, July 1828, 336.

8 Caroline H. Dall, "Lydia Maria Child," *Unitarian Review and Religious Magazine*, June 1883, 525–26.

9 Carolyn L. Karcher, *The First Woman in the Republic: A Cultural Biography of Lydia Maria Child* (Durham, NC: Duke University Press, 1994), 168–69.

10   Karcher, *First Woman in the Republic*, 66.

11   SJH, *Poems for Our Children* (Boston: Marsh, Capen & Lyon, 1830).

12   Lowell Mason, "Preface," in *Juvenile Lyre: Or, Hymns and Songs, Religious, Moral, and Cheerful, Set to Appropriate Music; For the Use of Primary and Common Schools* (Boston: Carter, Hendee, 1835), vi.

13   M. Sarah Smedman, "Sarah Josepha Hale," in *Dictionary of Literary Biography*, vol. 42 (Detroit, MI: Gale, 1985), 212–13.

14   *United States Magazine and Democratic Review* 12, January 1843, 111.

15   David E. Hale to SJH, February 10, 1831, mssHM 7160, Huntington Library.

16   Henry Williams, "Horatio Hale," *Memorials of the Class of 1837 of Harvard University: Prepared for the Fiftieth Anniversary of Their Graduation, by the Class Secretary, Henry Williams* (Boston: G.H. Ellis, 1887), 63.

17   Williams, "Horatio Hale," 63.

CHAPTER FIVE

Let the Ladies Do It

1   Unsigned but probably SJH, "Fatherless and Widows' Society, Boston," LM, January 1828.

2   SJH to Emma Willard, January 24, 1836, 46-M-016, Sarah Josepha Hale Collection, Athenaeum of Philadelphia (emphasis in original). The lines she quotes are from 1 Corinthians 13:7. The complete line, from the King James Version of the Bible is "Beareth all things, believeth all things, hopeth all things, endureth all things."

3   Karl Zinsmeister, "What Comes *Next*? How Private Givers Can Rescue America in an Era of Political Frustration," *Philanthropy*, Winter 2016: 14.

4   SJH to Mathew Carey, January 20, 1831, Historical Society of Pennsylvania, Philadelphia, Simon Gratz autograph collection (Coll. 250), American Literary, Miscellaneous (Case 6, Box 22).

5   Walt Whitman, *Prose Works* (Philadelphia: David McKay, 1892); accessed at www.bartleby.com/229.

6   Ralph Waldo Emerson, *The Heart of Emerson's Journals*, ed. Bliss Perry (New York: Dover Publication, 1995), 92.

7   SJH, *Fifth Annual Report of the Managers of the Seaman's Aid Society, of the City of Boston* (Boston: Marsh, Capen & Lyon, 1838), 5–6.

8   SJH, *Third Annual Report of the Managers of the Seaman's Aid Society of the City of Boston* (Boston: James B. Dow, 1836), 6.

9   SJH, *Sixth Annual Report of the Seaman's Aid Society, of the City of Boston* (Boston: James B. Dow, 1839), in "Supplement," 23.

10 SJH to Mathew Carey, January 20, 1831, Historical Society of Pennsylvania, Simon Gratz autograph collection (Coll. 250A), American Literary, Miscellaneous (Case 6, Box 22).

11 SJH, "Rights of Married Women," GLB, May 1837.

12 SJH, "Rights of Married Women."

13 George Washington Warren, *The History of the Bunker Hill Monument Association During the First Century of the United States of America* (Boston: James R. Osgood, 1877), 149.

14 Wheeler, *History of Newport*, 317.

15 SJH, "The Worth of Money," LM, February 1830.

16 SJH, "Worth of Money."

17 Warren, *History of the Bunker Hill Monument Association*, 290.

18 Warren, *History of the Bunker Hill Monument Association*, 295.

19 Warren, *History of the Bunker Hill Monument Association*, 300.

CHAPTER SIX
The Prince of Publishers

1   Frank Luther Mott, writing in *A History of American Magazines*, 1:580n, lists the various titles of Godey's magazine: (1) *The Lady's Book*, 1830–39; (2) *Godey's Lady's Book* and *Ladies' American Magazine*, 1840–43; (3) *Godey's Magazine and Lady's Book*, 1844–48; (4) *Godey's Lady's Book*, 1848–54, 1883–92; (5) *Godey's Lady's Book and Magazine*, 1854–83; (6) *Godey's Magazine*, 1892–98.

2   Lawrence Martin, "The Genesis of Godey's Lady's Book," *New England Quarterly* 1, no. 1 (January 1928): 41–70.

3   LAG, "Editor's Table," GLB, December 1835.

4   LAG, "Editor's Table," GLB, September 1836.

5   LAG, "Editor's Table," GLB, September 1836.

6   LAG, "Editor's Table," GLB, July 1836.

7   LAG, "Editor's Table," GLB, September 1836.

8   SJH, "The *Conversazione*," GLB, January 1837.

Notes

9   SJH, "Editor's Table," GLB, January 1837.

10   LAG, "Our Plates," GLB, May 1839.

11   LAG, "Publisher's Notice," GLB, December 1861.

12   "Godey's Lady's Book for 1850," advertisement, GLB, January 1850.

13   "Complimentary Notices," March 1871, quoting the *Times* (of Bath, ME).

14   "Complimentary Notices," quoting the *Telegraph* (of Gloucester, MA).

15   "Complimentary Notices," quoting the *Register* (of Rochelle, IL).

16   "Complimentary Notices," quoting the *Valley Echo* (Greensville, PA).

17   LAG, *Godey's Arm-Chair*, GLB, February 1858.

18   LAG, "We," GLB, February 1849.

19   SJH, "Literary Notices: 'Fanshawe,'" LM, November 1828.

20   Okker, *Our Sister Editors*, 89.

21   As quoted in "Our Copyright" in "Editors' Book Table," GLB, May 1845.

22   Edgar Allan Poe, "The Magazines," *Broadway Journal*, April 26, 1845, 268.

23   LAG to SJH, December 10, 1838, 46-M-006, Athenaeum.

24   LAG to SJH, December 16, 1837, 46-M-005, Athenaeum.

25   "Public Dinner to Louis A. Godey," GLB, March 1856.

26   According to the consumer price index of the Bureau of Labor Statistics, $5,000 in 1867 is equivalent in purchasing power to about $87,969 today.

27   David E. Hale to SJH, July 1, 1835, 46-M-171, Athenaeum.

28   SJH to Emma Willard, March 3, 1834, 46-M-014, Athenaeum. This letter is misdated on the Athenaeum's website as from 1824. The text makes it clear that it was written a decade later.

29   Henry Williams, "Horatio Hale," in *Memorials of the Class of 1837 of Harvard University, Prepared for the Fiftieth Anniversary of Their Graduation* (Boston: Geo. H. Ellis, 1887), 92–98.

30   In a letter to Willard, SJH reports that Horatio would have an annual salary of $2,000 plus rations and travel expenses. SJH to Emma Willard, January 10, 1837, 46-M-013, Athenaeum. The letter is dated 1836 but it is clear from the contents that it was written in 1837. Since the letter was written in January, it is likely that Hale, used to writing "1836," incorrectly dated it as that year.

31   Lieutenant-Colonel B.K. Pierce to Brigadier-General Roger Jones, May 1, 1839, 46-M-1289, 46-M-162, Athenaeum. This letter was enclosed in an envelope sent to SJH.

32   David E. Hale to Horatio Emmons Hale, January 1, 1836, 46-M-161, Athenaeum.

33 SJH to David E. Hale, October 5, 1829, 46-M-128, Athenaeum.

34 SJH to David E. Hale, March 18, 1839, 46-M-151, Athenaeum.

35 "Editor's Table," GLB, July 1839.

36 SJH, "Editors' Table," December 1877.

37 David E. Hale to SJH, February 10, 1830, 46-M-180, Athenaeum.

CHAPTER SEVEN
Literary Ladies

1 SJH, "Editor's Table," GLB, January 1838.

2 SJH, "Longfellow the Poet," GLB, October 1846. Hale's brief introduction to Longfellow's poem "It Is Not Always May," reads: "In brilliant fancy and elegant diction our American poet Longfellow will bear comparison with any who write at present in the English language. He has the additional merit, and that is not a small one, of having kept himself perfectly free from the nasal whine of the transcendental school; which is so much in vogue at the present day, and which is destined to be universally regarded with a feeling of nausea at no very distant future day. The peculiar twang of the transcendental poets is conventional and counterfeit. Longfellow's verses are classical—masculine. They have the clear, silver ring of the true coin."

3 Washington Irving, "England and America," GLB, January 1848.

4 SJH, "Editors' Book Table," GLB, January 1840.

5 Edgar Allan Poe, "REVIEWS: *Keeping House and House-Keeping. A Story of Domestic Life*," *Broadway Journal*, April 5, 1845, 211.

6 Finley, *Lady of Godey's*, 91.

7 GLB, June 1846.

8 Elaine Showalter, *A Jury of Her Peers* (New York: Vintage Books, 2010), 32–34.

9 SJH, *Traits of American Life* (Philadelphia: E.L. Carey & A. Hart, 1835).

10 Mott, *History of American Magazines*, 1:585.

11 Maria Edgeworth, "Soliloquy of Mary, Queen of Scots, on Leaving the Shores of France," GLB, September 1841.

12 Eliza Leslie, "Western New York: A Slight Sketch," GLB, November 1845.

13 SJH, "Stage-coach Adventures," GLB, September 1846.

14 Harriet Beecher Stowe, "The Canal Boat," GLB, October 1841.

15 Eliza Leslie, "The Center-Table," GLB, July 1844.

16 Showalter, *Jury of Her Peers*, 34.

17 SJH, "Editors' Book Table," GLB, January 1846.

18 Okker, *Our Sister Editors*, 85.

19 N.P. Willis to SJH, January 21, 1848, mssHM 6867-69, Huntington Library.

20 SJH, "Editor's Table," GLB, December 1839. "Editor's Table" became "Editors' Table" in 1840. Despite the use of the plural noun "Editors," Godey said that the column was written by Hale.

21 SJH, "To Correspondents," GLB, June 1841.

22 Okker, *Our Sister Editors*, 98.

23 Gretchen Holbrook Gerzina, *Frances Hodgson Burnett: The Unexpected Life of the Author of the Secret Garden* (New Brunswick, NJ: Rutgers University Press, 2004), 34–35.

24 Dr. Elizabeth Blackwell to SJH, 18 March 1851, 46-M-085, Athenaeum.

25 Harriet Beecher Stowe to SJH, undated but between 1850 and 1853, mssHM 24166, Huntington Library.

26 SJH, *Woman's Record*, xxxv.

27 Col. C.B. Phipps to Lord Clarendon, September 30, 1853, 46-M-104, Athenaeum.

CHAPTER EIGHT

The Dignity of Housekeeping

1 Sanford, "Mrs. Sarah J. Hale."

2 SJH, "Editors' Table: A Cry for Help," GLB, June 1876.

3 John Spaulding, "Introduction," in *Civil War Recipes: Receipts from the Pages of Godey's Lady's Book*, ed. Lily May Spaulding and John Spaulding (Lexington: University Press of Kentucky, 1999), 2.

4 SJH, "Editors' Table: National Normal Schools and Seminaries of Household Science for Young Women," GLB, January 1867.

5 SJH, "Literary Notices," LM, January 1830.

6 SJH, "Literary Notices," GLB, October 1864.

7 SJH, "Preface," in *The Ladies' New Book of Cookery: A Practical System for Private Families in Town and Country* (New York: H. Long & Brother, 1852), iv.

8   SJH, "Modern Cookery and Household Management," GLB, January 1863.

9   SJH, *Ladies' New Book of Cookery*, 149.

10   SJH, *Ladies' New Book of Cookery*, 145.

11   SJH, *The Good Housekeeper: Or the Way to Live Well and to Be Well While We Live* (Boston: Weeks, Jordan, 1839), 7.

12   W.J. Rorabaugh, *The Alcoholic Republic* (Oxford: Oxford University Press, 1979), 120.

13   "Receipts, &c.: Rich Bride or Christening Cake," GLB, April 1860.

14   SJH, "Editors' Table: The Sewing Machine," GLB, August 1860.

15   SJH, "Editors' Table: The Queen of Inventions—The Sewing Machine," GLB, July 1860.

16   SJH, "Editors' Table: The Queen of Inventions."

17   SJH, "Editors' Table: Sewing Machine Clubs," GLB, September 1860.

18   D.C. Bloomer, ed., *Life and Writings of Amelia Bloomer* (Boston: Arena Publishing, 1895).

19   C.T. Hinckley, "A Ramble Through the Mechanical Department of the 'Lady's Book,'" in *American Periodicals* 16, no. 1 (2006): 103–114.

20   Memorial to Congress, as quoted in SJH, "Editors' Table: Free National Normal Schools for Young Women," GLB, February 1870.

21   SJH, "Editors' Table: National Normal Schools and Seminaries of Domestic Science for Young Women: Another Plan," GLB, January 1868.

22   SJH, "Editors' Table: National Normal Schools."

23   SJH, *Keeping House and House Keeping: A Story of Domestic Life* (New York: Harper & Brothers, 1845).

24   SJH, "Editors' Table: A Noble Benefaction," GLB, February 1871.

CHAPTER NINE
A Suitable Job for a Woman

1   S. Margaret Fuller, *Woman in the Nineteenth Century* (New York: Greeley & McElrath, 1845), 159.

2   John Matteson, *The Lives of Margaret Fuller* (New York: W.W. Norton, 2012).

3   SJH, *Woman's Record*, 665–70.

4   SJH, "Literary Notices," LM, November 1828.

5   SJH, "Editors' Table," GLB, March 1852.

6   Okker, *Our Sister Editors*, 4.

7   SJH, "What Can Women Do?," LM, May 1834.

8   SJH, "Editors' Table: A Noble Benefaction," GLB, February 1871.

9   SJH, *My Cousin Mary: Or the Inebriate* (New York: Whipple and Damrell, 1839).
     While Hale is generally understood to have written *My Cousin Mary*, whose title page says only that it was written by "A Lady," there remains some question about the authorship. See "Sarah Josepha Buell Hale," in *Bibliography of American Literature*, vol. 3 (New Haven, CT: Yale University Press, 1959), 324.

10   SJH, "Editors' Table: Our Plates and Their Lessons," GLB, January 1861.

11   Finley, *Lady of Godey's*, 309–10.

12   Oliver Johnson, *A Home in the Woods: Oliver Johnson's Reminiscences of Early Marion County (As Related to Howard Johnson)* (Indianapolis: Indiana Historical Society, 1951), 175.

13   SJH, "An Authoress—No. II," LM, March 1829.

14   Horace Mann to SJH, September 16, 1850, 46-M-096, Athenaeum; emphasis in original.

15   SJH, "Editors' Table," GLB, August 1852; emphasis in original. And also, "Memorial to the Honorable Senate and House of Representatives, in Congress assembled," as quoted in "Editors' Table: Free Normal Schools for Female Teachers of Common Schools," GLB, February 1853.

16   SJH, "Editors' Table," GLB, August 1852; emphasis in original.

17   SJH, "Editors' Table," GLB, August 1852.

18   SJH, "Editors' Table," GLB, August 1852.

19   SJH to William Henry Seward, October 23, 1863, William Henry Seward Papers, A.S51, Rare Books, Special Collections, and Preservation, River Campus Libraries, University of Rochester.

20   SJH, "Editors' Table: Postmistress," GLB, September 1854.

21   SJH, "Editors' Table: Women in the Post-Office Department," GLB, October 1862.

22   SJH, "Women in the Post-Office Department."

23   SJH, "Women in the Post-Office Department."

24   SJH, "Women in the Post-Office Department."

25 SJH, "Editors' Table," GLB, March 1866.

26 SJH, "Editors' Table: Notes and Notices, Are American Women Citizens?," GLB, February 1866.

27 SJH, "Editors' Table: The Rights of American Women as Citizens," GLB, March 1866.

28 SJH, "The Rights of American Women as Citizens."

29 SJH, "Editors' Table," GLB, March 1852.

30 SJH, "An Appeal to American Medical Christians on Behalf of the Ladies' Medical Missionary Society," GLB, March 1852.

31 SJH, "Doings of the Ladies' Medical Missionary Society," GLB, June 1853.

32 Elizabeth Blackwell to SJH, March 18, 1851, 46-M-085, Athenaeum. By 1853, Hale was happy to report that public opinion supported the return of female midwives and "a man midwife will soon become an obsolete idea," but she could point to no positive practical result. Despite her exertions on behalf of midwives, it was a lost cause. While women continued to practice as midwives for the rest of the nineteenth century, especially in poor and immigrant communities, they mostly did so illegally. Midwifery was virtually abolished in the early part of the twentieth century, due to state licensing requirements. Midwives today are usually registered nurses with specialized training.

33 SJH, "Editors' Table: Diminutions of the English Language," GLB, May 1865.

CHAPTER TEN
Mrs. Hale's Magazine

1 LAG, "Godey's Arm-Chair," GLB, January 1853.

2 LAG, "To Our Old Friends," GLB, April 1850.

3 Okker, *Our Sister Editors*, 56.

4 Mark Twain, *Life on the Mississippi* (James R. Osgood, 1883). A copy of the *Lady's Book* may have been on the parlor table, but Twain wasn't a fan. He described the "chaste and innocuous Godey's 'Lady's Book,'" with painted fashion-plate of wax-figure women with mouths all alike—lips and eyelids the same size—each five-foot woman with a two-inch wedge sticking from under her dress and letting-on to be half of her foot." Hale, having retired in 1877 and died in 1879, was not the editor when Twain made his observations.

Notes

5   Geraldine Ellis, "Sarah Josepha Hale," unpublished manuscript, Geraldine Kane Ellis Papers, Madeleine Clare Wallace Library, Wheaton College (Massachusetts), 253.

6   SJH, "Editor's Table," GLB, November 1838.

7   "Etiquette of Trousseau," GLB, August 1849.

8   "To Correspondents," GLB, April 1858.

9   Princess Victoria, diary, December 24, 1832, as referenced in Rachel Knowles's "Did They Have Christmas Trees in the Regency?," https://www.regencyhistory.net/2012/12/did-they-have-christmas-trees-in-regency.html.

10 Prince Albert, writing in 1847, as quoted in "Christmas Tree," New World Encyclopedia, https://www.newworldencyclopedia.org/entry/Christmas_tree.

11 White House Historical Association, "White House Christmas Traditions," https://www.whitehousehistory.org/press-room/press-backgrounders/white-house-christmas-traditions (accessed October 30, 2020).

12 *Harper's Weekly*, December 1858.

13 SJH, "A Plea for Dancing," in *Manners: Or, Happy Homes and Good Society All the Year Round* (Boston: J.E. Tilton, 1868), 104. *Manners* is a collection of Hale's column "The Home Circle," which was published in the *Philadelphia Home Weekly*.

14 SJH, "Editors' Table: Polka Taught Without the Aid of a Master," GLB, November 1845.

15 Dr. Chas. P. Uhle, "Health Department," GLB, February 1869.

16 SJH, "Health and Beauty: Tight Lacing," GLB, July 1847.

17 SJH, "Editor's Table: Amiability—Mistakes Concerning It," GLB, January 1839.

18 SJH, "Amiability."

19 Quoted in Elswyth Thane, *Mount Vernon Is Ours: The Story of Its Preservation* (New York: Duell, Sloan, and Pearce, 1966), 16.

20 SJH to Susan Pellet, May 29, 1858, Fred W. Smith National Library for the Study of George Washington, Mount Vernon Ladies' Association.

21 SJH to Ann Pamela Cunningham, January 16, 1857, Mount Vernon Ladies' Association.

22 *Daily Morning Post* (Pittsburgh), August 1854, 2.

23 *North-Carolina Standard*, November 22, 1837, 3.

24 *Cincinnati Daily Star*, August 14, 1877, 2.

25 *Washington Evening Star*, August 11, 1855.

26 *Rutland (VT) Evening Herald*, May 25, 1871.

27 "Sarah Josepha Buell Hale," in *Bibliography of American Literature*, 3:319–40.

28 Laura Ingalls Wilder, *Little Town on the Prairie* (New York: Harper & Brothers, 1941).

29 Wilder, *Little Town on the Prairie*. Ma wasn't able to obtain a copy of *Godey's Lady's Book* before it came time for Mary to leave for college, so she made the skirt wide enough to accommodate a hoop if hoop skirts came back into style.

CHAPTER ELEVEN
Our Glorious Thanksgiving Day

1 President James Madison named Thanksgiving days after military victories during the War of 1812, as did Lincoln and Jefferson Davis of the Confederacy during the Civil War. Lincoln was the first president after Washington to name a day of general thanksgiving.

2 SJH, *Northwood; or, Life North and South: Showing the True Character of Both*, 2nd ed. (New York: H. Long & Brother, 1852).

3 SJH, "Sketches of American Character: The Thanksgiving of the Heart," LM, December 1829.

4 SJH, "Thanksgiving of the Heart."

5 SJH, "Our National Thanksgiving," GLB, September 1863.

6 SJH, "Editors' Table: Thanksgiving Day," GLB, October 1857.

7 When Hale's correspondence was sorted in 1916, her family found "innumerable" replies to her Thanksgiving correspondence, according to Finley. Those signed with nationally prominent names were sold at auction. The rest were destroyed.

8 SJH to William Seward, September 26, 1863, William Henry Seward Papers, A.S51, Rare Books, Special Collections, and Preservation, River Campus Libraries, University of Rochester.

9 SJH, "Editors' Table: Our Holidays," GLB, January 1847.

10 LAG, "Godey's Arm-Chair," GLB, October 1856.

11 S.G.B., "Thanksgiving," GLB, November 1863.

12 SJH, "Editors' Table: The National Thanksgiving," GLB, November 1857.

13 SJH, "Editors' Table: Our Thanksgiving Union," GLB, November 1859.

14 SJH, "Editors' Table: Thanksgiving—*the New National Holiday*," GLB, September 1860.

15 SJH, "Editors' Table: Thanksgiving Day: The Last Thursday in November," GLB, November 1861.

16 SJH, "Editors' Table: American Thanksgiving in Prussia," GLB, March 1860.

17 Townsend Harris to SJH, November 25, 1860, mssHM 20525, Huntington Library.

18 E.D. Morgan to SJH, October 4, 1859, mssHM 20519, Huntington Library.

19 Kingsley Bingham to SJH, September 30, 1856, mssHM 20514, Huntington Library.

20 As quoted in Barton H. Wise, *The Life of Henry A. Wise of Virginia, 1806–1876* (New York: Macmillan, 1899), 214–15.

21 Thomas Jefferson to Samuel Miller, January 23, 1808, Founders Online, National Archives, http://founders.archives.gov/documents/Jefferson/99-01-02-7257.

22 Zachary Taylor's letter, dated November 6, 1849, was reprinted in *The Republic* (Washington, D.C.) on November 19, 1849, under the heading "Letter from the President."

23 Millard Fillmore to SJH, November 15, 1852, mssHM 20515, Huntington Library.

24 Franklin Pierce to SJH, November 19, 1856, mssHM 20524, Huntington Library.

25 Finley, *Lady of Godey's*, 201.

26 Frederick W. Seward, *William H. Seward: An Autobiography from 1801–1846 with a Memoir of His Life, and Selections from His Letters from 1831–1846* (New York: D. Appleton, 1877), 511.

27 Seward, *William H. Seward*, 321.

28 SJH to Abraham Lincoln, October 3, 1863, Abraham Lincoln Papers, Library of Congress.

29 William H. Seward to SJH, September 29, 1863, mssHM 23546, Huntington Library.

30 "President Abraham Lincoln's Thanksgiving Day Proclamation of October 3, 1863 (Presidential Proclamation 106)," National Archives, Series: Presidential Proclamations, 1791–2016, Record Group 11: General Records of the United States Government, https://catalog.archives.gov/id/299960.

CHAPTER TWELVE
Hale's Civil War

1 LAG, "Godey's Armchair: Abraham Lincoln," GLB, July 1865.

2 SJH, "Editors' Table," GLB, June 1863.

3 SJH, "Editors' Table," GLB, December 1862.

4 SJH, "Eighteen Hundred and Sixty-Two," January 1862.

5 Delta (possibly a pseudonym for Henry W. Domett), "A Trip in the Street Cars," GLB, June 1865.

6 S.F. Flint, "The Soldier's Wayside Dream," GLB, August 1863.

7 LAG, "Godey's Arm-Chair: An Affecting Incident," GLB, November 1863. A few months later the soldier was identified as a man named Hummiston from Portville, New York. Godey wrote: "Large numbers of photographic copies of the picture upon which the dying eyes of the warrior-father closed have been sold, and the profits realized from their sale will be appropriated to the benefit of the children. It is hoped that a sufficient sum may be realized in this way, and by future sales, to aid materially in the education of the little ones who were made orphans at Gettysburg." LAG, "Godey's Arm-Chair: Identity Ascertained," GLB, March 1864.

8 SJH, "Editors' Table," GLB, December 1862. Hale's reference to a "lodge in the wilderness" comes from Psalm 55.

9 SJH to Mrs. Ronson, January 30, 1864, Historical Society of Pennsylvania, Simon Gratz autograph collection (Coll. 250B), alphabetical collection.

10 SJH, "Editors' Table: Our Plates and Their Lessons," GLB, January 1861.

11 Ellis, "Sarah Josepha Hale," 518.

12 SJH to H.N. Leech, March 12, 1861, Sarah Josepha Buell Hale Papers, Albert and Shirley Small Special Collections Library, University of Virginia.

13 Mott, *History of American Magazines*, 1:585.

14 LAG, "Godey's Arm-Chair," GLB, December 1860.

15 Isabelle Webb Entrikin, *Sarah Josepha Hale and Godey's Lady's Book* (Lancaster, PA: Lancaster Press, 1946), 121. According to Entrikin, the quality of the submissions improved after the publisher's plea.

16 SJH, "Editors' Table: Our National Thanksgiving—A Domestic Festival," GLB, November 1864.

17   Milo P. Jewett, *Origin of Vassar College* (1879), Vassar College Librar- ies, Archives and Special Collections, as quoted in Edward R. Linner, *Vassar: The Remarkable Growth of a Man and His College 1855–1865* (Poughkeepsie, New York: Vassar College, 1984), 18.

18   SJH to Matthew Vassar, September 30, 1860, Vassar College Libraries, Archives and Special Collections.

19   Matthew Vassar to SJH, May 8, 1860, in Elizabeth Hazelton Haight, ed., *The Autobiography and Letters of Matthew Vassar* (New York: Oxford University Press, 1916), 51.

20   SJH to Vassar, January 21, 1865, as quoted in Linner, *Vassar*, 117–18.

21   SJH to Vassar, January 21, 1865, as quoted in Linner, *Vassar*, 117–18.

22   Horatio Hale, writing anonymously, "Vassar College: The New Plan of Organization Examined; Only 'One Defect'; And This May Be Easily Amended," GLB, February 1864.

23   SJH to Milo H. Jewett, February 20, 1864, as quoted in Linner, *Vassar*, 132.

24   SJH, "Editors' Table: Vassar College—and Its Organization," GLB, May 1864.

25   Vassar to SJH, June 27, 1866, Vassar College Libraries, Archives and Special Collections.

26   SJH to Vassar, January 21, 1865, as quoted in Linner, *Vassar*, 118.

27   Linner, *Vassar*, 140.

28   "'The Best Human Benefactor of WOMAN,' Matthew Vassar and Sarah Josepha Hale," Vassar Encyclopedia, 2018, http://vcencyclopedia.vas- sar.edu/early-vassar/hale-vassar.html.

29   SJH, "Editors' Table: In Memoriam," GLB, November 1868.

30   SJH, "A Just Man Gone," GLB, September 1868.

CHAPTER THIRTEEN
Twilight Years

1   SJH, *Boarding Out: A Tale of Domestic Life* (New York: Harper & Brothers, 1846).

2   SJH to D.E. Wilson, June 15, 1846, 46-M-047, Athenaeum.

3   The description of Hale's workroom on Locust Street along with the reminiscences of her grandchildren are taken from Finley's *Lady of Godey's*.

4   John Raymond to Cornelia Raymond, November 30, 1864, as found in Harriett Raymond Lloyd, ed., *Life and Letters of John Howard Raymond* (New York: Fords, Howard & Hulbert, 1881), 527.

5   Sanford, "Mrs. Sarah J. Hale."

6   SJH to Ulysses S. Grant, October 24, 1876, mssHM 20526, Huntington Library. Hale's suggestion that Congress legislate a Thanksgiving Day was finally taken up in 1941, when Congress passed a resolution naming the fourth Thursday of November as the permanent date of the holiday. President Franklin Delano Roosevelt signed it into law.

7   "Women Prison Inspectors," *Evening Telegraph* (Philadelphia), July 16, 1869.

8   SJH, "Editors' Table: A New College for Women," GLB, March 1875.

9   The Episcopal Church, of which Hale was a member, recognizes Hale on its liturgical calendar on April 30, the date of her death, for her work on behalf of the deaconess movement and women's education. A line in a suggested prayer for that day reads, "Gracious God, we bless thy Name for the vision and witness of Sarah Hale, whose advocacy for the ministry of women helped to support the deaconess movement."

10   The Vassar letter is quoted in Linner, *Vassar*, 141.

11   SJH, "Editors' Table: Ought American Women to Have the Right of Suffrage?," GLB, October 1867.

12   Frances Dana Barker Gage writing as Aunt Fanny, "Letter from Mrs. Gage," *Lily*, August 1, 1852.

13   SJH, "Woman Suffrage," GLB, May 1871.

14   SJH, "Women in School Boards," GLB, February 1871.

15   SJH, "Equal Pay for Equal Work," GLB, April 1873.

16   SJH to Mrs. Brainerd, February 2, 1862, Historical Society of Pennsylvania, Simon Gratz autograph collection (Coll. 250A), American Poets (Case 7, Box 5).

17   The best discussion of Hale's work with missionary societies is "Our Medical Missionaries," GLB, December 1877.

18   Among Horatio's many publications is *The Iroquois Book of Rites*, available online. The William George Hale Papers reside at the Center for American History at the University of Texas at Austin.

19   LAG, "Godey's Arm-Chair: Leave Taking," GLB, December 1877.

20   SJH, "Editors' Table: Fifty Years of My Literary Life," GLB, December 1877. All subsequent citations in this chapter are to this source.

Notes

AFTERWORD
Sarah Who?

1   The controversy over Hale's authorship of "Mary's Lamb" followed her into the grave. A decade after her death, in 1889, Horatio Hale sprang to his mother's defense in a long article for the *Boston Evening Transcript*. (See "Mary's Lamb," *Boston Evening Transcript*, April 10, 1889, 5.) In 1904, *The Century* magazine published an article by Hale's great-nephew, Richard Walden Hale, defending his great-aunt as the author of "Mary's Lamb" ("'Mary Had a Little Lamb,' and Its Author," *The Century* 67, no. 5 [March 1904]: 738–42). The controversy flared up again in the 1920s, when Henry Ford, the car magnate and a collector of Americana, published a book contending that Hale was not the author of the nursery rhyme. The controversy was laid to rest not long after that, thanks in part to Finley's effective debunking of the claims against Hale in *The Lady of Godey's*, published in 1931. Today Hale's authorship of the poem is generally accepted.

2   SJH to Emily C. Judson, August 6, 1873, Princeton University Library, Department of Rare Books and Special Collections, C0140, Box 20.

3   Showalter, *Jury of Her Peers*, 84.

4   "Mrs. Sarah Josepha Hale," *Harper's Bazaar*, June 28, 1879, 416.

5   President Rutherford B. Hayes to SJH, May 26, 1877, as quoted in "Selections from the Correspondence of the Late Mrs. Sarah Josepha Hale," Sales Catalogue, Anderson Galleries, No. 1262, 1917, New York, 8.

6   "Sarah Josepha Hale," *Chicago Daily Tribune*, May 6, 1879, 5.

7   "General Intelligence: Personal Items," *New England Farmer* (Boston), May 10, 1890, 3.

8   "A Noted Woman," *The Times* (Philadelphia), May 2, 1879, 2.

9   "Mrs. Sarah Josepha Hale," *Cecil Whig* (Elkton, MD), June 9, 1871, 1.

10   "Obituary: Mrs. Sarah J.B. Hale," *New York Times*, May 2, 1879, 4.

11   "Sarah Josepha Buell Hale," *Philadelphia Inquirer*, May 1, 1879, 4.

12   Jennie June (1829–1901) is best known as the founder of the women's club Sorosis and a progenitor of the women's club movement overall.

13   Howells classified *Peterson's Magazine* in the same category as *Godey's*. The full quotation reads: "Philadelphia had long counted for nothing in the literary field. Graham's Magazine at one time showed a certain critical force, but it seemed to perish of this expression of vitality; and there remained Godey's Lady's Book and Peterson's Magazines, publications really incredible in their insipidity." This

criticism appears in a collection of Howells's essays on American literature and authors, *Literary Friends and Acquaintances*, published in 1900.

14   Mott, *History of American Magazines*, 1:583–84.

15   Other biographies of Hale include: Norma R. Fryatt, *Sarah Josepha Hale: The Life and Times of a Nineteenth-Century Career Woman* (New York: Hawthorne Books, 1975); Sherbrooke Rogers, *A New England Pioneer* (Grantham, NH: Tompson & Rutter, 1985); and Muriel L. Dubois, *To My Countrywomen* (Bedford, NH: Apprentice Books, 2006). Olive Burt is the author of *First Woman Editor*, a 1960 novel for young adults based on Hale's life (New York: Julian Messner, 1960). Sarah Josepha Hale figures prominently in Denise Kiernan's *We Gather Together* (New York: Dutton, 2020).

16   The first winner of the Sarah Josepha Hale Award was Robert Frost in 1956. Subsequent medalists have included David McCullough, Doris Kearns Goodwin, Ken Burns, Nathaniel Philbrick, and Jodi Picoult, among many other notable literary figures.

Index

Bingham, Kingsley, 195
"Birds" (SJH), 62
Black, Sarah, 158
Blackwell, Elizabeth, 129, 162–64, 207
Blake, John Lauris, 29
Bloomer, Amelia, 142, 225
bluestockings, term use, 36
Boarding Out (SJH), 127, 220
The Boston Book (gift book), 126
Boston Cooking-School Cook Book (Farmer), 136
Boston Spectator and Ladies' Album, 32
Bowles & Dearborn, 26
"The Boy, the Bee, and the Butterfly" (SJH), 62
"The Bright Hearth" (SJH), 62
Broadway Journal, 104
Bryant, William Cullen, xiii, 28, 45, 113
Buchanan, James, xvi, 130, 197
Buckingham, Joseph, 84
Buell, Abigail, 4
Buell, Charles Whittlesey (brother), 4, 22, 23
Buell, Freelove, 4
Buell, Gordon (father), 1, 4, 6–7, 10, 13, 22
Buell, Hannah, 4
Buell, Hepzibah, 4
Buell, Horatio Gates (brother), 4–5, 11, 15, 22, 29, 68, 90
Buell, Martha Maria (sister), 4, 13, 21
Buell, Martha Whittlesey (mother), 1, 4, 6, 8–10, 13, 20–21, 55

Buell, Matthew, 82
Buell, Mehitable, 4
Buell, Mindwell, 4
Buell, Samuel, 4
Buell, Thankful (paternal grandmother), 4
Buell, William, 3–4
Buell families, 2, 3
Buell family, 8, 16
Bunker Hill Monument, 25, 81–87, 105, 111, 179, 206
Bunyan, Paul, 9
Burnett, Frances Hodgson, xiii, 124
Burns, Robert, 9
Bush, Laura, xvii

Carey, Mathew, 78
"The Cask of Amontillado" (Poe), 115
"The Centre-Table" (Leslie), 120
"The Changing World" (SJH), 25
Charlotte, Queen, 172
Chaucer, Geoffrey, 165
Cheney, William, 16–17
Chicago Daily Tribune, 233
Child, Lydia Maria, 43–44, 57–58, 60, 127–28, 136
child advocacy
    day nurseries for poor working women, 77–78
    public children's playgrounds, 105
    urban parks, 222
children, education for
    dame schools, 11–13, 54–55
    of girls vs. boys, 12
    infant schools, 53–55

housekeeping, 131–32
influences on, 6–8
marriage, 14–15, 17–20
siblings, 4–5
widowhood, ix–xi, 50
Hale, Sarah Josepha (née Buell)
(SJH), characteristics
ability to connect with readers,
xvii
bright and sensible, 221
courteous and gracious, 221
culturally savvy, xvii
gift for delivering hard truths,
xvii
indefatigable, xvii, 59, 181, 221
intellectual curiosity, 131
kind and cordial, 225
in old age, 221
patriotic, xii, 6–7, 82–83, 192
positive spirit, 231–32
self-confident, xvii, 51, 123, 221
self-effacing, 5–6
a woman of her time, 33
youthful, 221
Hale, Sarah Josepha (née Buell)
(SJH), cultural influencer
on American cultural norms,
xiii–xiv, 177, 187
on American literary culture,
169
Christmas trees, 172–74
corsets, battle against, 175–76
lingerie, use of the term, 175
men's whiskers, 176–77
for the middle class, 169–70
popular culture, 174–75, 180–82
shaping a common American
aesthetic, xii–xiii, 7

white wedding gowns, 171–72
women's health, 175–76
Hale, Sarah Josepha (née Buell)
(SJH), employment
teaching, x, 11–13
in widowhood, x–xi, 22–24, 26,
46–47, 59–60
See also Hale, Sarah Josepha
(née Buell) (SJH), literary
career
Hale, Sarah Josepha (née Buell)
(SJH), legacy
authorship, redefining for
women, 122–23
child advocacy, xv, 53
labor-saving devices,
encouraged acceptance of, xv
as "Mary Had a Little Lamb"
author, xi, 60–63, 231
reshaping thought about
women and their place in
society, xi, xiv, xvii–xviii
terms coined, xv
women's march to equality,
xvii–xviii
See also Hale, Sarah Josepha:
philanthropy; Thanksgiving
Day campaign; women in the
workplace
Hale, Sarah Josepha (née Buell)
(SJH), literary career
admirers, xv–xvi
awards, 25
beginnings, 17–19, 23–24,
164–65
bylines, 181
correspondents, xvi
Coterie (literary society), 18–19

Index

Ladies' Magazine, editorials, (*cont.*)
"Female Education," 38
fundraising, Bunker Hill Monument, 83, 85
indigent widows and children, 71
on infant schools/educational theories, 55–56
"Literature for Ladies," 43
options for women who need to work, 150–51
treatment of women in Muslim countries, 66
women as teachers, 154
Ladies' Magazine, the editor
beginnings, 29–30, 32
on behalf of working women as teachers, 13
criticism for accepting the job, 30
emerging literary talent, xiii
an opinion leader, 95
philosophy, 32–33
"Progress of Society" (column), 38
shaping cultural attitudes, 95, 169
"Sketches of American Character," 40
spotting new talent, 44–45, 95
success as, 31
"The Village Schoolmistress" (sketch), 41–42
"Walter Wilson" (sketch), 41
Ladies' Magazine, themes and topics
Bunker Hill Monument, 25
death, 25
defense of intellectuals, 36

educational organizations and charities serving women, 71
education for girls, 39–40
education for women, xiv, 27, 32–39, 76, 88–89, 169
financial independence for women, 41
funding of institutions of higher education for women, 36
grief and mourning, 25
intellectual equality of women, xiv, 42, 44
marriage and motherhood as primary responsibilities and greatest satisfaction for women, 33
physical activity for women, 35–36
poverty, 40
in sketches, 40–41
women and men in separate spheres, 33
women in the workplace, xiv, 33–34, 36–37, 41–42
Ladies' Magazine and Literary Gazette, 88
The Ladies' Wreath (SJH), 96, 245–47
The Lady of Godey's (Finley), 235
Lady's Book. See *Godey's Lady's Book*
Lady's Dollar Newspaper, 202
Lafayette, Marquis de, 81
L.A. Godey & Co., 93
Lambdin, James, 236
Land-Grant College Act, 143–44
The Last of the Mohicans (Cooper), 45
Lawrence, Abbott, 68

Image Credits

Sarah Josepha Hale was sixty-two when this portrait was painted in 1850. Library of Congress, LC-USZ62-35926A. (From a portrait painted by W.H. Chambers and engraved by W.G. Armstrong for *Godey's Lady's Book*.)

. . .

The farmhouse where Hale grew up in Newport, New Hampshire. (From *The Book of Old Newport: Old Drawings and Photographs of Newport, New Hampshire*, compiled by Marcia J. and Samuel H. Edes; embellished by Martin W. Nourse, Hartford, CT [Newport, NH: Press of the Argus Spectator, 1909].)

The schoolhouse in Newport where Hale taught before her marriage. (From *The Book of Old Newport: Old Drawings and Photographs of Newport, New Hampshire*, compiled by Marcia J. and Samuel H. Edes; embellished by Martin W. Nourse, Hartford, CT [Newport, NH: Press of the Argus Spectator, 1909].)

. . .

The Rising Sun Tavern, where Sarah Buell met and married David Hale in 1813. Courtesy of the author.

Millions of first-graders learned Hale's poem "Mary Had a Little Lamb" in *McGuffey's First Reader*. (*McGuffey's First Reader*, 1836, 78–79.)

. . .

Louis A. Godey, publisher of *Godey's Lady's Book*. Wikimedia Commons.

Lydia Maria Child, whom Hale succeeded as editor of *Juvenile Miscellany*. Library of Congress, LC-DIG-ppmsca-54178. (Photograph by John Adams Whipple.)

An advertisement for the millinery shop Hale opened with her sister-in-law after her husband's death. From the *Claremont (NH) Spectator*.

. . .

Lydia Huntley Sigourney, poet, wrote for both of Hale's magazines. Brady-Handy photograph collection, Library of Congress, Prints and Photographs Division, LC-DIG-cwpbh-02751.

Edgar Allan Poe, 1848. Library of Congress, LC-USZ62-10610. (From a photo of a daguerreotype by W.S. Hartshorn 1848; copyright 1904 by C.T. Tatman.)

One of the poems by Henry Wadsworth Longfellow published in *Godey's Lady's Book*, 1850.

. . .

Dr. Elizabeth Blackwell, the first woman to receive a medical degree. Library of Congress, LC-USZ62-57850.

Oliver Wendell Holmes, poet and physician. Library of Congress, LC-DIG-pga-12887.

Hale published the work of the young Harriett Beecher Stowe. Library of Congress, LC-USZ62-11212.

A "Dinner Cap" from *Godey's Lady's Book*, 1861.

. . .

Image Credits

The white wedding gown caught on in America in the 1840s after Hale introduced it in *Godey's Lady's Book*. (From "Purity," *Godey's Lady's Book*, November 1850.)

· · ·

Hale published this illustration in 1849, launching Americans' devotion to the Christmas tree. Wikimedia Commons.

· · ·

Cover of *Godey's Lady's Book*, June 1867.

· · ·

A fashionable dinner dress from *Godey's Lady's Book*, 1862.

Abraham Lincoln's secretary of state, William Seward. Library of Congress, LC-DIG-cwpb-04948. (From Brady's National Photographic Portrait Galleries.)

· · ·

Matthew Vassar, founder of Vassar College. (Courtesy Archives & Special Collections, Vassar College Libraries.)

Thomas Edison recorded "Mary Had a Little Lamb" on his new phonograph invention in 1878. Library of Congress, LC-USZ62-98128.

· · ·

Sarah Josepha Hale at eighty-five. Library of Congress, LC-USZ62-29515. (From an engraving by J.C. Buttre. Published in Lillian C. Buttre, *The American Portrait Gallery*, vol. 3 [New York: J.C. Buttre, 1877–80].)